Grammar Links 3

A Theme-Based Course for Reference and Practice

Volume A

SECOND EDITION

Janis van Zante

Debra Daise
University of Colorado,
International English Center

Charl Norloff
University of Colorado,
International English Center

Randee Falk

M. Kathleen Mahnke
Series Editor
Saint Michael's College

Houghton Mifflin Company   Boston   New York

Publisher: Patricia A. Coryell
Director of ESL: Susan Maguire
Senior Development Editor: Kathleen Sands Boehmer
Editorial Assistant: Evangeline Bermas
Senior Project Editor: Margaret Park Bridges
Senior Manufacturing Coordinator: Marie Barnes
Marketing Manager: Annamarie Rice
Marketing Associate: Laura Hemrika

Cover image: Stock Illustration Source © 2003 David Ridley, *Multicultural Figures*

Printed in the U.S.A.

Library of Congress Control Number: 2003115026

ISBN: 0-618-27419-7

123456789-HES-08 07 06 05 04

Contents

Introduction

WELCOME TO *GRAMMAR LINKS*!

Grammar Links is a comprehensive five-level grammar reference and practice series for students of English as a second or foreign language. The series meets the needs of students from the beginning through advanced levels:

- *Grammar Links Basic*: beginning
- *Grammar Links, Book 1*: high beginning
- *Grammar Links, Book 2*: intermediate
- *Grammar Links, Book 3*: high intermediate
- *Grammar Links, Book 4*: advanced

Available with each *Grammar Links* student text are an audio program and printable Web-based teacher's notes; the teacher's notes are accompanied by the answer key and tapescripts for each book. Tests and other materials are also available on the Houghton Mifflin Website and are described below. In addition, *Grammar Links 1–4* feature workbooks for further practice of all grammar points introduced in the student books.

NEW IN THIS EDITION

- A fresh, new design with eye-catching art, realia, and a focus on ease of use
- Streamlined, easy-to-read grammar charts showing structures at a glance
- Succinct explanations of grammar points for easy understanding
- Simplified content coverage accompanied by vocabulary glosses to let students focus on grammar while learning about topics of interest
- An even greater number and variety of activities than before, now signaled with icons for easy reference:

  Listening activities for receptive practice of grammar structures in oral English

  Communicative activities that lead to fluent use of grammar in everyday speaking

  Writing activities for productive practice of targeted structures in extended written discourse

   Links to the World Wide Web for:
  - Model paragraphs for writing assignments
  - Practice tests, both self-check tests for student use and achievement tests for teacher use
  - Links to interesting sites related to unit themes for further reading and discussion
  - Vocabulary flashcards for review of the content-related vocabulary that is used in text readings and exercises
  - Much more! See for yourself at www.hmco.com/college/esl.

TO THE TEACHER

Series Approach

Recent research in applied linguistics tells us that when a well-designed communicative approach is coupled with a systematic treatment of grammatical form, the combination is a powerful pedagogical tool.

Grammar Links is such a tool. The grammar explanations in *Grammar Links* are clear, accurate, and carefully sequenced. All points that are introduced are practiced in exercises, and coverage is comprehensive and systematic. In addition, each grammar point is carefully recycled in a variety of contexts.

The communicative framework of *Grammar Links* is that of the theme-based approach to language learning. Unlike other approaches, theme-based models promote the development of both communicative and linguistic abilities through in-depth contextualization of language in extended discourse. The importance of this type of contextualization to grammar acquisition is now well documented. In *Grammar Links*, content serves as a backdrop for communication; high-interest topics are presented and developed along with the grammar of each chapter. As a result, *Grammar Links* exercises and activities are content-driven as well as grammar-driven. While learning about adjective clauses in Book 3, for example, students explore various aspects of the discipline of psychology. While they are practicing gerunds and infinitives in Book 2, they read about successful American entrepreneurs. And while practicing the simple present tense in Book 1, students learn about and discuss North American festivals and other celebrations. Throughout the series, students communicate about meaningful content, transferring their grammatical training to the English they need in their daily lives.

Complementing the communicative theme-based approach of the *Grammar Links* series is the inclusion of a range of successful methodological options for exercises and activities. In addition to more traditional, explicit rule presentation and practice, we have incorporated a number of less explicit, more inductive techniques. Foremost among these are our discovery exercises and activities, in which students are asked to notice general and specific grammatical features and think about them on their own, sometimes formulating their own hypotheses about how these features work and why they work the way they do. Discovery exercises are included in each unit opener. They are frequently used in chapter openers as well and are interspersed throughout the *Grammar Practice* sections, particularly at the higher levels.

In short, the *Grammar Links* approach provides students with the best of all possible language learning environments—a comprehensive, systematic treatment of grammar that employs a variety of methods for grammar learning within a communicative theme-based framework.

About the Books

Each book in the *Grammar Links* series is divided into approximately 10 units. Each unit looks at a well-defined area of grammar, and each unit has an overall theme. The chapters within a unit each focus on some part of the targeted unit grammar, and each chapter develops some specific aspect of the unit theme. In this way, chapters in a unit are linked in terms of both grammar coverage and theme, providing a highly contextualized base on which students can build and refine their grammatical skills.

Grammar coverage has been carefully designed to spiral across levels. Structures that are introduced in one book are recycled and built upon in the next. Students not only learn increasingly sophisticated information about the structures but also practice these structures in increasingly challenging contexts. Themes show a similar progression across levels, from less academic in Books 1 and 2 to more academic in Books 3 and 4.

Grammar Links is flexible in many ways and can be easily adapted to the particular needs of users. Although its careful spiraling makes it ideal as a series, the comprehensive grammar coverage at each level means that the individual books can also stand alone. The comprehensiveness and careful organization also make it possible for students to use their text as a reference after they have completed a course. The units in a book can be used in the order given or can be rearranged to fit the teacher's curriculum. Books can be used in their entirety or in part. In addition, the inclusion of ample practice allows teachers to be selective when choosing exercises and activities. All exercises are labeled for grammatical content, so structures can be practiced more or less extensively, depending on class and individual needs.

Unit and Chapter Components

- **Unit Objectives.** Each unit begins with a list of unit objectives so that teachers and students can preview the major grammar points covered in the unit. Objectives are accompanied by example sentences, which highlight the relevant structures.

- **Unit Introduction.** To illustrate grammar use in extended discourse, a reading and listening selection introduces both the unit grammar and the unit theme in a unit opener section entitled *Grammar in Action*. This material is followed by a grammar consciousness-raising or "noticing" task, *Think About Grammar*. In *Think About Grammar* tasks, students figure out some aspect of grammar by looking at words and sentences from the *Grammar in Action* selection, often working together to answer questions about them. Students induce grammatical rules themselves before having those rules given to them. *Think About Grammar* thus helps students to become independent grammar learners by promoting critical thinking and discussion about grammar.

- **Chapter Introduction.** Each chapter opens with a task. This task involves students in working receptively with the structures that are treated in the chapter and gives them the opportunity to begin thinking about the chapter theme.

- *Grammar Briefings.* The grammar is presented in *Grammar Briefings*. Chapters generally have three or four *Grammar Briefings* so that information is given in manageable chunks. The core of each *Grammar Briefing* is its **form** and **function** charts. In these charts, the form (the *what* of grammar) and the function (the *how, when,* and *why*) are presented in logical segments. These segments are manageable but large enough that students can see connections between related grammar points. Form and function are presented in separate charts when appropriate but together when the two are essentially inseparable. All grammatical descriptions in the form and function charts are comprehensive, concise, and clear. Sample sentences illustrate each point.

- *Grammar Hotspots.* *Grammar Hotspots* are a special feature of *Grammar Links*. They occur at one or more strategic points in each chapter. *Grammar Hotspots* focus on aspects of grammar that students are likely to find particularly troublesome. Some hotspots contain reminders about material that has already been presented in the form and function charts; others go beyond the charts.

- *Talking the Talk.* *Talking the Talk* is another special feature of the *Grammar Links* series. Our choice of grammar is often determined by our audience, whether we are writing or speaking, the situations in which we find ourselves, and other sociocultural factors. *Talking the Talk* treats these factors. Students become aware of differences between formal and informal English, between written and spoken English.

■ ***Grammar Practice.*** Each *Grammar Briefing* is followed by comprehensive and systematic practice of all grammar points introduced. The general progression within each *Grammar Practice* is from more controlled to less controlled, from easier to more difficult, and often from more receptive to more productive and/or more structured to more communicative. A wide variety of innovative exercise types is included in each of the four skill areas: listening, speaking, reading, and writing. The exercise types that are used are appropriate to the particular grammar points being practiced. For example, more drill-like exercises are often used for practice with form. More open-ended exercises often focus on function.

In many cases, drill-like practice of a particular grammar point is followed by open-ended communicative practice of the same point, often as pair or group work. Thus, a number of exercises have two parts.

The majority of exercises within each *Grammar Practice* section are related to the theme of the unit. However, some exercises depart from the theme to ensure that each grammar point is practiced in the most effective way.

■ **Unit Wrap-Ups.** Each unit ends with a series of activities that pull the unit grammar together and enable students to test, further practice, and apply what they have learned. These activities include an error correction task, which covers the errors students most commonly make in using the structures presented in the unit, as well as a series of innovative open-ended communicative tasks, which build on and go beyond the individual chapters.

■ **Appendixes.** Extensive appendixes supplement the grammar presented in the *Grammar Briefings*. They provide students with word lists, spelling and pronunciation rules, and other supplemental rules related to the structures that have been taught. The appendixes are a rich resource for students as they work through exercises and activities.

■ **Grammar Glossary.** A grammar glossary provides students and teachers with definitions of the grammar terms used in *Grammar Links* as well as example sentences to aid in understanding the meaning of each term.

Other Components

■ **Audio Program.** All *Grammar Links* listening exercises and all unit introductions are recorded on audio CDs and cassettes. The symbol 🎧 appears next to the title of each recorded segment.

■ **Workbook.** *Grammar Links 1–4* student texts are each accompanied by a workbook. The four workbooks contain a wide variety of exercise types, including paragraph and essay writing, and they provide extensive supplemental self-study practice of each grammar point presented in the student texts. Student self-tests with TOEFL® practice questions are also included in the workbooks.

■ **Teacher's Notes.** The *Grammar Links* teacher's notes for each student text can be downloaded from www.hmco.com/college/esl. Each contains an introduction to the series and some general and specific teaching guidelines.

■ **Tapescript and Answer Keys.** The tapescript and the answer key for the student text and the answer key for the workbook are also available at the *Grammar Links* Website.

■ **Links to the World Wide Web.** As was discussed above, the *Grammar Links* Website www.hmco.com/college/esl has been expanded for the second edition to include student and teacher tests, teacher notes, model writing assignments, content Web links and activities, and other material. Links are updated frequently to ensure that students and teachers can access the best information available on the Web.

TO THE STUDENT

Grammar Links is a five-level series that gives you all the rules and practice you need to learn and use English grammar. Each unit in this book focuses on an area of grammar. Each unit also develops a theme—for example, business or travel. Units are divided into two or three chapters.

Grammar Links has many special features that will help you to learn the grammar and to use it in speaking, listening, reading, and writing.

FEATURE	BENEFIT
Interesting Themes	Help you link grammar to the real world—the world of everyday English
Introductory Reading and Listening Selections	Introduce you to the theme and the grammar of the unit
Think About Grammar Activities	Help you to become an independent grammar learner
Chapter Opener Tasks	Get you started using the grammar
Grammar Briefings	Give you clear grammar rules in easy-to-read charts, with helpful example sentences
Grammar Hotspots	Focus on especially difficult grammar points for learners of English—points on which you might want to spend extra time
Talking the Talk	Helps you to understand the differences between formal and informal English and between written and spoken English
Grammar Practice	Gives you lots of practice, through listening, speaking, reading, and writing exercises and activities
Unit Wrap-Up Tasks	Provide you with interesting communicative activities that cover everything you have learned in the unit
Vocabulary Glosses	Define key words in readings and exercises so that you can concentrate on your grammar practice while still learning about interesting content
Grammar Glossary	Gives you definitions and example sentences for the most common words used to talk about English grammar—a handy reference for now and for later
Websites	Guide you to more information about topics of interest
	Provide you with self-tests with immediate correction and feedback, vocabulary flashcards for extra practice with words that might be new to you, models for writing assignments, and extra practice exercises

All of these features combine to make *Grammar Links* interesting and rewarding—and, I hope, FUN!

M. Kathleen Mahnke, Series Editor
Saint Michael's College
Colchester, VT USA

ACKNOWLEDGMENTS

▩ Series Editor Acknowledgments

This edition of *Grammar Links* would not have been possible without the thoughtful and enthusiastic feedback of teachers and students. Many thanks to you all!

I would also like to thank all of the *Grammar Links* authors, from whom I continue to learn so much every day. Many thanks as well to the dedicated staff at Houghton Mifflin: Joann Kozyrev, Evangeline Bermas, and Annamarie Rice.

A very special thanks to Kathy Sands Boehmer and to Susan Maguire for their vision, their sense of humor, their faith in all of us, their flexibility, their undying tenacity, and their willingness to take risks in order to move from the mundane to the truly inspirational.

M. Kathleen Mahnke, Series Editor

▩ Author Acknowledgments

Many people made valuable contributions to this book. We would like to acknowledge and thank the following:

The staff at Houghton Mifflin, for their constant patience and encouragement

Each other and the other *Grammar Links* authors, for inspiration, advice, and continued friendship throughout the writing and production process

Our students, for their willingness to test the material

Linda Butler, author of *Grammar Links Basic* and *Grammar Links 1*, for her many valuable insights based on her classroom experience with the first edition of this book

Michael Masyn, of the International English Center at the University of Colorado, for his experience and suggestions

Bob Jasperson, Director of the International English Center, for his support

Len Neufeld, for ensuring that the *Grammar Briefings* were presented in the clearest and best possible way.

In addition, we thank the following reviewers:

Brian McClung, North Lake College

Janet Selitto, Valencia Community College

Finally, we are immensely grateful for the support, encouragement, and patience of our close friends and families, especially Lakhdar Benkobi, Len Neufeld, Richard, Jonathan, and Joshua Norloff, and Peter van Zante.

Debra Daise, Randee Falk, Charl Norloff, and Janis van Zante

Present and Past: Simple and Progressive

TOPIC FOCUS
Natural Time and Clock Time

UNIT OBJECTIVES

- **the simple present and present progressive**
  (The earth *revolves* around the sun. We *are studying* the solar system this year.)

- **verbs with stative meanings**
  (We *own* four clocks and several watches.)

- **the simple past and past progressive**
  (I *called* a friend last night. He *was eating* dinner.)

- **time clauses**
  (*Before she went to school,* she drank a cup of coffee.)

- **used to and would**
  (People *used to tell* time by the sun. They *would follow* the sun's shadow on a dial.)

Grammar in Action

Read and listen to this article.

When Did Time Begin?

Did time **have** a beginning? If it did, how **did** it **begin**? When **did** it **begin**? Scientists (think) that our universe **began** from a very small point of space-time. About 14 billion years ago, this point suddenly **exploded**

An Explosion

outward. We **call** this gigantic explosion the big bang. **Did** time **exist** before the big bang? No one **knows**. But the big bang **was** the beginning of time as humans **are** able to understand it now.

At the moment of the big bang, the universe **began** to expand and change. It **is** still **expanding** and **is** still **changing**. Nowadays, scientists **are observing** distant parts of the universe, and they **are learning** more about its early history. About 10 billion years ago, galaxies **were forming** from clouds of stars, dust, and gas. While our galaxy, the Milky Way, **was moving** through space, our solar system

formed within it. Our solar system **includes** the sun and the planets that **revolve** around it. The motions of our planet, Earth, **give** us natural time cycles—days, nights, and seasons of the year. These cycles **repeat** themselves regularly, over and over again.

Natural time cycles **had** an important influence in the development of life on earth. From the beginning, the activities of living things **followed** earth's patterns of daylight and darkness and the seasons of the year. As a result, all living things, including human bodies, **follow** these natural time cycles. Our daily pattern of sleeping and waking is one of our natural cycles.

Long ago, people everywhere **lived** in a way that was closely connected to the cycles of nature. They **depended** on natural time, measured by changes in the sun, moon, and

A Galaxy

stars. But now we **have** a mechanical measure of time, clock time, and people often **schedule** their lives according to it.

Are you feeling sleepy or hungry now, even though the clock **says** it**'s** not time to sleep or eat? What **is** your body **telling** you? Perhaps it**'s trying** to follow nature instead of the clock.

Our Solar System

> *gigantic* = very, very big. *expand* = grow bigger. *observe* = look at. *revolve* = move around. *have an influence* = cause an effect. *mechanical* = operated by a machine.

Think About Grammar

A. Work with a partner. Look at the boldfaced verbs in the article. Underline the verbs that describe an action or state that finished in the past or that was in progress at a time in the past. Circle the verbs that describe an action or state that includes the present or that is in progress in the present.

B. Some of the verbs that you underlined or circled describe an action in progress in the present or in the past. These verbs are in the present progressive or past progressive tense. Write *past progressive* or *present progressive* next to each of the verbs.

1. is expanding _____
2. is changing _____
3. are observing _____
4. are learning _____

5. were forming _____
6. was moving _____
7. is telling _____
8. is trying _____

C. Answer the questions.

1. Progressive verbs all end in the same three letters. What are they? _____
2. Progressive verbs all have the same auxiliary (helping) verb. What is it? _____

D. The other verbs are in the simple present or the simple past tense. Write *simple present* or *simple past* next to each of the verbs.

1. think _____
2. exploded _____
3. says _____
4. had _____

5. began _____
6. were _____
7. followed _____
8. revolve _____

Chapter 1

Simple Present and Present Progressive

Introductory Task: True or False?

A. Work with a partner. Read the statements about a group of students. Then answer the questions.

    a. Most people in the group **use** an alarm clock to wake up on weekdays.
    b. Only two people **are wearing** contact lenses at the moment.
    c. Everyone **sleeps** more than six hours every night.
    d. Three people **are feeling** sleepy now.
    e. Most people **wear** a watch every day.
    f. Right now, fewer than half of the students **are thinking** about food.

1. Habits are things that people do regularly or routinely. Which statements describe people's habits? _a_____ _____ _____

   Are the boldfaced verbs in these statements in the simple present or the present progressive? _____

2. Which statements describe things people are doing at this moment in time?

   _____ _____ _____

   Are these boldfaced verbs in the simple present or the present progressive?

   _____

B. Follow these steps to find out if the statements in Part A are true or false for your class:

1. Work together as a class to write a question for each statement. The questions should be ones that can be answered *yes* or *no*. Follow these examples: *Do you use an alarm clock to wake up on weekdays? Are you wearing contact lenses?*

2. Each student goes around the class asking the other students the questions. Keep track of the number of *yes* and *no* answers.

3. What are your results? Are the statements true or false for your class?

Simple Present and Present Progressive I

FORM

A. Affirmative Statements

SIMPLE PRESENT				PRESENT PROGRESSIVE		
SUBJECT	BASE FORM OF VERB (+ -S/-ES)			SUBJECT	BE + BASE FORM OF VERB + -ING*	
I	**play**	every day.		I	**am playing**	now.
Joe	**plays**	every day.		He	**is playing**	now.
They	**play**	every day.		We	**are playing**	now.

(See Appendix 1 for spelling rules for the -s/-es form of the verb. See Appendix 2 for pronunciation rules for the third person singular form of the simple present tense.)

(See Appendix 3 for spelling rules for the -ing form of the verb.)

B. Negative Statements

SIMPLE PRESENT				PRESENT PROGRESSIVE		
SUBJECT	DO + NOT + BASE FORM OF VERB*			SUBJECT	DO + NOT + BASE FORM OF VERB + -ING*	
I	**do not work**	every day.		I	**am not working**	now.
She	**does not work**	every day.		She	**is not working**	now.
You	**do not work**	every day.		You	**are not working**	now.

C. *Yes/No* Questions and Short Answers

SIMPLE PRESENT			PRESENT PROGRESSIVE	
QUESTIONS	SHORT ANSWERS		QUESTIONS	SHORT ANSWERS
Do they **work** every semester?	Yes, they **do**.		**Am** I **working** this semester?	Yes, you **are**.
	No, they **don't**.			No, you **aren't**.
Does he **work** every evening?	Yes, he **does**.		**Is** he **working** this evening?	Yes, he **is**.
	No, he **doesn't**.			No, he **isn't**.
Do you **work** every semester?	Yes, I **do**.		**Are** you **working** this evening?	Yes, I **am**.
	No, I **don't**.			No, I'm **not**.

(continued on next page)

D. Wh- Questions

Wh- Questions About the Subject

SIMPLE PRESENT	PRESENT PROGRESSIVE
Who works with you?	**Who is working** with you?
What usually **happens**?	**What is happening**?

Other Wh- Questions

SIMPLE PRESENT	PRESENT PROGRESSIVE
Where do you **play**?	**When am** I **playing**?
How long does she **play**?	**Why is** Anna **playing**?
	Who are you **playing** with?

*CONTRACTIONS: SIMPLE PRESENT	*CONTRACTIONS: PRESENT PROGRESSIVE
do + not → don't does + not → doesn't	I + am → I'm he/she/it + is → he's/she's/it's we/you/they + are → we're/you're/they're is + not → isn't are + not → aren't he/she/it + is + not → he's/she's/it's not OR he/she/it isn't we/you/they + are + not → we're/you're/they're not OR we/you/they aren't

GRAMMAR **HOT**SPOT!

1. In conversation, these contractions are common:

   - *Do/be* + *not* (e.g., *don't*, *aren't*)
   - Subject pronoun + *be* (e.g., *he's*, *we're*)
   - *Wh-* word + *is* (e.g., *who's* and *what's*)

   In some formal writing, contractions are avoided.

Tina and Bob **don't** play baseball.
They're playing basketball.
Why's she playing?
Why is the climate changing?

2. Affirmative short answers are never contracted.

Yes, I am.   **NOT:** Yes, ~~I'm.~~

3. When two verbs with the same subject are connected with *and* or *but,* it isn't necessary to repeat the subject.

She **works** and **plays** every day.
She **works** but **doesn't play**.

4. When these verbs include a form of *be* (or of *have*; see Unit Two), it isn't necessary to repeat that form.

She is **working** and **playing**.
She is **working** but **not playing**.

Simple Present and Present Progressive I

1 Simple Present—Form: A Conversation About Time

A student and an astronomer are getting acquainted. Use the words in parentheses to complete the statements and questions in the simple present. Complete the short answers. Use contractions with subject pronouns and with *not*.

Q: <u>Do you work</u> at an observatory?
        1 (you, work)

A: Yes, <u>I do</u>.
          2

Q: I <u>don't know</u> much about astronomy. What <u>does your work involve</u>?
      3 (not, know)   4 (your work, involve)

A: Well, I _____ about measuring time, motion, and space.
           5 (think)

Q: What _____ between astronomy and the measurement of time?
         6 (the connection, be)

A: We _____ our ability to measure time from observing the motions of
         7 (get)

the stars, the earth, and the moon. These motions _____ us natural time
                                         8 (give)

periods, that is, days and nights and the seasons of the year.

Q: If we have natural time, why _____ clock time, too?
                         9 (we, use)

A: Natural time _____ us small or precise enough units of time.
           10 (not, give)

Q: _____ on both natural time and clock time?
        11 (I, live)

A: Yes, _____. Your body and some of your activities
           12

_____ regular natural time cycles, or patterns. However,
      13 (follow)

in our culture, most people _____ the feeling that clock time
                     14 (have)

_____ their lives and routines. For example, they
      15 (control)

_____ when their body tells them to. They
      16 (not, eat)

_____ when the clock says it's lunch or dinner time.
      17 (eat)

Q: Well, my English teacher _____ the clock, and it
                  18 (watch)

_____ time for me to go to class. Thanks for answering my questions!
      19 (be)

---

astronomy = the science that deals with the study of the sun, moon, planets, stars, etc.
observatory = a building built for the purpose of looking at the sky through a
telescope. *precise* = correct, accurate.

 For more information about astronomers and astronomy, go to the *Grammar Links* Website.

2 **Simple Present—*Yes/No* and *Wh-* Questions:** Where Does Natural Time Come From?

A. Use the cues to write questions about the information in each paragraph.

I. The earth and other planets move around the sun. It takes the earth about 365¼ days to orbit the sun. When we talk about the solar system, we call 365 days an "Earth year."

Yes/No Questions:

1. <u>Does the earth move around the sun</u> ?
   (the earth / move / around the sun)

2. _____ ?
   (it / take / the earth / about 365¼ days / to orbit the sun)

Wh- Questions:

1. What <u>do we call 365 days</u> ?
   (we / call / 365 days)

2. How long _____ ?
   (an "Earth year" / be)

3. How long _____ ?
   (it / take / the earth / to orbit / the sun)

II. The length of a planet's year depends on the planet's distance from the sun. So years on Venus aren't as long as Earth years, but years on Mars are longer than Earth years. It takes Venus 224½ Earth days to orbit the sun. It takes Mars 687 Earth days to orbit the sun.

Yes/No Questions:

1. _____ ?
   (years on Venus / be / as long as / Earth years)

2. _____ ?
   (years on Mars / be / longer than / years on Venus)

Wh- Questions:

1. What _____ ?
   (the length of a planet's year / depend on)

2. How long _____ ?
   (it / take / Venus / to orbit the sun)

3. How long _____ ?
   (it / take / Mars / to orbit the sun)

III. The planets rotate as they orbit the sun. The earth rotates on its axis once every 24 hours. This rotation makes day and night on Earth. When one side of the earth faces the sun, it is daytime on that side. When that side turns away from the sun, it is night.

Yes/No Questions:

1. _____ ?
   (the planets / rotate / as they orbit the sun)

2. _____ ?
   (the earth / rotate / on its axis / once every year)

Wh- Questions:

1. How often _____ ?
   (earth / rotate / on its axis)

2. What _____ ?
   (make / day and night / on earth)

3. When _____ ?
   (it / be / daytime / on one side of the earth)

B. Work with a partner. Take turns asking and answering the questions you wrote in Part A. Give short answers to *yes/no* questions.

Example: Student A: *Does the earth move around the sun?*   Student B: *Yes, it does.*
Student B: *What do we call 365 days?*   Student A: *An Earth year.*

🌐 See the *Grammar Links* Website to find out more about our solar system and natural time.

3 Present Progressive—Form: Time Talk

A. Use the words in parentheses to complete the statements and questions in the present progressive. Complete the short answer. Use contractions with subject pronouns and with *not*.

I. A mother and son:

A: Peter, why __aren't you doing__ anything?
       1 (you, not, do)

B: I __'m doing__ something. I _____ here and
       2 (do)   3 (sit)

_____ .
4 (think)

A: You _____ . You _____ television!
     5 (not, think)   6 (watch)

B: I _____ a nature program. It _____
    7 (watch)   8 (help)

me think about serious environmental problems.

A: That nature program _____ you do your homework. You
               9 (not, help)

_____ time!
10 (waste)

II. Three young men:

A: Hey, guys! What's up? Why _____ here on the sidewalk with all this stuff?
           1 (you, sit)

B: We _____ to buy concert tickets. The line
     2 (wait)

_____ very fast.
3 (not, move)

C: We _____ to entertain ourselves while we wait. We
     4 (try)

_____ to the radio and _____ card games.
5 (listen)   6 (play)

A: I get it. You _____ time.
      7 (kill)

III. Three grandmothers:

    A: How _____ nowadays, Mildred?
                  1 (your children, get along)

    B: They _____ just fine. Jennie _____
               2 (get along)   3 (work)

       in Chicago, and Carl _____ to be a lawyer. And the
                                4 (study)

       grandchildren _____ fast!
                       5 (grow)

    C: Good morning! _____ anything important?
                       6 (I, interrupt)

    B: No, _____ . We _____ the time of day
                  7   8 (pass)

       chatting about our families. Please join us.

  B. Work in pairs or small groups. In Part A, people are "wasting time," "killing time," and "passing the time of day." Discuss these idioms and think of other examples of each. Then choose one and work together to write a dialogue that uses it. Use the present progressive at least four times. Present your dialogue to the class.

See the *Grammar Links* Website for a model dialogue for this assignment.

GRAMMAR BRIEFING 2

Simple Present and Present Progressive II
■ Simple Present

FUNCTION

A. Uses of the Simple Present

1. Use the simple present to talk about habitual and repeated actions in the present. These actions started in the past and will probably occur in the future.

   | Farmers **get up** early every morning. |
   | They sometimes **go out** with friends. |

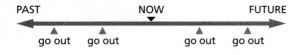

PAST   NOW   FUTURE

go out go out   go out go out

2. Use the simple present to talk about things that are generally accepted as true, including scientific facts.

   | Farmers **grow** crops. |
   | The earth **revolves** around the sun. |

3. The simple present is also used with verbs with stative meaning.
   (See Grammar Briefing 3, page 17.)

   | They **know** about the test. |
   | She **has** a new car. |

(continued on next page)

1. Time expressions used with the simple present include *every day* (*week, month, year,* etc.), *on Mondays* (*weekends, holidays,* etc.), *in the morning* (*the fall, the first semester,* etc.), and *at noon* (*3:00 p.m., the end of the day,* etc.).

He works **every week.**

I go **on weekends.**

Classes begin **in the fall.**

We finish **at 3:00 p.m.**

2. Adverbs of frequency ([*almost*] *always, usually, often, sometimes, seldom, rarely,* [*almost*] *never,* etc.) are also often used with the simple present.

(See Appendix 4 for the position of adverbs of frequency in a sentence.)

We **sometimes** work on the weekend.

I **usually** drink tea.

She is **almost never** at home in the evening.

Present Progressive

FUNCTION

A. Uses of the Present Progressive

1. Use the present progressive to talk about actions in progress at this moment.

Right now, the sun **is shining.**

We **are sitting** in the park now.

2. Use the present progressive to talk about actions in progress through a period of time including the present. The actions began before now and will probably continue after now, but they do not have to be happening at this moment.

Rosa **is taking** an astronomy course this semester.

At present, scientists **are studying** new methods to measure time.

3. The present progressive can be used to emphasize that a situation is temporary. The simple present indicates a more permanent situation.

They **are living** in Chicago this summer. (temporary situation)

They **live** in New York. (more permanent situation)

She**'s** not **earning** much money now. (temporary situation)

She **doesn't earn** much money. (more permanent situation)

(continued on next page)

B. Time Expressions with the Present Progressive

1. *Now*, *right now*, and *at the moment* can be used with the present progressive to talk about a point in time or a period of time.	I'm working **right now**. He's studying **at the moment**.
2. *Nowadays, at this time, at present, these days,* and *this week (month,* etc.*)* are used to talk about a period of time.	They're working at a lab **these days**. We're studying the solar system **this week**.

TALKING THE TALK

The present progressive can be used with *always* to express a complaint.	Dudley **is** always **arriving** late. I'm tired of waiting for him.

GRAMMAR PRACTICE 2

Simple Present and Present Progressive II

4 **Simple Present and Present Progressive—Uses: Watches**

Why is the simple present or the present progressive used in these sentences? For each boldfaced verb, choose a reason.

Digital Watch

Simple Present
Habitual or repeated action
Scientific fact, thing generally accepted as true

Present Progressive
Action in progress at this moment
Action in progress through a period of time including the present

1. Tiny batteries **provide** the power for digital electronic watches.
   Scientific fact, thing generally accepted as true

2. Please don't interrupt me! I'**m trying** to set my watch.
   Action in progress at this moment

3. Megan never **wears** a watch.
   Habitual

4. Rachel's watch has been running slow for a while. Its battery **is wearing out**.
   Action in progress through a period of time

5. How often **do** you **look** at your watch each day?

_____

6. Why **are** you **looking** at your watch? Are we late?

_____

7. Our watches have beepers, so we sometimes **use** them as alarms.

_____

8. Keith's watch **is beeping**. It's lunch time.

_____

9. Watches come in many different styles these days. Some people **are wearing** colorful ones.

_____

10. A watch is one type of chronometer. Chronometers **measure** time.

_____

5 **Adverbs of Frequency and Time Expressions with Simple Present:** Routines

A. Use the adverbs of frequency and time expressions to write true statements about your routines.

1. usually + in the evening _I usually drink a cup of hot tea in the evening_____.

2. often + in the morning _____.

3. seldom + at night _____.

4. always + once a day _____.

5. usually + once a week _____.

6. sometimes + on weekends _____.

7. always + every semester _____.

8. almost never + in the summer _____.

B. Now change one (any one) of the sentences so that it tells a lie. That is, the routine it states is not true for you.

> _a glass of hot milk_
> Example: "I usually drink ~~a cup of hot tea~~ in the evening."

C. 1. Work with a partner. Use the cues in 2–8 of Part A to ask a question about each of your partner's routines. Student A uses "*What do you* + adverb of frequency + *do* + time expression?" in each question. Student B answers the questions, pretending that the lie is one of his or her routines.

Example:
Student A asks: *What do you usually do in the evening?*
Student B answers: *I usually drink a glass of hot milk in the evening.*

2. Which of your partner's routines is the lie? Find out by asking *yes/no* questions. Try to detect the lie with as few questions as possible.

Example:
Student A asks: *Is it true? Do you usually drink a glass of hot milk in the evening?*
If the routine is a true one, Student B answers, *Yes, I do.*
If the routine is the lie, Student B answers, *No, I don't. In fact, I usually drink a cup of hot tea in the evening.*

3. Now switch roles. Student B asks questions and Student A answers. Who is a better lie detector?

6   Simple Present Versus Present Progressive: Usually, but Not Today

A. Work in pairs. People sometimes change their routines temporarily. Use the cues to write questions in the simple present. Then answer each question, using your own ideas and following the pattern in the example. In each answer, include *usually* and the time expression given and use the simple present and the present progressive.

1. Q: _Where do Arthur and Nancy eat dinner_____?
   (where / Arthur and Nancy / eat dinner)

   A: _They usually eat dinner at home, but tonight they're eating dinner at a restaurant._
   (tonight)

2. Q: _____?
   (what kind of clothes / Flora / wear)

   A: _____
   (today)

3. Q: _____?
   (which language / Elena and Frank / speak)

   A: _____
   (right now)

4. Q: _____?
   (how / Theresa / get to school)

   A: _____
   (these days)

5. Q: _____?
   (when / the neighbors / go on vacation)

   A: _____
   (this year)

 B. Now work on your own. What about your own routines? Write three statements like those in Part A about temporary changes in your habits or situation. In each statement, include *usually* and a time expression such as *now, today, these days, this semester,* and *this year,* and use the simple present and the present progressive.

Example: *I usually live in Mexico, but this year I'm living in the United States.*

7 **Simple Present Versus Present Progressive; Present Progressive with _Always_:** Dudley's Driving Me Crazy!

A. Complete the e-mail message with the simple present or the present progressive of the verbs in parentheses. Use contractions with subject pronouns and with *not*.

From: Chris
Sent: October 2   7:16 p.m.
To: Max
Subject: Dudley's Driving Me Crazy!

Hi, Max! College __is__ great! I __'m enjoying__ my classes this
      1 (be)   2 (enjoy)

semester. Also, I _____ along well with all my housemates these days, except
                        3 (get)

for Dudley. Everyday life with Dudley _____ very well right now. Let me tell
                                            4 (not, go)

you about his habits. First of all, Dudley often _____ other people's food and
                                                      5 (eat)

even _____ their cookies! Not only that, but he usually
        6 (steal)

_____ his dirty dishes in the sink for someone else to wash. In fact, Greg
      7 (put)

_____ Dudley's breakfast, lunch, and dinner dishes now.
      8 (wash)

Dudley and his friends _____ parties here almost every night.
                              9 (have)

At the moment, they _____ CDs very loudly and
                          10 (play)

_____ on the telephone, too.
      11 (talk)

On top of that, Dudley often _____ our things without asking.
                                  12 (borrow)

He _____ my favorite sweater today.
      13 (wear)

Finally, Dudley _____ our mail sometimes.
                    14 (read)

I _____ this message quickly, just in case he comes in.
      15 (type)

Dudley won't change his bad habits. Slowly but surely, he _____
                                                                16 (drive)

me crazy!

Your buddy, Chris

B. Work with a partner. Imagine that you are Dudley's housemates. Dudley is driving you crazy, too. Use the information in Chris's message to complain to each other about Dudley's bad habits. Use the present progressive and *always*.

Example: *He's always eating my food!*

8 Simple Present Versus Present Progressive: Studying the Universe and Time

Matt just ran into an old friend from high school. Use the words in parentheses to complete the statements and questions in the simple present or the present progressive. Use contractions with subject pronouns and with *not*.

Matt: Hi, Ashley! It's good to see you again. What **are you doing** back here?
1 (you, do)

_____ Are you visiting _____ your parents?
2 (you, visit)

Ashley: I _____ am living _____ at home with them this summer, and I
3 (live)

_____ am working _____ as a waitress at night. But I _____ am looking _____
4 (work)   5 (look)

for a day job, too, because part-time waitresses _____ ~~are not~~ don't earn _____
6 (not earn)

enough money.

Matt: Why _____ are you working _____ so hard this summer?
7 (you, work)

Ashley: I 'm _____ trying _____ to save money for my second year of college.
8 (try)

_____ Are you going _____ to college these days?
9 (you, go)

Matt: Not yet. At this point, I _____ try _____ to figure out what subjects would
10 (try)

interest me.

Ashley: I _____ get _____ interested in astronomy and cosmology.
11 (get)

Matt: Let's see, astronomers _____ observe _____ the planets and the stars. But what
12 (observe)

_____ do cosmologists do _____?
13 (cosmologists, do)

Ashley: They _____ study _____ the universe as a whole. These days cosmologists
14 (study)

_____ are trying _____ to understand the beginning of the universe and the nature
15 (try)

of time. They're my heroes.

Matt: Really? Maybe I should consider studying cosmology, too!

Verbs with Stative Meaning

FORM and FUNCTION

A. Overview

1. Verbs with stative meaning refer to states. They occur in the simple tenses, rather than the progressive, even for uses where other verbs occur in the progressive.

   We **know** more about the moon these days.
   NOT: We ~~are knowing~~ more about the moon these days.

   The sky **seems** dark now.
   NOT: The sky ~~is seeming~~ dark now.

2. Verbs with stative meaning often concern thoughts, attitudes, emotions, possession, the senses, or description. Common verbs with stative meaning include:

THOUGHTS	ATTITUDES	EMOTIONS	POSSESSION	SENSES	DESCRIPTION
believe	appreciate	fear	belong to	feel	appear
feel (= think)	(dis)agree	(dis)like	have	hear	be
forget	doubt	hate	owe	see	cost
know	hope	love	own	smell	look (like)
mean	mind		possess	taste	seem
realize	need				sound (like)
remember	prefer				tend
suppose	want				weigh
think	wish				
understand					

B. Verbs with Stative and Active Meanings

1. Some of the verbs above have both a stative meaning and an active meaning:

STATIVE MEANING	ACTIVE MEANING
People **think** astronomy is exciting. (opinion)	People **are thinking** about solutions to environmental problems. (mental action)
She **doesn't see** well at night. (sense)	He's **seeing** a client at the moment. (meeting with)
The air **smells** good. (sense)	They **are smelling** the roses. (action)
The soup **tastes** salty. (sense)	The chef **is tasting** the soup. (action)
The pillow **feels** soft. (sense)	She's **feeling** the bath water. (action of touching)
They **look** happy. (description)	They **are looking** for their mother. (action)
He **weighs** 180 pounds. (state)	He **is weighing** himself on the scale. (action)
I **have** a good watch. (possession)	I'm **having** a good time. (experience)
She **has** a lot of strength. (quality)	We're **having** dinner. (action)

2. In their active meaning, these verbs can occur in the progressive and simple tenses.

   He **is thinking** about his future now.
   He often **thinks** about his future.

In conversation, certain verbs with stative meaning are sometimes used in the progressive. The present progressive emphasizes emotion or a sense of a process or change.

They **love** it here.

They**'re loving** it here! (emphasis on the emotion)

Digital watches **cost** less these days.

Digital watches **are costing** less these days. (emphasis on change in cost)

GRAMMAR **HOT**SPOT!

1. The verb *be* can have an active meaning, and occur in the progressive, when followed by an adjective describing a behavior that can change. These adjectives include *bad, careful, foolish, good, impolite, kind, lazy, nice, patient, polite, rude,* and *silly.*

   Tom **is** rude. (Tom is generally rude.)

   Tom **is being** rude. (Tom is behaving in a rude way now.)

2. In addition to the uses shown above, *feel* can be followed by an adjective describing health or emotions (e.g., *fine, happy, lonely, sick, strange, tired, well*). In this use, *feel* can occur in the simple or progressive.

   Peter **is feeling** pretty lonely today. = Peter **feels** pretty lonely today.

   Andrew **is feeling** sick. = Andrew **feels** sick.

GRAMMAR PRACTICE 3

Verbs with Stative Meaning

9 **Identifying Verbs with Active Meaning and Verbs with Stative Meaning: Astronomy Class I**

Mark the boldfaced verbs that have active meaning with an *A* and the verbs that have stative meaning with an *S*.

         A   S   A

    [1]Calvin**'s taking** an astronomy class this semester. [2]He **hates** the class. [3]He often **complains**

                          S   a

about it. [4]Calvin **needs** help. [5]Patricia's **studying** astronomy this semester, too. [6]She really

    A   S   A

enjoys the class. [7]She **likes** the professor, too. [8]Patricia often **tries** to help Calvin. [9]She

  A   A   AS

explains things to him. [10]He **listens** to her carefully. [11]He **understands** her explanations.

               S

[12]Calvin **appreciates** Patricia's help.

10 Verbs with Both Active and Stative Meanings: Astronomy Class II

In each pair of sentences, mark the boldfaced verb with active meaning with an *A* and the boldfaced verb with stative meaning with an *S*.

1. a. Calvin **is** shy. *S*

    b. He**'s being** foolish about his problems. *A*

2. a. Calvin doesn't need glasses. He **sees** well. *S*

    b. Calvin**'s seeing** the professor in his office now. *A*   *meeting with.*

3. a. We **think** about time and space in astronomy class. *A*

    b. I **think** astronomy is fascinating. *S* *believe*

4. a. The observatory **has** two telescopes. *S*

    b. We **have** astronomy class in the observatory once a week. *A*

5. a. We **look** for distant stars and planets with the telescopes. *A*

    b. There's Venus! It **looks** beautiful. *S*

11 Simple Present Versus Present Progressive; Stative Versus Active Meaning: Astronomy Class III

Use the words in parentheses to complete the statements and questions in the simple present and present progressive. Use contractions with subject pronouns and with *not*.

I. Teacher: I <u>have</u> something interesting to show you. I <u>'m holding</u> a
                1 (have)   2 (hold)

rock that came from the moon. It _____ to the university museum
                                   3 (belong)

now. Sylvia, let me hand the rock to you.

Sylvia: Wow, I _____ this. I _____ a real moon
                    4 (not, believe)   5 (feel)

rock! Actually, it _____ much different from an Earth rock.
                    6 (not, feel)

Raymond: Hey, Sylvia. You _____ too much time with that rock. Let me hold it
                              7 (spend)

now. I _____ with Sylvia. I _____
        8 (not, agree)   9 (think)

that it _____ lighter than an Earth rock. It _____
          10 (feel)   11 (look)

different, too. It _____ to have a slightly different color.
                    12 (appear)

II. Sylvia: Raymond, what _____ to that rock now?
                                  1 (you, do)

Raymond: I _____ it. It _____ different from an Earth rock, too.
            2 (smell)   3 (smell)

Sylvia: I _____ that. Rocks _____.
                    4 (doubt)   5 (not, smell)

_____ about tasting it, too?
            6 (you, think)

Raymond: Of course. I _____ in using all my senses to experience
                              7 (believe)

nature. I _____ this rock _____
              8 (suppose)   9 (be)

pretty old, so it probably _____ very good.
                                      10 (not, taste)

Sylvia: Raymond, you _____ silly today!
                              11 (be)

12 Using Verbs with Stative Meaning and Verbs with Active Meaning: Are You a Lark or an Owl?

> All humans naturally tend to be awake during the day and to sleep at night. However, some people tend to be "day people" (morning larks), while others tend to be "night people" (night owls).

A. A typical lark and a typical owl are speaking about themselves at two different times of one day. Use the simple present or the present progressive of the words in parentheses to complete the statements. Use contractions with subject pronouns and with *not*.

Lark

Owl

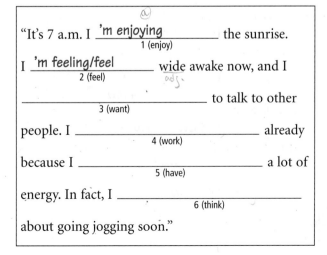

"It's 7 a.m. I **'m enjoying** the sunrise.
                      1 (enjoy)

I **'m feeling/feel** wide awake now, and I
          2 (feel)

_____ to talk to other
          3 (want)

people. I _____ already
                  4 (work)

because I _____ a lot of
                  5 (have)

energy. In fact, I _____
                        6 (think)

about going jogging soon."

"It's 7 a.m. I **'m enjoying** my bed.
                      1 (enjoy)

I **'m feeling/feel** really tired now, and I
          2 (feel)

_____ to talk to anyone.
          3 (not, want)

I _____ yet because I
          4 (not, move)

_____ much energy.
          5 (not, have)

I _____ about
          6 (not, think)

exercising at this hour."

"It's 10 p.m. At this moment, I _____ _____ exhausted and grumpy. In fact,
7 (feel)

I _____ asleep. I
8 (fall)

_____ to get into my nice,
9 (need)

warm bed. I _____ to go
10 (not, want)

anywhere now."

"It's 10 p.m. I _____
7 (not, feel)

sleepy at all now. I _____
8 (start)

to feel alert, cheerful, and energetic!

I _____ hard now.
9 (study)

I _____ to go out with
10 (plan)

some friends soon."

B. 1. Work with a partner. Interview each other. Ask questions about your partner's tendencies.

Examples: *How do you usually feel at 7 a.m.? At what time of day do you have the most energy? Do you prefer to go to bed early or late?*

2. Compare your partner's tendencies to those of the lark and the owl in Part A. Is your partner a lark or an owl or in between?

Check out the *Grammar Links* Website to find out more about larks, owls, and the sleep-wake cycle.

C. 1. Now work with a partner whose tendencies are different from yours. Role-play a telephone conversation between a lark and an owl. Imagine that it is now 7 a.m. The lark tries to persuade the owl to go out and do something. Or imagine that it is now 10 p.m. The owl tries to persuade the lark to go out and do something.

Example: Lark: *Good morning!*
　　　　Owl: *Why are you calling so early? I'm still sleeping. I feel so tired.*
　　　　Lark: *I want to go out now. . . .*

2. Perform your role-play for the class.

Check your progress! Go to the Self-Test for Chapter 1 on the *Grammar Links* Website.

Chapter 2

Simple Past and Past Progressive

Introductory Task: What Were You Doing?

A. Work with a partner. Find out what your partner was doing at various times yesterday. Take turns using the cues to ask and answer questions. Use the past progressive (e.g., *was/were working, was/were eating*) in each question and answer.

Example: Student A: What were you doing yesterday at 6 a.m.?
Student B: I was sleeping. What were you doing yesterday at 6 a.m.?
Student A: I was studying.

1. 6 a.m.
2. 9 a.m.
3. noon

4. 3 p.m.
5. 6 p.m.
6. 9 p.m.

B. Report to the class about the different things you and your partner were doing at the same time. Use the past progressive and *while*.

Example: At 6 a.m., while I was sleeping, Natalie was studying.

C. Work on your own. Write short sentences about five things you did yesterday. Use the simple past (e.g., *worked, ate*).

Example: Yesterday, I studied English. I talked to a friend.

1. _____
2. _____
3. _____
4. _____
5. _____

Simple Past and Past Progressive I

FORM

A. Affirmative Statements

SIMPLE PAST				PAST PROGRESSIVE		

SUBJECT	BASE FORM OF VERB + -ED	
I	**played**	yesterday.
Joe	**played**	yesterday.
They	**played**	yesterday.

SUBJECT	BE + BASE FORM OF VERB + -ING	
I	**was playing**	then.
He	**was playing**	then.
We	**were playing**	then.

(See Appendix 5 for spelling rules for the -ed form of the verb. See Appendix 6 for pronunciation rules for the -ed form of the verb. Some verbs have irregular forms in the simple past; see Appendix 7 for these irregular verbs.)

(See Appendix 3 for spelling rules for the -ing form of the verb.)

B. Negative Statements

SIMPLE PAST			PAST PROGRESSIVE		

SUBJECT	DID + NOT + BASE FORM OF VERB*	
I	**did not work**	at night.
She	**did not work**	at all.
You	**did not work**	on Mondays.

SUBJECT	BE + NOT + BASE FORM OF VERB + -ING*	
I	**was not working**	then.
She	**was not working**	then.
You	**were not working**	then.

C. *Yes/No* Questions and Short Answers

SIMPLE PAST		PAST PROGRESSIVE	
QUESTIONS	SHORT ANSWERS	QUESTIONS	SHORT ANSWERS
Did they **work** every semester?	Yes, they **did.**	**Was** I **working** here then?	Yes, you **were.**
	No, they **didn't.**		No, you **weren't.**
Did he **work** every evening?	Yes, he **did.**	**Was** he **working** that evening?	Yes, he **was.**
	No, he **didn't.**		No, he **wasn't.**
Did you **work** every semester?	Yes, I **did.**	**Were** you **working** here then?	Yes, I **was.**
	No, I **didn't.**		No, I **wasn't.**

(continued on next page)

D. Wh- Questions

Wh- Questions About the Subject

SIMPLE PAST	PAST PROGRESSIVE
Who worked with you?	**Who was working** with you?
What happened?	**What was happening** at that time?

Other Wh- Questions

SIMPLE PAST	PAST PROGRESSIVE
Where did you **work**?	**Who were** you **working** with?
How did Joan **work**?	**Why was** Joan **working**?

*CONTRACTIONS: SIMPLE PAST	*CONTRACTIONS: PAST PROGRESSIVE
did + not → didn't	was + not → wasn't were + not → weren't

GRAMMAR PRACTICE 1

Simple Past and Past Progressive I

1 **Simple Past—Form:** Natural Time

Use the words in parentheses to complete the statements and questions in the simple past. Complete the short answers. Use contractions with *not*.

Child: Tell me about the old days, Grandpa. How __did people live__ a long time ago?

                                          1 (people, live)

Grandfather: Life __was__ very different then.

                                   2 (be)

Child: How _____ their time?

                         3 (people, spend)

Grandfather: In those days, most people _____ farmers. A farmer

                                          4 (be)

               _____ hard from early morning until night.

                   5 (work)

Child: _____ alarm clocks?

                      6 (the farmers, have)

Grandfather: No, _____. They _____ them.

                     7   8 (not, need)

            Their life _____ nature's cycles of day and night. People

                          9 (follow)

            _____ at sunrise. They _____ late,

                10 (wake up)   11 (not, stay up)

            because they _____ electricity.

                          12 (not, have)

Child: _____ alive in those days, Grandpa?

                      13 (you, be)

Grandfather: No, _____.

                     14

Child: How _____ about life in the old days, Grandpa?
                        15 (you, learn)

Grandfather: I _____ about it from *my* grandpa.
                        16 (learn)

2 Simple Past—Irregular Verbs; Questions: Clock Time

A. Debbie's busy life is ruled by the clock. Yesterday her alarm clock rang at 5:45 a.m. and she raced through the day. Use the cues in the box to tell your version of what Debbie did at each time listed below. Use the simple past.

begin working	~~get out of bed~~	read business reports
fall asleep	have dinner with her sister	speak to her boss
drive to work	leave her office	take a shower
eat some french fries	make some phone calls	write some letters
drink a cup of instant coffee	put on her clothes and makeup	see a movie with her boyfriend

1. 5:55 a.m. *She got out of bed at 5:55.*
2. 6:10
3. 6:30
4. 6:40
5. 7:05
6. 8:00
7. 9:15
8. 11:20

9. 12:35 p.m.
10. 1:00
11. 3:45
12. 5:45
13. 6:00
14. 8:20
15. 11:30

B. Work with a partner. Compare your versions of Debbie's schedule by asking and answering *yes/no* and *wh-* questions.

Example: *What time did Debbie get out of bed? She got out of bed at 5:55 a.m.*
Did Debbie and her boyfriend see the movie at 3:45 p.m.? No, they didn't. They saw the movie at 8:20.

3 Past Progressive—Form: Observing Mr. Doe

A. Two men who live in Washington, D.C., are getting acquainted. Use the words in parentheses to complete the statements and questions in the past progressive. Complete the short answers. Use contractions with *not*.

Q: It's nice to meet you. What kind of work do you do?

A: Well, mostly I observe people and write reports about them. For example, last week I

    was observing _____ a man, John Doe.
                    1 (observe)

Q: That sounds interesting. What _was Mr. Doe doing_____ last week?
                                        2 (Mr. Doe, do)

A: Well, last Monday at noon, Mr. Doe _____. When I checked at
                                              3 (sleep)

   2 p.m., though, he _____ anymore.
                          4 (not, sleep)

Q: _____ at 2:00?
                        5 (Mr. Doe, work)

A: No, _____. But he _____ ready
           6   7 (get)

   to start working. He _____ off his beard. And by 4 p.m. he
                              8 (shave)

   _____ with some other men.
           9 (meet)

Q: What _____ about?
                          10 (they, talk)

A: I'm not sure. They _____ loudly enough for me to hear.
                            11 (not, speak)

   I think they _____ something. Mr. Doe
                      12 (plan)

   _____ much then. At midnight, though, Mr. Doe was very
           13 (not, say)

   alert, and he _____ a lot of phone calls from a hotel room.
                        14 (make)

Q: Making phone calls at midnight? That isn't normal! I'm suspicious. Are you a spy?

   _____ Mr. Doe because he's a spy?
                        15 (you, watch)

A: No, _____. I'm a scientist. Last week I
             16

   _____ the effects of air travel across many time zones. Mr. Doe
           17 (study)

   is a businessman from Honolulu. He flew to Washington on Sunday night. While he

   _____ here, he _____
           18 (stay)   19 (experience)

   jet lag. That's normal!

> *jet lag* = a tired and confused feeling resulting from high-speed air travel through
> several time zones.

 B. While Mr. Doe was staying in Washington, he was thinking about home. What was
happening in Honolulu? What was his family doing? Write three sentences about
what was happening at each time.

1. When it was noon in Washington, it was 7 a.m. in Honolulu.

   Example: *People were driving to work. Mrs. Doe was fixing breakfast. . . .*

2. When it was 9 p.m. in Washington, it was 4 p.m. in Honolulu.

3. When it was 3 a.m. in Washington, it was 10 p.m. in Honolulu.

Simple Past and Past Progressive II
▪ Simple Past

FUNCTION

A. Uses of the Simple Past

1. Use the simple past to talk about actions that began and ended in the past:

   - The actions can be single actions, or they can be repeated actions.

     | She **left** her office at 5:00. (single action) |
     | They **milked** the cows every day. (repeated action) |

     PAST   NOW   FUTURE
     left

     PAST   NOW   FUTURE
     milked   milked

   - They can take place at a moment of time or over a period of time.

     | I **was** there yesterday. (moment of time) |
     | He **lived** in New York for three years. (period of time) |

     PAST   NOW   FUTURE
     was there

     PAST   NOW   FUTURE
     lived in New York

2. The simple past is also used with verbs with stative meaning to talk about states in the past.
   (See Chapter 1, Grammar Briefing 3, page 17.)

   | Galileo **was** a scientist. |

B. Time Expressions and Adverbs of Frequency with the Simple Past

1. Time expressions used with the simple past include *yesterday, last Monday* (*week, year,* etc.), *a month* (*a year, a day,* etc.) *ago, in 1980* (*January, the fall,* etc.), *on Sunday* (*March 1, the weekend,* etc.), *at 8:00 a.m.* (*night, the end of the month,* etc.).

   | I stayed home **last weekend.** |
   | I was there **two months ago.** |
   | Classes began **in the fall.** |

2. Adverbs of frequency ([*almost*] *always, usually, often, sometimes, seldom, rarely,* [*almost*] *never,* etc.) are also used with simple past.
   (See Appendix 4 for the position of adverbs of frequency in a sentence.)

   | We **sometimes** worked on the weekend. |
   | I **usually** drank tea. |
   | She was **almost never** on time. |

(continued on next page)

■ Past Progressive

A. Uses of the Past Progressive

1. Use the past progressive to talk about actions in progress at a particular moment or over a period of time in the past. The past progressive emphasizes that the action was in progress.

   At nine o'clock last night, I **was studying** for a math test. (particular moment)

   During the 1990s, he **was working** at that company. (period of time)

2. In contrast to the simple past, the past progressive doesn't specify whether the action was completed. (The simple past emphasizes completion of the action.)

   She **was writing** a paper last night. (She might or might not have finished writing the paper.) *Compare*: She **wrote** a paper last night. (She finished writing the paper.)

3. Use the past progressive in stories to give background information. This information sets the scene for the action which is in the simple past.

   The wind **was blowing** fiercely and the rain **was beating** against the house. (background) Suddenly, the lights **went out**. (action)

B. Time Expressions with the Past Progressive

1. The past progressive is often used in time clauses with *when* and *while*.

   (See Grammar Briefing 3, page 31.)

   He was doing the dishes **while** she was studying.

2. Time expressions used with the past progressive include *then, at that moment, at that time, during the fall (the past year, that period, etc.), last Monday (week, year, etc.).*

   He was studying **at that moment**.

   We were living in the United States **last year**.

Simple Past and Past Progressive II

4 **Simple Past and Past Progressive—Meaning:** Spring Forward

Nell made the following statements. Read each statement and the sentence that follows it. If the sentence is true, mark it with a ✓. If there isn't enough information to decide whether or not it is true, mark it with a ?.

1. I **was explaining** something to a friend last week.

   Nell finished the explanation. _____?_____

2. An event **happened** last April.

   The event ended in April. _____✓_____

3. I **was teaching** English at that time.

   Nell began teaching before that time. _____

4. That Sunday, I didn't read the newspaper, watch television, or listen to the radio because I **was preparing** for my class.

   Nell finished preparing on Sunday. _____

5. I **wrote** several letters that evening.

   Nell finished writing the letters. _____

6. My students are sometimes a little late for class. But that Monday morning I came to class, and all of them **were sitting** in the classroom.

   All the students arrived before Nell. _____

7. They were tired of waiting and wanted to leave, so they **were writing** a note to me.

   The students finished the note. _____

8. They **explained** the reason. I felt really embarrassed about forgetting!

   They finished the explanation. _____

Nell was late because she forgot something that starts on the first Sunday of every April in

most of the United States. What is it? _____

5 **Using Simple Past and Past Progressive in Stories:** Setting the Scene and Telling the Story

A. Work in pairs. Write sentences in the past progressive to continue setting the scene for the action that follows.

I.

My friends and I were having a party. _People were laughing and singing._
                                         1

_____
                      2

_____
                      3

Suddenly, the music stopped. . . .

II.

Henry was sitting at his desk. _____
                                              1

_____
                      2

_____
                      3

Then the door opened. . . .

B. Write sentences in the simple past to tell the actions in the story.

I.

It was getting dark, and snow was beginning to fall. I was hurrying home.

Then I heard footsteps behind me.
                      1

_____
                      2

_____ . . .
                      3

II.

Andrea was working in the art studio. She was painting and listening to the radio.

_____
                      1

_____
                      2

_____ . . .
                      3

C. Write a one-paragraph story of your own. Use the past progressive to set the scene and the simple past to tell the actions.

 See the Grammar Links Website for a model story for this assignment.

Simple Past and Past Progressive in Time Clauses

FORM

TIME CLAUSE	MAIN CLAUSE
When he woke up,	he took a shower.

1. A clause has a subject and a verb.

    > S   V
    > John took a shower.

2. A time clause begins with a time word like *when, while, before,* or *after.* A time clause cannot stand alone; it must be used with a main clause.

    >   time clause   main clause
    > **When** he woke up, he took a shower.
    > NOT: ~~When he woke up.~~

3. The time clause can come before or after the main clause, with no difference in meaning. Use a comma between clauses when the time clause is first but not when the main clause is first.

    > When he woke up, he took a shower.
    > = He took a shower when he woke up.

FORM and FUNCTION

A. Simple Past + Simple Past in Sentences with Time Clauses

Use simple past for two completed actions. Use *before, after, when,* or *while* in the time clause. These actions can occur:

*   One before the other.

>   later action   earlier action
> He **took** a bath **when/after** he **woke up.**
>
> earlier action   later action
> He **shaved before** he **ate** breakfast.

*   At the same time.

>   same time
> **When/While** he had breakfast,
>   same time
> he **listened** to the radio.

(continued on next page)

B. Simple Past + Past Progressive in Sentences with Time Clauses

Use simple past + past progressive to talk about an action that began and ended while another action was in progress. Use the simple past for the completed action and the past progressive for the action that was in progress.

Use *while* or *when* in the time clause:

- Clauses with the past progressive can begin with *while* or *when*.

- Clauses with the simple past must begin with *when*.

action in progress
While/When <u>he **was working**</u>,
completed action
<u>Charlie **spilled**</u> his coffee.

action in progress	completed action
He **was working when** he **spilled** his coffee.

NOT: He was working ~~while~~ he spilled his coffee.

C. Past Progressive + Past Progressive in Sentences with Time Clauses

Use past progressive + past progressive to talk about two actions that were in progress at the same time. Use *when* or *while* in the time clause.

PAST ◄──────── NOW ▼ ──────► FUTURE

was eating
was thinking

action in progress
While/When <u>she **was eating**</u>,
action in progress
<u>she **was thinking**</u> about her homework.

Simple Past and Past Progressive in Time Clauses

Time Zones

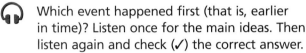

6 The Simple Past and Time Clauses—Meaning: Standard Time

Which event happened first (that is, earlier in time)? Listen once for the main ideas. Then listen again and check (✓) the correct answer.

1. ❏ First, most people were farmers.
   ❏ First, it wasn't important for them to know the exact time.
   ✓ Both at the same time.

2. ❏ First, clock time became important.
   ❏ First, modern transportation and communications began to develop.
   ❏ Both at the same time.

3. ❏ First, the United States had standard time.
   ❏ First, each town or city had its own time.
   ❏ Both at the same time.

4. ❏ First, it was 7:00 a.m. in Philadelphia.
   ❏ First, it was 7:16 a.m. in Boston.
   ❏ Both at the same time.

5. ❏ First, the railroads spread throughout the country.
   ❏ First, the differences in times became a problem.
   ❏ Both at the same time.

6. ❏ First, the passengers traveled across the country.
   ❏ First, they changed their watches.
   ❏ Both at the same time.

The railroads spread throughout the country in the 1880s.

7. ❏ First, train schedules were confusing.
   ❏ First, railroad officials decided to set their clocks to a standard time.
   ❏ Both at the same time.

8. ❏ First, standard time started.
   ❏ First, officials divided the United States into four time zones.
   ❏ Both at the same time.

9. ❏ First, it was 7:00 a.m. in Philadelphia.
   ❏ First, it was 7:00 a.m. in Boston.
   ❏ Both at the same time.

See the *Grammar Links* Website for more information about standard time and time zones.

7 The Simple Past and Past Progressive in Time Clauses; Combining Sentences: Early Calendars

Use the time expressions to combine the sentences into a sentence with two clauses. You must use the time expression with the right clause. Use a comma when necessary.

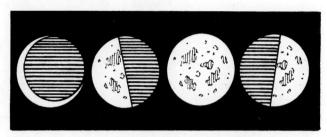

A Moon (Lunar) Cycle

1. Ancient peoples needed to be able to predict the seasons.

   Ancient peoples began to farm.

   + (after)
   After ancient peoples began to farm, they needed to be able to predict the seasons. OR Ancient peoples needed to be able to predict the seasons after they began to farm.

2. They learned to recognize the moon's patterns.

   They observed the moon's changes for a long time.

   + (before)

3. They recorded the moon's cycles.

   They were observing the moon.

   + (while)

4. They made a calendar based on lunar months.

   They understood the cycles of the moon.

   + (after)

5. They were using the lunar calendar.

   They found a problem with the lunar calendar.

   + (while)

6. A few years passed.

   The calendar and the seasons didn't match anymore.

   + (after)

7. The calendar became more accurate.

   They added days to the year.

   + (when)

A lunar month averages 29½ days. A year equals 365 days. Approximately how many days did they need to add to 12 lunar months to make the calendar more accurate?

To learn more about the history of calendars, go to the *Grammar Links* Website.

8 **The Simple Past Versus Past Progressive in Time Clauses:**
A Night Person's Bad Day

A. Complete the sentences with the simple past or past progressive of the verbs in parentheses.

1. When Charlie's alarm clock __rang_____ (ring), he

   __felt_____ (feel) sleepy and confused.

2. After Charlie _____ (wake up), he _____ (remember)

   that he had an early appointment with the dentist.

3. Charlie _____ (drop) his watch into the tub while he

   _____ (take) his bath.

4. When Charlie _____ (ride) the bus, he

   _____ (fall) asleep and _____ (miss)

   his stop.

5. While Charlie _____ (run) back to the dentist's office, he

   _____ (trip) and _____ (hurt) his knee.

6. While Charlie _____ (have) lunch, he

   _____ (spill) coffee on his new shirt.

7. Charlie finally _____ (start) to feel more alert before he

   _____ (leave) to go to work at the observatory.

8. After it _____ (get) dark, Charlie

   _____ (begin) to observe the stars.

9. While he _____ (look) through the telescope, an idea

   _____ (hit) him: He was definitely a night person.

10. Before the sun _____ (come up), Charlie

    _____ (make) a decision: He would always be an astronomer.

 B. Think of times when things went wrong for you. Write three kinds of sentences about those times.

1. Write two sentences using *when*, *before*, or *after* and the simple past for two completed actions.

Example: After I got to class, I realized that my homework was at home. OR
I remembered the answer when the test was over.

2. Write two sentences using *when* or *while* and the simple past and past progressive for action that occurred when another action was in progress.

Example: When I was traveling to the United States, the airline lost my luggage. OR I cut myself while I was shaving.

3. Write two sentences using *when* or *while* and the past progressive for two actions in progress at the same time. Then add sentences that tell what happened.

Example: I was studying while I was eating lunch. I spilled my soup on my book. OR When I was driving to class, I was putting on my makeup. I almost had an accident.

---

9 **Simple Past, Past Progressive, and Time Clauses:** A Legend of Discovery

Complete the paragraph with the simple past or the past progressive of the words in parentheses. In some cases, either tense is possible.

Galileo Galilei ___was_____
                        1 (be)

an Italian scientist. He _____
                              2 (live)

from 1564 to 1642. Galileo _____
                                   3 (make)

one of his first discoveries while he

_____ a service at
    4 (attend)

the cathedral in Pisa. During the service, he

_____ a hanging
    5 (notice)

lamp. Air currents _____
                         6 (blow)

gently through the cathedral at the time, and the

lamp _____ back and
         7 (swing)

forth. While Galileo _____
                           8 (watch)

the lamp, he _____
                  9 (realize)

that each swing took an equal amount of time,

no matter how wide it was. After he

_____ home, he
    10 (go)

_____ experiments, using weights and strings. In this way, he
    11 (make)

_____ the principle of the pendulum (from a Latin word meaning
    12 (discover)

"hanging" or "swinging"). In 1656, a Dutch astronomer, Christiaan Huygens,

_____ Galileo's discovery to build the first pendulum clock.
    13 (use)

Used To

FORM

A. Affirmative Statements

We **used to believe** in the man in the moon.

B. Negative Statements

They **didn't use to have** clocks.

C. Yes/No Questions

Did you **use to play** every day?

D. Wh- Questions

Where **did** you **use to play**?

Who **used to play** with you?

FUNCTION

Talking About Past Actions and States: *Used To* Versus *Would*

1. Use *used to* to talk about actions and states that existed in the past but don't exist anymore. *Used to* emphasizes a contrast between the past and present.

   People **used to tell** time by the sun (but they don't anymore).

   People **didn't use to have** digital watches (but now they do).

2. *Would*, like *used to*, can be used to talk about repeated actions in the past. *Would* can't be used to talk about states.

   When I was young, I **would go/used to go** swimming every chance I got.

   I **used to be** a good swimmer.
   NOT: I ~~would be~~ a good swimmer.

   I **used to like** going to the beach.
   NOT: I ~~would like~~ going to the beach.

GRAMMAR **HOT**SPOT!

Use *used to* except in sentences with *did* (negatives, *yes/no* questions, and *wh-* questions with *did*). In those sentences, use *use to*.

What **did** you **use to do**?
NOT: What did you ~~used to~~ do?

Used To

10 **Used To—Form:** Long, Long Ago

An Hourglass

A Water Clock

A Sundial

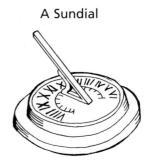

Rewrite the following sentences. Use *used to*.

1. People didn't know as much about the solar system and the universe as we do now.

    People didn't use to know as much about the solar system and the universe as we do now.

2. What did people believe about the earth?

    _____

3. People believed the earth was the center of the universe.

    _____

4. They didn't know that the universe has no center.

    _____

5. How did people measure time?

    _____

6. People didn't have mechanical clocks or watches.

    _____

7. They used the natural motion of the sun to measure time with sundials.

    _____

8. The Greeks had water clocks for measuring time.

    _____

9. What other kinds of clocks did people use?

    _____

10. Some of them kept time with sand clocks, or hourglasses.

    _____

11 *Used To* Versus *Would*: When We Were Children

A. Replace *used to* with *would* in the sentences where it can be used. If *would* can't be used, write NC (no change).

                     NC
1. My older brother used to want to be a firefighter.

         would
2. He ~~used to~~ play with his toy fire trucks for hours at a time.

3. In the summer time, my brother used to pretend that the plants in our garden were on fire.

4. He used to spray water on the plants to put out the pretend fire.

5. I used to like to watch him spray water all over the place.

6. Our neighbors used to complain whenever he sprayed water into their garden.

7. We didn't use to understand why they minded getting wet.

8. We used to think that grownups didn't know how to have fun.

B. Write three pairs of sentences about things that you did in your childhood but don't do any longer. In each pair of sentences, use *used to* in the first sentence. Then use *would*, if possible, or *used to* in the next sentence.

Example: I used to spend a lot of time with my grandmother in the summers.
         She would tell me about life in the old days.

12 *Used To; Wh-* and *Yes/No* Questions: Did You Use To . . . ?

Work with a partner. Using the verbs in the box, write three *yes/no* and three *wh-* questions to ask your partner about his or her past. Take turns asking and answering the questions.

drink	go	have	play	use	want
eat	hate	like	study	visit	wear

Example: What did you use to want to be? OR
        Did you use to want to be an astronomer?

Now tell the class one thing about your partner's past.

Example: Anna used to want to be a race car driver.

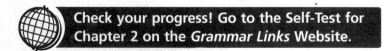

Check your progress! Go to the Self-Test for Chapter 2 on the *Grammar Links* Website.

Wrap-up Activities

1 **A Telescope in Space:** EDITING

Correct the 13 errors in the article. There are errors in verb forms and tenses. Some errors can be corrected in more than one way. The first error is corrected for you.

A Telescope in Space

Astronomers didn't ~~used~~ **use** to have powerful telescopes to look into space and observe distant parts of the universe. Most scientists use to believe that the universe was static. (In this case, the word "static" is meaning "not becoming larger or smaller.") Then, in the 1920s, an American astronomer, Edwin Hubble, was having the opportunity to use a big new telescope in California to observe nearby galaxies. In 1929, he made a discovery. The galaxies were moving away from each other. The universe were expanding. This meant that it once was very, very small. Hubble's discovery helped cosmologists to develop the theory of the big bang.

But in order to learn more about the beginning of the universe, scientists were needing a telescope outside Earth's atmosphere to provide a clear view of distant galaxies. After years of planning, a team of scientists and engineers at the National Aeronautics and Space Administration (NASA) sended a large telescope into space in 1990. They were naming it the Hubble Space Telescope (HST) after Edwin Hubble. After they were putting HST into orbit, they got an unpleasant surprise. HST didn't worked correctly. Why was this? They were building HST, while they made an error. In 1993, astronauts correct the error. In simple terms, NASA corrected the telescope's vision by fitting it with contact lenses. These days, HST sending clear, beautiful images to Earth. So now we are learning more about the expansion of the universe, the big bang, and the beginning of time.

2 What Was the Question? WRITING/SPEAKING

The following are the answers that a student gave to questions asked in an interview.

Step 1 Work with a partner. Write questions that fit the answers.

1. Q: _How old are you?_

   A: Twenty, almost twenty-one.

2. Q: _____

   A: One brother and two sisters.

3. Q: _____

   A: Two. My native language and English.

4. Q: _____

   A: Swim, play the guitar, and go to movies.

5. Q: _____

   A: Yes, this semester I'm doing that.

6. Q: _____

   A: Three years ago.

7. Q: _____

   A: A year ago today, I was working and thinking about going back to school.

8. Q: _____

   A: Yes, I used to, but not now.

Step 2 Now work with a different partner. Use the questions you wrote in Step 1 to interview each other. Then report to the class. Tell the most interesting thing you learned about your partner.

3 Origin Story: WRITING

The big bang is the scientific explanation of the origin of the universe and the beginning of time. Read the beginning of an origin story from some of the first people who lived in Australia:

> In the beginning, the earth was an endless cloudy plain. It was separated from both the sky and the sea and covered by shadowy twilight. Above the earth, there were no stars or sun or moon. On the surface of the earth, there were no plants or animals. But underneath the surface, the stars were twinkling, the sun was shining, and the moon was becoming larger and smaller while all the forms of life were sleeping and waiting to come to life. Then, on the morning of the first day, the sun burst through the earth's surface and covered the land with its light....

Adapted from: Chatwin, Bruce. *The Songlines*. London: Jonathan Cape Ltd., 1987, p. 72.

Write a one-paragraph origin story. You can write a story that you know or make one up. Use the simple past and past progressive. Include at least two sentences with time clauses.

 See the *Grammar Links* Website for a model story for this assignment.

4 Terratoo: SPEAKING

Step 1 Work in small groups. Imagine that you and your partners now live on Terratoo, an Earth-like planet in a distant galaxy. Discuss what your imaginary planet is like and what is going on there. Decide on the answers to these questions about it:

1. *Time*: How long are the days, nights, seasons, and years? What other measures of time do you use?

2. *The planet*: How does it look? What is the weather like? What kinds of plants and animals live there?

3. *Daily life*: What kind of language do you speak? What kind of food do you eat? What do you like to do for fun?

4. *Activities*: What time is it on your part of the planet right now? What's happening? What are the people around you doing?

Step 2 Describe your version of Terratoo to the class.

Step 3 Now imagine that you must all go to live on one planet together. As a class, discuss the different versions of Terratoo and decide which one you want to live on.

Present and Past: Perfect and Perfect Progressive

TOPIC FOCUS
The Pace of Life

UNIT OBJECTIVES

- **the present perfect and the present perfect progressive**
  (Many people *have learned* to use computers. We *have been working* with them for years.)

- **the present perfect versus the simple past**
  (I *have been* to Egypt. I *went* there several years ago.)

- **the past perfect and the past perfect progressive**
  (Before he came to the United States, he *had studied* English. He *had been taking* classes for several months before he decided to study abroad.)

Grammar in Action

🎧 Reading and Listening: The Pace of Life

Read and listen to this passage from a textbook.

The pace, or speed, of life **hasn't** always **been** as fast as it is now. In the last 200 years, there **have been** important changes in technology. The first changes led to the industrial age, which lasted from the early 1800s to the mid-1900s. More recent changes **have led** to the information age, which continues today. In the industrial age, the pace of life became much faster. That trend **has continued** in the information age.

Transportation in the Industrial Age

Before the industrial age began, people **had followed** the cycles of nature. They lived as their parents and grandparents **had lived**. People and information **had** never **moved** faster than the speed of a fast horse or sailing ship. The pace of life **had stayed** much the same for thousands of years. But during the 1800s, new technology, such as trains and the telegraph, changed everything. By the late 1800s, the speed of transportation and communications **had increased** greatly. And because the new technology **had made** it possible for people to do more in less time, the pace of life started to speed up, too.

Since the middle of the 1900s, we **have been experiencing** an important and rapid change in information technology. Before the 1960s, very few people **had** ever **worked** with a computer. Since then, millions of people **have become** computer users. The computer **has given** us the ability to store, send, and receive very large amounts of information instantly. In the information age, the speed of change **has** also **speeded up**—lately, things **have been changing** faster than ever before. And it seems that time and life **have been moving** faster, too.

Communication in the Information Age

How **have** people **reacted** to the new technology and new speeds? Some people believe that the new technology **has brought** us many benefits and **made** our lives more convenient and exciting. Others believe that our lives **haven't improved** because the fast pace isn't natural and it **has caused** us too much stress.

How **have** you **been feeling** about the pace of your life recently? **Has** it **been** too fast, just right, or too slow?

---

technology = the use of scientific knowledge for practical purposes. *age* = a period of time in history. *trend* = a general direction or tendency. *telegraph* = a system for sending messages electrically over a wire.

Think About Grammar

A. Read each pair of sentences. Circle the boldfaced verbs that talk about actions that occurred before a time in the past. Underline the boldfaced verbs that talk about actions that began in the past but continue to the present.

1. a. Since the information age began, people **have experienced** many changes.

   b. Before the industrial age began, people **had experienced** few changes.

2. a. By the late 1800s, the speed of communications **had gotten** much faster.

   b. Since the beginning of the information age, the speed of communications **has gotten** much faster.

3. a. In recent times, many people **have worked** with computers.

   b. Before the 1960s, only a few people **had worked** with computers.

4. a. The speed of technological change **has increased** since computers were introduced.

   b. The speed of technological change **had increased** by the 1990s.

5. a. Until the early 1800s, the pace of life **had stayed** slow.

   b. Lately, the pace of life **has stayed** fast.

B. Work with a partner. Compare and discuss your answers to Part A. The circled verbs are in the past perfect. The underlined verbs are in the present perfect. How are the forms for these tenses similar? How are they different?

 To learn more about the industrial age and the information age, go to the *Grammar Links* Website.

Present Perfect and Present Perfect Progressive

Introductory Task: Quiz: What Is Your Time Type?

A. Write sentences with a verb in the present perfect (e.g., *have become*) to answer the following questions. In each sentence, include the adverb of frequency that is most appropriate for you: *often*, *sometimes*, or *rarely*.

Example: I have sometimes become irritated when I had to wait in line. OR I have rarely gotten angry when traffic was moving slowly.

Your Time Type Quiz

1. How frequently have you become irritated when you had to wait in line?

   _____

2. How frequently have you gotten angry when traffic was moving slowly?

   _____

3. How frequently have you worried about being late for a party?

   _____

4. How frequently have you felt anxious when you didn't have anything to do?

   _____

5. How frequently have you wanted to make every moment of your life count?

   _____

6. How frequently have you wished that you had more time in a day?

   _____

B. Work with a partner. Find out your partner's time type. Read your partner's answers and give 3 points for each answer with *often*, 2 points for each *sometimes*, and 1 point for each *rarely*. Then add up the points and look at page A-1 to learn what the score means.

C. Report to the class. What have you learned about your partner? Is your partner a "fast" or "slow" person?

Present Perfect and Present Perfect Progressive I

FORM

A. Affirmative Statements

PRESENT PERFECT			PRESENT PERFECT PROGRESSIVE		
SUBJECT	*HAVE/HAS + PAST PARTICIPLE**		SUBJECT	*HAVE/HAS + BEEN + PRESENT PARTICIPLE**	
I	**have done**	that.	I	**have been doing**	that.
She	**has done**	that.	She	**has been doing**	that.

(See Appendix 7 for the past participles of irregular verbs.)

(See Appendix 3 for spelling rules for the *-ing* form of the verb.)

B. Negative Statements

PRESENT PERFECT			PRESENT PERFECT PROGRESSIVE		
SUBJECT	*HAVE/HAS + NOT + PAST PARTICIPLE**		SUBJECT	*HAVE/HAS + NOT + BEEN + PRESENT PARTICIPLE**	
Bob	**has not done**	that.	Bob	**has not been doing**	that.
We	**have not done**	that.	We	**have not been doing**	that.

C. *Yes/No* Questions and Short Answers

PRESENT PERFECT		PRESENT PERFECT PROGRESSIVE	
QUESTIONS	SHORT ANSWERS	QUESTIONS	SHORT ANSWERS
Have you **done** that?	Yes, I **have**.	**Have** you **been doing** that?	Yes, I **have (been)**.
	No, I **haven't**.		No, I **haven't (been)**.
Has he **done** that?	Yes, he **has**.	**Has** he **been doing** that?	Yes, he **has (been)**.
	No, he **hasn't**.		No, he **hasn't (been)**.

(continued on next page)

D. Wh- Questions

Wh- Questions About the Subject

PRESENT PERFECT*	PRESENT PERFECT PROGRESSIVE*
Who has done that?	**Who has been doing** that?
What has happened?	**What has been happening**?

Other Wh- Questions

PRESENT PERFECT*	PRESENT PERFECT PROGRESSIVE*
What have they **done**?	**What have** they **been doing**?
Where has it **gone**?	**Why has** she **been doing** that?

*CONTRACTIONS

I + have → I've
he/she/it + has → he's/she's/it's
we/you/they + have → we've/you've/they've
wh- word + has → who's, what's, where's, etc.

have + not → haven't
has + not → hasn't

GRAMMAR **HOT**SPOT!

The contraction 's can be *is* or *has*:

- 's + present participle = *is*.

  > She**'s climbing** Mount Everest. (present progressive, *'s = is*; *climbing* is the present participle of *climb*)

- 's + past participle = *has*.

  > She**'s climbed** Mount McKinley. (present perfect, *'s = has*; *climbed* is the past participle of *climb*)

  > She**'s been climbing** mountains for a long time. (present perfect progressive, *'s = has*; *been* is the past participle of *be*)

Present Perfect and Present Perfect Progressive I

1 Present Perfect—Form: A Conference on the Pace of Life

Use the words in parentheses to complete the statements and questions in the present perfect. Complete the short answers. Use contractions with subject pronouns and with *not*.

Moderator: People used to live according to natural time, but they don't anymore. What

 __has happened_____ as a result? _____ their
 1 (happen)   2 (people, lose)

 sense of natural time?

Participant 1: Yes, _____. Natural time _____.
 3   4 (not, change)

 However, people's ideas and feelings about time _____.
 5 (change)

Moderator: Why _____?
 6 (this, happen)

Participant 2: Modern technology _____ many changes.
 7 (cause)

Moderator: Time _____, but it seems to go faster.
 8 (not, speed up)

 _____?
 9 (life, speed up)

Participant 3: Yes, _____. And some people
 10

 _____ well to the fast pace of life.
 11 (not, react)

 They _____ a lot of stress.
 12 (feel)

Participant 1: I agree. Lately, we Americans _____ the feeling that we don't
 13 (have)

 have enough time.

Moderator: But new technology _____ to many products to help us save
 14 (lead)

 time: microwave ovens, personal computers, cell phones, and so on.

Participant 2: That's true. But it _____ that way. In the end,
 15 (not, work out)

 the new technology _____ more time than
 16 (take)

 it _____ us.
 17 (give)

> *conference* = a meeting to discuss a subject. *moderator* = the person who directs
> a discussion.

 Go to the *Grammar Links* Website to find out more about technology and the
pace of life.

2 Present Perfect Progressive—Form: What Have People Been Doing? I

Use the words in parentheses to write statements and questions. Use present perfect progressive. Complete the short answers. Use contractions with subject pronouns and with *not*.

Lauren, who is from a small town, has been visiting the big city where her friend Shelly lives. They planned to meet in the park at noon. It's now 12:30.

Lauren: Hi, Shelly. You look tired. <u>Have you been running</u>_____?
                                                    1 (you / run)

Shelly: Yes, _____. I'm sorry I'm late.
                             2

Lauren: That's okay. _____.
                                        3 (I / have / a good time)

Shelly: Really? _____?
                                4 (what / you / do)

Lauren: _____. It's been interesting.
                         5 (I / watch / all the people)

Shelly: Interesting? _____?
                               6 (what / the people / do)

_____?
                           7 (they / relax / in the park)

Lauren: No, _____. Everyone has been really busy. Do you
                            8

see that guy sitting on the bench over there?

Shelly: The one with the laptop computer? _____?
                                    9 (he / work)

Lauren: Yes, _____.
                         10

_____.
                      11 (he / eat / lunch / at the same time)

_____.
                 12 (that woman / make / calls on her cell phone)

_____.
                 13 (everything / move / fast)

Except for the traffic. _____.
                          14 (the traffic / not / move / at all)

3 Contractions with Present Progressive, Present Perfect, and Present Perfect Progressive: Answering Questions

Listen and complete the answer to each question. Use *is* or *has*. Then listen again to check your answers.

1. Lisa <u>has</u>_____.

2. The stress <u>is</u>_____.

3. Someone else _____.

4. I think her father _____.

5. His job _____.

6. I'm not sure, but something _____.

7. The computer _____.

8. Something _____.

9. Another person _____.

10. Her job _____.

11. I don't know, but something _____.

12. The boredom _____.

13. I think his mother _____.

14. Jason _____.

15. The printer _____.

16. Everything _____.

Present Perfect and Present Perfect Progressive II
■ Present Perfect

FUNCTION

A. Actions and States at an Unspecified Time in the Past

1. Use the present perfect to talk about actions and states that occurred at an unspecified time in the past. The actions and states can be single or repeated:

We **have read** the paper.

I **have rewritten** the paper three times.

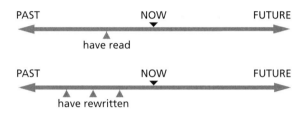

2. The present perfect indicates that the past action or state is connected to the present in some way. For example:

- It occurred recently.

I've just **graduated** from college.

- The speaker thinks it could happen again.

I've **played** tennis a few times.

- It is relevant to the present situation.

I can do the job because I've **had** experience with those machines.

Time Expressions and Adverbs of Frequency

1. When used to talk about actions and states at an unspecified time in the past, the present perfect can occur with time expressions including:

- *Already, yet* (in questions and negatives), *so far*, and *still*.

She has **already** graduated from college.

I haven't finished **yet**.

- *Just, recently*, and *lately*, if the action or state was recent.

We have **just** eaten in that restaurant.

2. The present perfect can also occur with adverbs of frequency, including *ever* (in questions and negatives); *never, sometimes, always*, etc.; and *once* (*three times*, etc.).

Have you **ever** been to Spain?

He has **never** eaten in that restaurant.

I've been there **twice**.

(continued on next page)

B. Actions and States Continuing to the Present

Use the present perfect with a time expression of duration (see below) to talk about actions and states that began in the past and continue to the present.	They **have lived** here **for 10 years**.

```
PAST              NOW              FUTURE
◄─────────────────▼───────────────────►
       10 years
       lived here
```

Time Expressions of Duration

Time expressions of duration begin with *for*, *since*, or *all*. They tell how long an action or state has been occurring:

- *For* and *all* tell the length of time. (*For* can sometimes be omitted.)

I have taught **(for) five years**.

They've lived here **all their lives**.

```
PAST              NOW              FUTURE
◄─────────────────▼───────────────────►
    5 years
    taught
```

- *Since* tells the beginning of the time period.

He's been sick **since Monday**.

```
PAST              NOW              FUTURE
◄─────────────────▼───────────────────►
    ▲
  Monday
  got sick
```

■ Present Perfect Progressive

FUNCTION

Actions Continuing to the Present

Use the present perfect progressive to talk about actions that began in the past and continue to the present. It often emphasizes that the action is ongoing.	She**'s been working**. We**'ve been taking** the kids to school.

```
PAST              NOW              FUTURE
◄─────────────────▼───────────────────►
    's been working
```

The present perfect progressive can occur with *for*, *since*, or *all* and with the other time expressions used with the present perfect (*recently*, *lately*, etc.). It is **not** used with adverbs of frequency.	I've been snowboarding **for three years**. We've been singing in a band **since 1996**. Joe**'s** been practicing a lot **lately**. **NOT**: Joe's been practicing ~~often/three times~~.

Present Perfect and Present Perfect Progressive II

4   Present Perfect—Actions at Unspecified Past Times: Free Time

A. Work in pairs. Student A uses the cues in List A to ask Student B questions. Then Student B uses the cues in List B to ask Student A questions. Use the present perfect and *ever* in each question.

Example: Student A: *Have you ever been to Disneyland?*
                    Student B: *No, I haven't. I've never been to Disneyland. OR No, I haven't been there yet.*
                                      OR Yes, I have. I've been to Disneyland once (twice/many times).

List A	List B
1. be to Disneyland	9. go on a vacation in India
2. build a campfire	10. get lost in a forest
3. drive a sports car	11. ride a camel
4. eat Korean food	12. drink carrot juice
5. read a novel in English	13. write a poem
6. swim across a lake	14. sleep on a beach
7. meet a movie star	15. see a comet
8. take a photo of a sunrise	16. draw a picture of your own face

B. Now ask your partner questions again. Use the verbs in the cues, but change what follows the verbs.

Example: Student A: *Have you ever been to Las Vegas?*
                    Student B: *No, I haven't. I've never been to Las Vegas. OR Yes, I have.*
                                      I've been to Las Vegas once (twice/many times).

5   Present Perfect—Actions and States Continuing to the Present: Tell Me About Yourself

A. Work in pairs. Ask each other these questions. When your partner answers *yes* to a question, ask a second question, using the present perfect, to find out *how long* the fact has been true about him or her. Your partner answers using the present perfect and *since, for,* or *all*.

Example: A: *Do you live in Rockville?* B: *Yes, I do.* A: *How long have you lived here?*
                    B: *I've lived here since 2001/for three months/all my life.*

1. Do you live in _____?
   (name of city or town)

2. Are you a student at _____?
   (name of your school)

3. Are you married?

4. Are you a parent?

5. Do you have a job?

6. Do you know _____?
   (name of another student)

7. Do you drive?

8. Do you own a car?

9. Do you play _____?
   (a game or sport)

10. Do you like _____?
    (a kind of music, a certain food, etc.)

B. Tell the class two things about your partner. Use the present perfect and time expressions of duration.

Example: Leticia has lived in Rockville for three months.

6 **Using Present Perfect Progressive:** What Have People Been Doing? II

For Student A.

Café

 A. Work in pairs to role-play two cell-phone conversations. First, Student A looks at the picture on this page. Then Student B looks at the picture on page A-1. Imagine that you have spent thirty minutes in the place shown in your picture. Your partner calls you and wants to know what's been happening. Tell your partner what all the people have been doing. You can use your imagination to add details. Use the present perfect progressive. Use time expressions in some of your sentences.

Example: Student A: Hello.
Student B: Hi. Where are you? What have you been doing?
Student A: I'm in a café. I've been watching all the people here.
Student B: Who's there? What have they been doing?
Student A: Well, there are two women here. They've been eating. They've also been talking about their husbands for the last 10 minutes. And there's . . .

B. Write five sentences about what the people in one of the pictures have been doing. Use a time expression in each sentence.

Example: The women have been talking about their husbands for 10 minutes.

Present Perfect Versus Present Perfect Progressive

FUNCTION

A. Talking About Completed Actions and States

To talk about completed actions and states, use the present perfect. Do not use the present perfect progressive.

She **has graduated** from college.
NOT: She ~~has been graduating~~ from college.

I've **studied** French several times.
NOT: I've ~~been studying~~ French several times.

B. Talking About Actions and States Continuing to the Present

1. For **actions** continuing to the present:

   • Use the **present perfect** with a time expression of duration (*for, since, all*).

   They**'ve watched** TV **since this morning**.

   • Use the **present perfect progressive** alone or with a time expression of duration.

   They**'ve been watching** TV.

   They**'ve been watching** TV **since this morning**.

   With time expressions of duration, there is little difference in meaning between the present perfect and present perfect progressive.

   We**'ve worked all day**. = We**'ve been working all day**.

2. For **states** continuing to the present, use only the **present perfect**. Progressives are not usually used with verbs that have stative meaning.

   This summer **has seemed** hotter than usual.
   NOT USUALLY: This summer ~~has been seeming~~ hotter than usual.

GRAMMAR **HOT**SPOT!

1. With some verbs, verb + object indicates progress toward a result (*write a paper, read a book, build a house*). In these cases, use the present perfect progressive to talk about actions continuing to the present. The present perfect **cannot** be used.

   She**'s been writing** a novel for five years. (end result = a written novel)
   NOT: She**'s** ~~written~~ a novel for five years.

2. In sentences without time expressions of duration, the present perfect and present perfect progressive have different meanings: The present perfect talks about completed events; the present perfect progressive talks about events continuing to the present.

   I**'ve studied** chemistry. (I studied it at some time in the past.)

   I**'ve been studying** chemistry. (I'm still studying it.)

Present Perfect Versus Present Perfect Progressive

7 **Present Perfect and Present Perfect Progressive—Meaning:** People, Places, and Paces

Work with a partner. Decide whether **a** or **b** is the correct explanation of the meaning of the first sentence. Circle the letter.

1. Bruce **has been working** on a report about the pace of life in big cities.

   a. He finished the report at some time in the past.

   b. He's still working on the report. *(circled)*

2. Greta **has worked** in a big city.

   a. She worked in a big city at some time in the past, but she doesn't work there now.

   b. She's still working in a big city.

3. Andy **has worked** all week on his paper about the pace of life in small towns.

   a. He finished his paper at some time in the past.

   b. He's still working on his paper.

4. Gail and Brad **have lived** in the country since they finished school.

   a. They lived in the country at some time in the past, but they don't live there now.

   b. They're still living in the country.

5. James **has been living** in a small town for two years.

   a. He lived in a small town at some time in the past, but he doesn't live there now.

   b. He's still living in a small town.

6. Lesley and I **have lived** on a farm.

   a. We lived on a farm at some time in the past, but we don't live there now.

   b. We're still living on a farm.

8 **Present Perfect Versus Present Perfect Progressive:** Living in the Past in the Present

The Amish people immigrated to North America in the 1700s. Since then, their way of life has changed very little. Read about an Amish couple on a typical day in their lives. Use the words in parentheses to complete the sentences. Use the present perfect progressive where possible. Use the present perfect elsewhere. Use contractions with *not*.

10 a.m.: Jacob is working in a field on his farm. He __has been working__ since 8 a.m., but he
                                                        1 (work)

__hasn't finished__ plowing the field yet. As usual, he is using horses to pull the plow.
   2 (not, finish)

Because Amish farmers don't often use modern technology, Jacob _____
                                                                 3 (not, ever, use)

a tractor. His twelve-year-old son, Amos, is with him in the field.

He _____ 4 (help) his father this morning. Over the years, Amos

_____ 5 (help) his father many times. Amos _____ 6 (always, know)

that someday he, too, will be a farmer and farm in the traditional way.

Noon: Rebecca is working in the house. She _____ 7 (sew) by hand all

morning. She _____ 8 (make) a quilt

for the past few weeks, and so far she

_____ 9 (finish) half of it. Rebecca's

young daughter Rachel _____ 10 (be)

at her side all morning. For the past six months,

Rebecca _____ 11 (teach) Rachel how

to sew. Although Rachel isn't ready to make a quilt yet,

she _____ 12 (already, make) three dresses, and she wears them often.

8 p.m.: The Fishers are returning home from a visit to friends. Jacob is driving them in a buggy pulled by a

horse. He _____ 13 (drive) for half an hour. Jacob _____ 14 (ride)

in a car several times in his life, but he _____ 15 (not, drive) a car even once. He

_____ 16 (not, ever, want) to own a car. He believes that cars and other forms of modern

technology make it too easy for family members to spend time away from one another. The Fishers

_____ 17 (always, prefer) to live their lives at a slow pace and keep their family close.

 See the *Grammar Links* Website to learn more about the Amish and their way of life.

Present Perfect Versus Simple Past

FUNCTION

A. Talking About Actions and States Continuing to the Present

To talk about a past action or state that continues to the present, use the **present perfect**. (The simple past is used only for completed actions.)	I **have taught** for 10 years (I still teach.) *Compare*: I **taught** for 10 years. (I don't teach anymore.)

B. Talking About Completed Actions and States

1. **If you mention when** a completed past action or state occurred, you must use the **simple past**.

   I **went** to France **in 1999/a few years ago.**
 NOT: I~~'ve gone~~ to France in 1999/a few years ago.

2. **If you don't mention when** a completed past action or state occurred:

   - You can use either the simple past or present perfect if the action or state **can** occur again.

     I**'ve lived** in France. OR I **lived** in France.

 I**'ve skied** several times. OR I **skied** several times.

   - You must use the simple past if the action or state **cannot** occur again.

     My son really **enjoyed** his high school graduation. (The graduation can't occur again.)

 Marilyn Monroe **made** many movies. (She's dead—she can't make more movies.)
 Compare: Jennifer Lopez **has made** many movies. (She can make more movies.)

GRAMMAR **HOT**SPOT!

1. In talking about completed actions or states, the present perfect expresses a connection to the present. The simple past does not.

   I **have seen** the Picasso exhibit. (implies that the exhibit is still there)
 Compare: I **saw** the Picasso exhibit. (implies that the exhibit is finished)

2. The simple past can be used instead of the present perfect with many time expressions, including *just*, *already*, and *yet*.

   Did you **eat yet?** = **Have** you **eaten yet?**

 I **already ate**, but Carolyn **didn't**. = I**'ve already eaten**, but Carolyn **hasn't**.

Present Perfect Versus Simple Past

9 Present Perfect Versus Simple Past: Timelines

Use the words in parentheses and the information from the timelines to complete the sentences. Use present perfect or simple past.

1. Joanna, <u>have you seen</u> the art exhibit?
(you, see)

2. Joanna, <u>did you see</u> the art exhibit?
(you, see)

3. In his lifetime, Neil Andersen _____ many important discoveries.
(make)

4. In her lifetime, Stephanie Chang _____ many important discoveries.
(make)

5. Greg, _____ Shirley this morning?
(you, see)

6. Greg, _____ Shirley this morning?
(you, see)

7. Professor Sanders _____ for
(teach)
_____ years.

8. Professor Marsh _____ for
(teach)
_____ years.

10 Present Perfect Versus Simple Past: Have You Ever . . . ?

Use the words in parentheses to complete the statements and questions. Use the present perfect where possible. Use the simple past elsewhere. Use contractions with subject pronouns and with *not*.

Born 1564
Died 1616

Born 1974

Tyler: <u>Have you ever been</u> to a Shakespeare play?
　　　　 ⎯⎯⎯⎯⎯⎯⎯⎯⎯⎯
　　　　 1 (you, ever, be)

Annie: Yes, ⎯⎯⎯⎯⎯⎯⎯⎯⎯⎯ .
　　　　　　　　　　2

　　　　 I ⎯⎯⎯⎯⎯⎯⎯⎯⎯⎯ several plays by Shakespeare.
　　　　　　　　3 (see)

Tyler: How many plays ⎯⎯⎯⎯⎯⎯⎯⎯⎯⎯ ?
　　　　　　　　　　　　　　4 (he, write)

Annie: I don't know exactly how many, but he ⎯⎯⎯⎯⎯⎯⎯⎯⎯⎯ a lot of them.
　　　　　　　　　　　　　　　　　　　　　　　　5 (write)

Tyler: I ⎯⎯⎯⎯⎯⎯⎯⎯⎯⎯ *Romeo and Juliet* in August.
　　　　　　6 (saw)

　　　　 ⎯⎯⎯⎯⎯⎯⎯⎯⎯⎯ it?
　　　　 7 (you, ever, see)

Annie: I ⎯⎯⎯⎯⎯⎯⎯⎯⎯⎯ the play yet, but I ⎯⎯⎯⎯⎯⎯⎯⎯⎯⎯
　　　　　　8 (not, see)　　　　　　　　　　　　　　　9 (see)

　　　　 the movie.

Tyler: When?

Annie: I ⎯⎯⎯⎯⎯⎯⎯⎯⎯⎯ it in a theater a few years ago. Actually, I
　　　　　　10 (see)

　　　　 ⎯⎯⎯⎯⎯⎯⎯⎯⎯⎯ it on video several times since then, too. Leonardo DiCaprio
　　　　 11 (watch)

　　　　 ⎯⎯⎯⎯⎯⎯⎯⎯⎯⎯ the part of Romeo in the movie. I
　　　　 12 (play)

　　　　 ⎯⎯⎯⎯⎯⎯⎯⎯⎯⎯ in love with him since I first saw it.
　　　　 13 (be)

Tyler: ⎯⎯⎯⎯⎯⎯⎯⎯⎯⎯ many movies?
　　　　 14 (Leonardo DiCaprio, make)

Annie: He ⎯⎯⎯⎯⎯⎯⎯⎯⎯⎯ enough for me. I hope he makes another one soon!
　　　　　　15 (not, make)

11 **Present Perfect and Simple Past:** Telling About Your Experiences

 A. Write a paragraph about four exciting, interesting, or unusual experiences you have had. Use the first sentence in the example. Then write two sentences about each experience. In the first, use the present perfect to tell what experience you have had. In the second, use the simple past to tell when it happened.

Example:

    Several of the experiences in my life have been exciting, interesting, or unusual. For example, I have been to New York City. I went there when I was sixteen years old. Also, I have seen a World Cup soccer game. It was in Japan in 2002. . . .

 See the *Grammar Links* Website for a complete model paragraph for this assignment.

B. Work in small groups. Read your paragraph to your group. Have the students in the group had very similar or very different experiences?

> **Check your progress! Go to the Self-Test for Chapter 3 on the *Grammar Links* Website.**

Chapter 4

Past Perfect and Past Perfect Progressive

Introductory Task: New Experiences

A. Sam left his country to come to the United States last year. Since then, he has had many new experiences. For each of his new experiences, write a follow-up sentence in the past perfect (*had* + past participle of the verb—e.g., *had been*). Use *never* and *before*.

1. Last year, Sam was away from his family. _He had never been away from his family before._

2. In August, he flew in an airplane. _He had never flown in an airplane before._

3. In September, he drank cranberry juice. _____

4. In December, he saw snow. _____

5. Last winter, he wore a heavy coat. _____

6. In February, he went skiing. _____

7. In March, he ate granola. _____

8. In May, he rode a horse. _____ ✗

B. Now write pairs of sentences about three new experiences of your own. Follow the pattern in Part A.

Example: _Last year, I tasted caviar. I had never tasted caviar before._

1. _____

2. _____

3. _____

Report to the class about your most interesting new experience.

---

granola = a mixture of oats with dried fruits and nuts, often used as a breakfast cereal. *caviar* = the eggs of fish prepared with salt.

Past Perfect and Past Perfect Progressive

FORM

A. Affirmative Statements

PAST PERFECT				PAST PERFECT PROGRESSIVE		
SUBJECT	*HAD + PAST PARTICIPLE**			SUBJECT	*HAD + BEEN + PRESENT PARTICIPLE**	
I	**had eaten**	before she arrived.		I	**had been eating**	before she arrived.
Emily	**had eaten**	before she arrived.		He	**had been eating**	before she arrived.

(See Appendix 7 for the past participles of irregular verbs.)

(See Appendix 3 for spelling rules for the *-ing* form of the verb.)

B. Negative Statements

PAST PERFECT				PAST PERFECT PROGRESSIVE		
SUBJECT	*HAD + NOT + PAST PARTICIPLE**			SUBJECT	*HAD + NOT + BEEN + PRESENT PARTICIPLE**	
He	**had not studied**	that yet.		I	**had not been studying**	before dinner.
We	**had not studied**	that yet.		He	**had not been studying**	before dinner.

C. *Yes/No* Questions and Short Answers

PAST PERFECT			PAST PERFECT PROGRESSIVE	
QUESTIONS	SHORT ANSWERS		QUESTIONS	SHORT ANSWERS
Had they **done** that before she arrived?	Yes, they **had.**		**Had** you **been doing** that before she arrived?	Yes, I **had (been).**
	No, they **hadn't.**			No, I **hadn't (been).**

D. *Wh-* Questions

Wh- Questions About the Subject

PAST PERFECT	PRESENT PERFECT PROGRESSIVE
Who had done that?	**Who had been doing** that?
Which student had done that?	**Which students had been doing** that?

Other Wh- Questions

PAST PERFECT	PAST PERFECT PROGRESSIVE
What had Joe **done** before she arrived?	**What had** Joe **been doing** before she arrived?
Where had they **gone?**	**Where had** they **been going?**

*CONTRACTIONS

I/he/she/you/we/they + had → I'd/he'd/she'd/you'd/we'd/they'd
had + not → hadn't

Past Perfect and Past Perfect Progressive

1 Past Perfect—Form: An Exchange Student—A Different Place

Use the words in parentheses to complete the statements and questions in the past perfect. Complete the short answers. Use contractions with subject pronouns and with *not*.

Jim: Hey, Dan. I heard that you spent last year as an exchange student. Tell me about your

experiences. __Had you studied_____ the language before you left?
      1 (you, study)

Dan: Yes, _____. I _____ it pretty well. And all
          2   3 (learn)

the students in my group _____ a lot of books about our host
                              4 (read)

country. But most of us _____ in any country with a really different
                            5 (not, live)

culture before. We experienced some differences there that we _____
                                                                 6 (not, be)

aware of before we left the United States.

Jim: What do you mean?

Dan: Well, until I went away, I _____ the importance of cultural differences
                                   7 (not, understand)

in how people think about time. By the time I left, I _____ lots of
                                                         8 (have)

experiences that taught me a different way of thinking about time.

Jim: Really? What kind of experiences?

Dan: Well, for example, one night I was really worried about being late. Earlier that day some students

_____ me and another American to a party at eight o'clock. The two
    9 (invite)

of us _____ lost on the way to the party, and when we got there it
          10 (got)

was almost nine.

Jim: _____ by then?
      11 (the other guests, already, arrive)

Dan: No, _____. The host _____ getting ready
            12   13 (not, finish)

for the party yet. He was really surprised that we _____ so early.
                                                      14 (come)

By the end of the year, he _____ me a lot about his culture's time
                              15 (teach)

customs. And now that I'm back home, I'm experiencing culture shock here. I'm always late!

---

exchange student = a person who studies in another country.

---

2 Past Perfect Progressive—Form: Two Views on the Pace of Life

Use the words in parentheses to complete the statements and questions. Use the past perfect progressive. Complete the short answer. Use contractions with subject pronouns and with *not*.

Frank: Last summer, I went with Paul to visit his family in the country. Before that, Paul

____had been staying____ in the city with me.
            1 (stay)

We ____'d been rushing____ around day and night.
            2 (rush)

We _____ a great time.
            3 (have)

Paul: Well, Frank _____ a great time, but I
            4 (have)

_____ it that much. The pace of life in the city was
     5 (not, enjoy)

too fast for me.

Frank: Anyway, we took a bus to the country and back. Going there was okay, but the trip back

was terrible because the bus was late.

Nuria: How long _____ by the time the bus came?
         6 (you, wait)

Frank: We _____ forever—two whole hours!
       7 (wait)

Paul: That's not true! We _____ long at all—only two hours.
        8 (not, wait)

But Frank _____ the whole time about being late.
       9 (worry)

Nuria: What about you, Paul? _____?
            10 (you, worry)

Paul: No, _____. My cousins _____
        11   12 (sit)

with us and _____ to us. It was a great, relaxing afternoon!
       13 (talk)

Past Perfect

FUNCTION

A. Overview

Use the past perfect to talk about a past action or state that occurred before another past action or state or before a specified time in the past. (Note that the action or state can be repeated.)

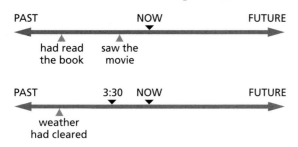

- The later past action or state is expressed with a simple past verb, often in a sentence with a time clause.

  (For information on time clauses, see Chapter 2, Grammar Briefing 3, page 31.)

- The two past actions or states don't have to be in the same sentence.

She **had read** the book (several times) before she saw the movie.

By 3:30, the weather **had cleared**.

                           time clause
She **had been** there three times before he **went**.

He **didn't recognize** her. She **had changed**.

B. Past Perfect in Sentences with Time Clauses

1. When the time clause begins with *before* or *until*, the verb in the main clause expresses the earlier action and is in the past perfect.

     earlier action   later action
   We'**d lived** there **before/until** it **became too expensive**.

2. When the time clause begins with *after*, the verb in the time clause expresses the earlier action and is in the past perfect.

       later action   earlier action
   We **got** to the theater **after** the movie **had started**.

3. When the time clause begins with *when*, either verb may express the earlier action and be in the past perfect.

       later action   earlier action
   When we **got** there, he **had eaten**.
       earlier action   later action
   When he **had eaten**, he **left**.

(continued on next page)

4. With *before*, *until*, and *after*, the simple past is often used in place of the past perfect, because these time expressions make the order of the actions clear.

He **studied** the language before he left. = He **had studied** the language before he left.

With *when*, the past perfect is needed, to make the order of the actions clear.

When they went to Rome, they **had gone** to Paris. (first Paris, then Rome)

When they **had gone** to Rome, they went to Paris. (first Rome, then Paris)

C. Time Expressions and Adverbs of Frequency

1. Time expressions such as *by/up to/before/until then* (*that time*, *three o'clock*, *the next day*, *2004*, etc.) are used in sentences with the past perfect to specify the later time.

We had eaten **by eight o'clock.**

Had you been there **before then**?

2. The past perfect is also used with:

   • Other time expressions including *already*, *just*, *yet* (in questions and negatives), and *still*.

   We had **already** eaten by that time.

   • Adverbs of frequency including *ever* (in questions and negatives); *never*, *sometimes*, *always*, etc.; and *three times* (*many times*, etc.).

   Had Jon **ever** driven there alone?

GRAMMAR **HOT**SPOT!

Use the past perfect only when an action or state occurred before another action, state, or time in the past. When there is no second action, state, or time, do **not** use the past perfect.

I **had given** him the key **before he left.**

I **had given** him the key **by then.**

Last night I **gave** him the key.
   NOT: Last night I ~~had given~~ him the key.

Past Perfect

3 **Past Perfect and Simple Past:** "Rip Van Winkle"—A Different Time

A. Use the words in parentheses to complete the sentences in the simple past and past perfect. Use contractions with *not*.

"Rip Van Winkle" is a well-known American story set in the late 1700s. While Rip Van Winkle was out hunting one day, he drank a strange liquor and fell asleep. When he woke up, he thought that he had slept for one night. But when he looked around, he discovered that things had changed. . . .

1. Rip's gun <u>had gotten</u> old and rusty, so it <u>didn't work</u>
   (get)   (not, work)
   anymore.

2. His faithful dog _____ no longer beside him.
                        (be)

   It _____.
      (run away)

3. He _____ at his beard. It _____
        (look)   (grow)
   long and gray.

4. The clothes worn by the people in his village _____ strange
                                                      (seem)
   to him because fashions _____.
                              (change)

5. He _____ surprised at the terrible condition of his house.
        (be)

   It _____.
      (fall apart)

6. His children _____, so he _____ them.
                   (grow up)   (not, recognize)

7. His daughter _____ a child in her arms. Rip
                   (have)

   _____ a grandfather.
      (become)

8. His wife _____ there any longer.
               (not, be)

   She _____.
       (die)

9. His friends and neighbors

   _____ him,
      (forget)

   so they _____
              (think)

   he was a stranger.

10. The United States _____ its independence.
    (win)

    It _____ no longer a British colony.
    (be)

11. Finally, Rip _____ that he _____
    (discover)   (be)

    asleep for 20 years.

🌐 Check out the *Grammar Links* Website to learn more about the story of Rip Van Winkle.

✍ **B.** Write a one-paragraph story about the experiences of someone like Rip who awoke after sleeping for a long time. You can write a story that you know or make one up. Use the past perfect and the simple past.

🌐 See the *Grammar Links* Website for a model story for this assignment.

4 **Past Perfect and Simple Past; Combining Sentences**: A New Experience

For each pair of sentences in this story, decide the order of events. Then combine the pair into one sentence using the time word shown, the simple past, and the past perfect. The order of events determines which verb is past perfect.

1. after: Sandra decided to study abroad. ____1____

    She applied to the university. ____2____

    After Sandra had decided to study abroad, she applied to the university.
    OR Sandra applied to the university after she had decided to study abroad.

2. before: She didn't fly in an airplane. _____

    She traveled to her host country. _____

3. until: She didn't experience another culture. _____

    She went to her host country. _____

4. before: She adapted to the customs of the new culture. _____

    She made a few embarrassing mistakes. _____

5. after: She learned the language well. _____

    She studied hard and practiced often. _____

6. when: She lived in the country for a while. _____

    She became more flexible. _____

7. after: She understood her own culture much better. _____

    She stayed in her host country for a few months. _____

---

adapt = change oneself so as to be right for a situation. *flexible* = being able or willing to change.

---

5 Past Perfect and Simple Past—Order of Actions: Place and Time

A. Listen to the sentences once for the main ideas. Then listen again and circle the letter of the state or action that occurred earlier.

1. a. Robert Levine taught at a university in the United States.
   b. He went to Brazil to teach as a visiting professor.

2. a. Professor Levine went to Brazil.
   b. He was aware of differences in time customs between the North American and Brazilian cultures.

3. a. The professor didn't realize that the cultural differences were so confusing.
   b. He arrived at the Brazilian university.

4. a. Many of the students came to class.
   b. He began to lecture at 10 a.m.

5. a. Professor Levine's students got ready to leave.
   b. The class ended.

6. a. Quite a few of the students asked questions and listened to him.
   b. The class ended.

7. a. Professor Levine was in Brazil for a while.
   b. He became interested in studying cultural differences in people's sense of time and in the pace of life.

8. a. He began to study differences in the pace of life.
   b. He compared North American and Brazilian ideas about what it means to be on time or to be late.

9. a. Professor Levine thought a lot about how to measure the pace of life.
   b. He and his students began making observations in cities all over the world.

10. a. They measured the walking and working speeds of people in many cities.
    b. Professor Levine analyzed the differences.

11. a. He evaluated the data.
    b. He found that there were differences in the pace of life on every level.

See the *Grammar Links* Website for more information about cultural differences in the pace of life and people's sense of time.

B. In his book *A Geography of Time*, Professor Levine has described cultural differences in the pace of life and in the way that people think about time. We often don't realize that people in another culture might not think about time in the same way that we do. Have you ever been confused by a different culture's sense of time? What happened? What had you thought before? What hadn't you realized until that happened? What did you learn about yourself and your own culture? Write a paragraph. Use the past perfect three or more times.

Example: *People in different cultures have different ideas about the best ways to use their time. I hadn't realized this until I came to the United States. I had been here for only a few days when I . . .*

6 Past Perfect Versus Simple Past: Speed

Use the words in parentheses to complete the sentences. Use the simple past or the past perfect. In cases in which both tenses are possible, use the past perfect.

1800   1860

It was around the year 1800 that Rip Van Winkle woke up and discovered that he

had been asleep for 20 years.

After Rip ___had woken up___ , he ___noticed___
            1 (wake up)   2 (notice)

some kinds of changes, but he probably ___didn't notice___ any
                                          3 (not, notice)

technological changes. Not much technological change _____
                                                 4 (happen)

by that time in history. Before the beginning of the 1800s, nothing

_____ faster than the speed of a sailing ship or a horse.
   5 (move)

After 1800, many changes _____ in the United States.
6 (happen)

By the mid-1800s, steamboats and trains _____ operating in
7 (begin)

many parts of the country. By 1860, the speed of transportation _____
8 (increase)

by twenty times. As a result, Americans of the 1860s _____ much
9 (travel)

more rapidly to distant places.

Communications _____ much faster by 1860, too.
10 (get)

In 1800, it _____ six weeks for a message from St. Louis,
11 (take)

Missouri, to reach Washington, D.C. However, by the 1850s, the telegraph

_____ an important means of communication. So, in the 1860s,
12 (become)

a message from St. Louis _____ Washington in a few seconds.
13 (reach)

To learn more about these changes, go to the *Grammar Links* Website.

7 Using Simple Past and Past Perfect: Milestones

Childhood is often measured by important accomplishments or "milestones": starting
school, learning how to read and write, learning how to ride a bike and play sports,
getting a first job, traveling alone for the first time, graduating, and so on.

1. Think about important milestones in your childhood and teenage years and the
ages at which you reached them. Mark three of these milestones, including the ages,
on the timeline.

BIRTH   NOW

2. Work with a partner. Tell your partner about the milestones you marked. Use the
simple past and the past perfect. Answer questions that your partner has about your
milestones. Then reverse roles.

Example: I started first grade when I was six. Before then, I had already learned how
to count and write my name. I hadn't learned to read yet. When I was
eight years old, I began playing soccer. By the time I was 10, I had become
a very good soccer player. . . .

3. Report to the class about what you learned about your partner.

Past Perfect Progressive; Past Perfect Progressive Versus Past Perfect

FUNCTION

A. Past Perfect Progressive

1. Use the past perfect progressive to talk about past actions that began before and continued to another past action or state or a specified time in the past. Use the simple past for the second action or state.

| I **had been running** a lot until I **hurt** my foot. |
| I **had been sleeping** late every day. But then I got a new work schedule. |
| At 3:00, she **had been talking** on the phone for five hours! |

2. Sentences with the past perfect progressive often include a time clause. The time clause can start with *before*, *when*, or *until*. The main clause verb is in the past perfect progressive; the time clause verb is in the simple past.

   (For information on time clauses, see Chapter 2, Grammar Briefing 3, page 31.)

| time clause |
| She **had been sleeping** <u>when he arrived.</u> |
| time clause |
| He **hadn't been studying** <u>until he failed that test.</u> |

Time Expressions

Time expressions used with the past perfect (see Grammar Briefing 2, page 66) can also be used with the past perfect progressive.

| Had you been planning your vacation **yet**? |
| I'd **already** been having problems with the car. |

B. Past Perfect Progressive Versus Past Perfect

1. The past perfect progressive is used to talk about past actions that were **in progress** up to another past action, state, or time.

   Remember! For past states (i.e., with verbs that have stative meaning), do not use the progressive. Use the past perfect.

| He**'d been doing** his homework when they arrived. (homework was in progress up to the time they arrived) |
| The summer **had seemed** hot before August. **NOT:** The summer ~~had been seeming~~ hot before August. |

2. The past perfect is used to talk about past actions or states that were **completed** before another past action, state, or time.

| He**'d done** his homework when they arrived. (homework was completed before they arrived) |

Past Perfect Progressive; Past Perfect Versus Past Perfect Progressive

8 **Past Perfect Progressive and Time Clauses:** Once Upon a Time: Sleeping Beauty

Use the words in parentheses to complete the story. Use the simple past and the past perfect progressive. If the past perfect progressive is not possible, use the past perfect. Use contractions with subject pronouns and with *not*.

A beautiful baby girl was born to a king and queen.

Soon after her birth, an evil fairy put a curse on the

little princess. The princess __had been living__
                                    1 (live)

happily in a big castle with her parents until they

__went_____ away for a day.
      2 (go)

Then she was free to do as she wished.

She _____ the castle
          3 (explore)

for hours when she _____ to go into the tower.
                          4 (decide)

Until she _____ to the top of the tower,
              5 (climb)

she _____ about the little room there. She found an old
        6 (not, know)

woman in the room. The woman _____ thread when the
                                      7 (spin)

princess _____ in. The moment the princess pricked her
            8 (come)

finger on the old woman's spindle, the curse came true: The princess and everyone else in

the castle fell into a deep sleep. Handsome princes _____
                                                          9 (try)

to rescue Sleeping Beauty for a long time before the curse finally

_____. She _____ asleep
     10 (end)   11 (be)

for a hundred years before a brave and charming prince _____
                                                              12 (ride)

into the castle and _____ her. He kissed her, and she and
                        13 (find)

everyone else woke up.

---

curse = a promise that something bad will happen. *spindle* = a sharp tool for winding thread.

---

9 Past Perfect Versus Past Perfect Progressive: At the Stroke of Midnight

Use the verbs in parentheses to complete the story. Use past perfect progressive where possible. Use past perfect elsewhere.

1. When Cinderella's cruel stepmother came home, she saw Cinderella on the floor on her hands and knees. Part of the floor was clean and wet. When her stepmother came home, Cinderella _had been scrubbing_ the floor.
   (scrub)

2. Cinderella's mean stepsisters were very happy because the prince _had invited_ them to a ball at his castle.
   (invite)

3. Soon after the stepsisters had left for the ball, Cinderella's fairy godmother appeared and looked closely at her. Cinderella's eyes had tears in them. Cinderella _____.
   (cry)

4. After the fairy godmother _____ her a beautiful dress, Cinderella
   (give)
   was able to go to the ball, too.

5. Cinderella was shocked when the clock struck midnight.
   Long before, she _____ the time.
   (forget about)

6. Cinderella rushed home, but then she realized that she had only one shoe. She
   _____ the other one.
   (lose)

7. Finally, the prince found Cinderella. He
   _____ her since he met her at the ball.
   (search for)

8. After they were married, Cinderella lived in the castle. On his birthday, the prince went into the kitchen, where he saw Cinderella stirring flour, butter, sugar, and eggs.
   She _____ a cake for him.
   (make)

9. Cinderella looked into the prince's library. He was holding a pen and looking thoughtfully at a piece of paper with a few words on it. The prince _____ a poem for her.
   (write)

10. When the fairy godmother visited Cinderella and the prince recently, they thanked her and told her that they _____ very happily since their marriage.
    (live)

Check your progress! Go to the Self-Test for Chapter 4 on the *Grammar Links* Website.

Wrap-up Activities

1 Time for Life: EDITING

Correct the 13 errors in the article. There are errors in verb forms and tenses. Some errors can be corrected in more than one way. The first error is corrected for you.

For many years, John Robinson ~~had~~ **has** been interested in how people use their time. He is now the director of the Americans' Use of Time Project. Robinson has first asked Americans to take part in a use-of-time survey in 1965. He has been repeating the surveys three times since then. Robinson has used the results of his surveys to answer two questions: How has Americans been spending their time recently? How they've been feeling about it?

Ten thousand people had taken part in the 1995 use-of-time survey. In 1995, the study participants have wrote down their activities in a "time diary" every day. In addition, they reported on their feelings about their amount of free time.

After the participants had completed the 1995 survey, Robinson had analyzed the results and compared them to previous survey results. He found some interesting changes in people's use of time. Americans actually spent less time working in 1995 than in 1985. By 1995, they have gotten more free time. However, many people believed that they had less time, and they felt more rushed and stressed. In 1997, Robinson has published a book, *Time for Life*, about the results of his surveys.

Why does it seem that we have so little time for life nowadays? According to Robinson, there are two reasons for this. First, since 1965, we spend more and more of our free time watching television. Most of us usually say that television is unnecessary or a waste of time. But in recent years we had spent more time on it than any other free time activity. Second, since Robinson did his first survey, we have been having many more opportunities and choices. We have been feeling more rushed because we want to do everything.

2 A Question Challenge—WRITING

Work in teams of two. Write questions for each of the answers below. The questions must be logical and grammatically correct. Each team must write at least three questions for each answer. The winning team is the one that writes the most correct questions within the time limit set by your teacher.

1. They've made new friends.
   What have the students done since the beginning of the semester?
   Why haven't Christina and Patrick been coming to our parties?
   Why are the visitors so happy?
2. Since I was a child.
3. Yes, they have many times.
4. For a very short time.
5. I've been setting my alarm clock.
6. Yes, she has been, but she hasn't been enjoying it.
7. We'd gotten lost.
8. Everything had changed.
9. Yes, he already had.
10. She'd been falling asleep.
11. No, when we arrived, they'd already finished.

3 Things Have Changed Since I Was a Child—SPEAKING

Step 1 Working in small groups, choose three areas that interest you. For example, you might choose from science, technology, communications, transportation, business, politics, art, movies, music, fashion, and sports.

Step 2 For each area, think of changes that have happened in your lifetimes. Talk about changes that occurred before some time in the past and changes that started in the past.

Example: *Most people hadn't used the Internet before the 1990s. The Internet has gotten much bigger and more important.*

Be sure to mention changes that are continuing now.

Example: *People have been finding new ways to use the Internet.*

Step 3 Make notes on the changes—past and ongoing—in each area that you discuss.

Step 4 Report to the class about the changes in those areas. Refer to your notes as necessary. Use sentences with the past perfect, past perfect progressive, present perfect, and present perfect progressive.

> When you sit with a nice girl for two hours, it seems like two minutes; when you sit on a hot stove for two minutes, it seems like two hours. That's relativity. —ALBERT EINSTEIN
>
> *Sad hours seem long.* —William Shakespeare, *Romeo and Juliet*

Have you ever had the feeling that time was racing by, dragging very slowly, moving in slow motion, or standing still? What caused this? Were you happy, sad, bored, busy, waiting, cold, hot, sick, nervous, frightened, or in love? Or have you ever had the feeling that you had experienced an event before it happened, even though you knew it wasn't possible? (This kind of experience is called *déjà vu.*)

Write a paragraph about a situation in which you experienced a changed feeling about the passage of time. Include the present perfect, past perfect, and past perfect progressive in your paragraph. Then read your paragraph to the class.

Example:

I'd been out on a date with a girl I really liked. We'd been having a very nice time, but the evening was passing much too quickly for me. It had been snowing all night, and I was driving home on a snowy street. Suddenly, a tree appeared right in front the car. I stamped on the brake, but the car kept moving forward. Time seemed to stretch out in slow motion while the car slid into the tree. With a big jolt, the car hit the tree, I broke the steering wheel with my chin, and time jumped back to normal. I've never forgotten that experience.

 See the *Grammar Links* Website for another model for this paragraph.

Future; Phrasal Verbs; Tag Questions

TOPIC FOCUS
Travel

UNIT OBJECTIVES

■ **expressing future time with *will* and *be going to***
(Your tour ***will*** be interesting. The guide ***is going to*** show you the museum.)

■ **expressing future time with the present progressive, the simple present, and *be about to***
(Lisa ***is touring*** the Capitol on Tuesday afternoon. Her tour ***starts*** at 1:00. It's 1:00 now, and the tour ***is about to*** start.)

■ **the future progressive with *will* and *be going to***
(The plane ***will be taking off*** soon. It ***is going to be leaving*** on time.)

■ **the future perfect with *will* and *be going to***
(The spacecraft ***will have reached*** Mars by the end of this month. You ***are going to have seen*** new photos of the planet before the end of the year.)

■ **the future perfect progressive with *will* and *be going to***
They ***will have been preparing*** for their trip. They ***are going to have been traveling*** for a long time by then.)

■ **phrasal verbs and verb–preposition combinations**
(An explorer ***set off*** for the South Pole. He ***was looking for*** adventure.)

■ **tag questions**
(Columbus was an explorer, ***wasn't he?***)

Grammar in Action

🎧 Reading and Listening: Travel Bulletin Board

Read and listen to the advertisements and announcements.

TRAVEL BULLETIN BOARD

1 Outdoor Adventures Unlimited:

How **are** you **going to spend** your next summer vacation? We specialize in planning trips to national parks. You **will take** the outdoor vacation of your dreams at Mesa Verde or Yellowstone. Call us at 1-800-OUT-DOOR.

2 *Tri-City Recreation Department:*

*We've planned the ultimate shopping escape for you. A bus **is taking** a group to the Mall of America next Saturday. When you **see** the mall, you**'re going to be** amazed. It's big enough to hold seven baseball stadiums or 32 Boeing 747s! The bus **leaves** at 7:00 on Saturday morning and **returns** at midnight.*

3 CULTURAL TRAVEL, INC:

You **will experience** the best in New York or Washington, D.C., when you **take** a city museum vacation with us.

Tours **are departing** on June 18th and July 7th.

For further details, call 222-694-3000.

4 Travel Lecture—Exploration: On April 24th a noted space-science researcher **will talk** about a plan for the exploration of Mars. He believes that we **are going to send** successful human missions to Mars soon by using the strategies of past explorers like the explorers of the Americas and Antarctica. The lecture **begins** at 8:00 p.m. in Olin Hall.

5 **Destination Mars:**
The earth seems pretty crowded these days, doesn't it? In the years to come, it **is going to be getting** even more crowded. What does this mean for the 21st century? **Will** we **have found** a solution to our population problems before the end of the 21st century? Don't worry: The answer is yes, thanks to Mars! By the end of the 21st century we **will have built** colonies on Mars, and in the 22nd century many people **will be living** there. Check out this website: www.marssociety.org.

mission = an assignment that a person or group is sent to complete. *strategy* = a plan of action. *colony* = a group of people who settle in a distant place.

Think About Grammar

The boldfaced verbs in the advertisements and announcements express a future time meaning.

A. Work with a partner. Look at the boldfaced verbs in 1, 2, 3, and 4.

1. In 1–4, four different forms are used to express the future. Give an example of a verb in each form. _are going to spend_ _____

   _____

   _____

   _____

2. a. Which two of the examples also can express another time?

   _____

   _____

   b. What other time do they express? _____

B. Look at the boldfaced verbs in 5.

1. Which two verbs express actions that will be ongoing at some time in the future?

   _____

   _____

2. Which two verbs express actions that will have happened before a time in the future?

   _____

   _____

5

Future Time

Introductory Task: Vacation Plans and Predictions

A. Listen to the first part of the conversation. The speakers are talking about their future vacation **plans**. Then listen again and fill in the blanks with the verbs you hear.

A: This summer I __'m taking__ an outdoor vacation with my family.
   1

We __'re going to go__ to a national park in Colorado.
   2

B: That sounds great! When _____ you _____?
   3

A: We _____ there on June 15th. What are your plans?
   4

B: I _____ to Washington, D.C., in July. I _____
   5   6

the National Gallery of Art and other museums there.

A: _____ your brother _____ to Washington with you?
   7

B: Oh, no! He hates museums. He _____ his vacation at a shopping mall.
   8

B. Listen to the second part of the conversation. The speakers are making **predictions** about their vacations. Then listen again and fill in the blanks with the verbs you hear.

A: A vacation in a shopping mall? Do you think he __'ll have__ a good time?
   1

B: It's not just any mall. It's the Mall of America. It has lots of things to do for fun, so I think

he __'s going to enjoy__ it. And he _____ cool, too,
   2   3

because the mall _____ air-conditioned. In Washington, the weather
   4

_____ probably _____ hot and humid in July.
   5

A: Yeah, but Washington is interesting. You _____ have a great trip!
   6

Forms used to talk about the future include *will*, *be going to*, and the present progressive.

Which two of these forms are used to talk about future plans?

_____   _____

Which two are used to make predictions?

_____   _____

Will and *Be Going To* I

FORM

A. Affirmative Statements

WILL		
SUBJECT	*WILL* + BASE FORM OF VERB*	
I	**will leave**	tomorrow.

BE GOING TO		
SUBJECT	*BE + GOING TO +* BASE FORM OF VERB*	
I	**am going to leave**	tomorrow.

B. Negative Statements

WILL		
SUBJECT	*WILL + NOT +* BASE FORM OF VERB*	
We	**will not leave**	in July.

BE GOING TO		
SUBJECT	*BE + NOT + GOING TO +* BASE FORM OF VERB*	
We	**are not going to leave**	in July.

C. *Yes/No* Questions and Short Answers

WILL	
QUESTIONS	SHORT ANSWERS
Will Jill **leave** this summer?	Yes, she **will.**
	No, she **won't.**

BE GOING TO	
QUESTIONS	SHORT ANSWERS
Is Jill **going to leave** this summer?	Yes, she **is.**
	No, she **isn't.**

D. *Wh-* Questions

Wh- *Questions About the Subject*

WILL	*BE GOING TO**
Who will leave next year?	**Who is going to leave** next year?

Other Wh- *Questions*

WILL	*BE GOING TO**
When will they **leave?**	**When are** they **going to leave?**

---

*CONTRACTIONS: WILL	*CONTRACTIONS: BE GOING TO
I/he/she/it/we/you/they + will → I'll/he'll/she'll/it'll/we'll/you'll/they'll will + not → won't	I + am + going to → I'm going to he/she/it + is + going to → he's/she's/it's going to we/you/they + are + going to → we're/you're/they're going to is + not + going to → isn't going to are + not + going to → aren't going to he/she/it + is + not + going to → he's/she's/it's not going to 　OR he/she/it isn't going to we/you/they + are + not + going to → we're/you're/they're not going to 　OR we/you/they aren't going to wh- word + be going to → who's going to, etc.

Will and *Be Going To* I

1 *Will*—Form: An Outdoor Vacation—Mesa Verde National Park

Use *will* and the words in parentheses to complete the statements and questions.
Complete the short answer. Use contractions with subject pronouns and with *not*.

Four Corners Heritage Tours
Durango, CO 81301

Utah | Colorado
Mesa Verde • *Durango*
Arizona | New Mexico

Thank you for making a reservation to tour the ancient Native American

village, or "pueblo," at Mesa Verde National Park. We promise that you

__won't be_____ disappointed. Your tour __will be_____
___ 1 (not, be) ___   ___ 2 (be) ___

an educational and enjoyable experience—one that you _____!
                                                          3 (not, forget)

This information sheet answers the questions that our guests frequently ask.

Q: At what time _____?
                              4 (the tour, begin)

A: The tour _____ at 8 a.m. The driver
                    5 (begin)

   _____ for you, so please be ready. The trip from Durango
            6 (not, wait)

   to Mesa Verde _____ more than an hour.
                        7 (not, take)

Q: _____ small?
              8 (my tour group, be)

A: Yes, _____. There _____ more
                  9   10 (not, be)

   than eight people in your group.

Q: How long _____?
                        11 (the tour, last)

A: About four hours. You _____ plenty of time to
                                  12 (have)

   explore Mesa Verde's "cliff dwellings"—homes built high on the sides of steep,

   flat-topped mountains.

Native Americans = people who were living in the Americas before the arrival of Europeans.

 To learn more about Mesa Verde and other national parks, go to the *Grammar Links* Website.

2 ***Be Going To*—Form:** A Shopping Vacation—The Mall of America

Use *be going to* and the words in parentheses to complete the statements and questions. Complete the short answer. Use contractions with subject pronouns.

Roger: Hey, Nick. I <u>'m going to go</u> on a one-day vacation
                           1 (go)

next Saturday. Do you want to come along?

Nick: Where <u>are you going to go</u>   ?
                           2 (you, go)

Roger: Believe it or not, I _____ the day at the
                                                   3 (spend)

Mall of America, near Minneapolis. You should come.

It _____ a lot of fun.
                     4 (be)

Nick: I don't believe it. Why _____ so far just to go
                                                      5 (you, travel)

to a mall? _____ there?
                           6 (you, shop)

Roger: Yes, _____. Of course. The Mall of America is
                     7

the biggest indoor mall in the United States—it has over 500 stores.

Nick: Over 500 stores? No, no way. I hate shopping.

I _____ with you.
           8 (not, come)

Roger: That's OK. I _____ lonely. My nephew Jeremy
                                       9 (not, feel)

and his friend Tyrone _____.
                                       10 (come)

We _____ Camp Snoopy, a huge amusement park
           11 (visit)

in the mall. Tyrone _____ at the golf course there.
                                 12 (play)

Nick: Golf! I _____ coming after all!
                     13 (think about)

Will and *Be Going To* II; Future Time Clauses

FUNCTION

A. Uses of Both *Will* and *Be Going To*

Use *will* or *be going to* to:

- Talk about future events that are (almost) certain.

- Make predictions and state expectations.

The sun **will rise/is going to rise** at six o'clock tomorrow.	
He'll **be/'s going to be** famous someday.	
The mail **will** probably **get/is** probably **going to get** here around three o'clock.	

(See Chapter 14, Grammar Briefing 4, page 274, for other modals used to express predictions and expectations.)

B. Other Uses of *Will*

1. *Will* is usually used to express willingness (the idea that you are ready and able to do something). It is used to:

   - Make offers.

   - Make promises.

   - Make requests (ask about willingness).

   - Refuse to do something (express lack of willingness).

   If you want, I'll **mail** those letters.

   We'll **be** there promptly at 8:00 a.m.

   Will you **take** these packages to the post office?

   She **won't tell** me what's bothering her.

2. *Will* is often used in formal situations if both *will* and *be going to* could be used. For example, *will* is almost always used in written notices.

   The train **will depart** at ten o'clock (formal announcement)
   Compare: The train**'s going to leave** at ten o'clock. (less formal)

C. Other Uses of *Be Going To*

1. *Be going to* is usually used to talk about an intention or plan.

   She**'s going to discuss** the problem with the travel agent. (intention)

   They**'re going to go** on vacation next month. (plan)

2. *Be going to* is usually used to make a prediction about what will happen in the immediate future. Often the prediction is based on evidence in the present situation.

   That boy**'s going to spill** his drink. Grab it! (He's not paying attention and is moving his arm toward the glass.)

(continued on next page)

D. Time Expressions

Time expressions used in talking about future time include *tomorrow, tonight, next week* (*spring, Monday,* etc.), and *in two hours* (*a few days,* etc.).

> He will help us **tomorrow**.
>
> I'm going to go **next fall**.
>
> We're going to leave **in two hours**.

FORM and FUNCTION

Expressing Future Time in Sentences with Time Clauses

In sentences about the future with time clauses:

- The time clause begins with expressions including *before, after, when, as soon as, until,* and *by the time*.
- Use a **present** form in the time clause.
- Use a future form in the main clause.

(See Chapter 2, Grammar Briefing 3, page 31, for more about time clauses.)

time clause	main clause
Before he **comes**, we'll **eat** dinner.
   NOT: Before he ~~will come~~, we'll eat dinner.

time clause	main clause
When they**'re traveling**, they**'ll stay** in a hotel.
   NOT: When they~~'ll travel~~, they'll stay in a hotel.

TALKING THE TALK

In speech, *going to* is usually pronounced "gonna." "Gonna" is not used in writing.

Joe: Where are you gonna go on your vacation?
Hal: We're gonna go to Tahiti.

GRAMMAR PRACTICE 2

Will and *Be Going To* II; Future Time Clauses

3 *Will* and *Be Going To*—Predictions: What Next?

A. Work with a partner. Discuss what you think will happen next in each of the following situations. Write two predictions for each situation. Use *will* for one prediction and *be going to* for the other one.

1. Len and Miranda have spent their vacation at Mesa Verde. Now they're on a plane, trying to get home. The plane is sitting on the runway. It was ready to take off an hour ago, but snow has been falling steadily since then.

   The passengers will get very nervous about the weather and ask to get off the plane.

   Len and Miranda aren't going to make it home tonight.

2. Mr. and Mrs. Miller and their six-year-old son, Ricky, are at the Mall of America. Mr. and Mrs. Miller have decided to separate for a few hours and meet later. Mr. Miller thinks that Ricky is with his mother. Mrs. Miller thinks that Ricky is with his father. Ricky is all alone in the biggest mall in the United States.

3. Vicky and Doug are driving to Yellowstone National Park in Wyoming. Doug decided to take a small road through the mountains to save time. He made a wrong turn, and they've been lost for hours. It's dark and late, and they haven't seen anyone else for a long time. Suddenly, their car sputters to a stop, out of gas.

4. Adrian and Marta have just arrived in New York City. They are planning to go to museums, the theater, and the opera. They're checking into their hotel now. Marta has just opened her purse and realized that she left all their cash, traveler's checks, and credit cards in the taxi that brought them from the airport.

B. Work in pairs or small groups to write two short paragraphs describing travel situations like the ones in Part A. Read your paragraphs to the class. The class should make predictions about each paragraph.

4 *Will* Versus *Be Going To*: Before an Outdoor Vacation

Decide whether each item expresses willingness (offers, refusals, etc.), a plan, or a prediction about the immediate future. Complete the items with the words in parentheses and *will/won't* or *be going to*. Use contractions with subject pronouns.

I. Pam: Do you know where the newspaper is?

Ryan: It's still on the porch. I __'ll get_____ it for you.

1 (get)

II. Ryan: Pam, why are you reading travel articles?

Pam: I've been thinking about our summer vacation.

I __'m going to find_____ something exciting for us to do.

2 (find)

III. Pam: How about taking a trip to New York City?

Ryan: No, Pam. I refuse to spend my vacation in a city.

I _____ there.

4 (go)

IV. Ryan: I want to make a phone call, but I can't find the phone book.

_____ me look for it?

4 (you, help)

Pam: Sure. I _____ you.

5 (help)

Who _____?

6 (you, call)

Ryan: I _____ the travel agent to make reservations

7 (call)

for our vacation.

V. Ryan: I'm making a tuna fish sandwich for myself for lunch. If you want,

I _____ one for you, too.

8 (make)

Pam: That sounds good. . . . Uh-oh, Ryan, the cat's in the kitchen.

It _____ onto the table. Quick!

9 (jump)

Catch it before it eats our tuna!

VI. Pam: Ryan made reservations for our vacation yesterday.

Diane: Where _____ ?

10 (you, go)

Pam: We _____ a trip to Yellowstone National Park.

11 (take)

_____ our cat for us while we're gone?

12 (you, look after)

---

5 | *Will* **and** *Be Going To*: What Will They Say Next?

You're staying at a motel that has only one television, in the lobby. You want to watch the weather forecast, but a man has the remote control. He watches each show for a few seconds and then changes channels. Although these changes come in the middle of sentences, you have a good idea of how each sentence ends.

Listen once for the main ideas. Then listen again and circle *will* or *be going to* or both.

1. *Nature Program:* . . . the universe (will) / (is going to) end in a big crunch.

2. *Quiz Show:* . . . We ['ll / 're going to] get married next June.

3. *Soap Opera:* . . . I ['ll / 'm going to] change.

4. *News:* . . . prices [will / are going to] rise.

5. *Hospital Drama:* . . . Your son [is going to / will] be okay.

6. *Auto Racing:* . . . Renzo [will / is going to] win the race!

7. *Situation Comedy:* . . . [won't / 'm not going to] eat your food anymore.

8. *Prison Drama:* . . . Yeah, a shovel. [I'll / I'm going to] dig a tunnel.

9. *Weather Forecast:* . . . the sky [will / is going to] remain clear next week.

6 **Expressing the Future in Sentences with Time Clauses:**
A City Museum Vacation—The Cloisters

A. The Cloisters is a museum in New York City. Before a tour, the guide gives an introduction. Complete the introduction with the *will* future or simple present form of the words in parentheses. Use contractions with subject pronouns.

A Cloister

1. Before we __start__ the tour,
   (start)

   I __'ll describe__ the museum to you.
   (describe)

2. When we _____ the museum,
   (tour)

   you _____ three cloisters, or courtyards,
   (see)

   three chapels, and many tapestries and other works

   of art from the Middle Ages.

3. As soon as you _____ into the first cloister,
   (walk)

   you _____ some beautiful stone carvings.
   (see)

4. I _____ you into the first chapel after
   (take)

   everyone _____ at the carvings in the cloister.
   (look)

5. You _____ a recording of music from the
   (hear)

   Middle Ages as soon as we _____ the chapel.
   (enter)

Stone Carvings and Chapel

B. Combine the pairs of sentences into one sentence using the time word given, the simple present, and *be going to*. In each pair, the action in the first sentence happens earlier in time.

Unicorn Tapestry

1. as soon as: We're going to leave the chapel.

   We're going to look at the unicorn tapestries.

   <u>As soon as we leave the chapel, we're going to look at the</u>

   <u>unicorn tapestries. OR We're going to look at the unicorn</u>

   <u>tapestries as soon as we leave the chapel.</u>

2. after: I'm going to point out flowers and plants that were grown during the Middle Ages.

   We're going to go into the second cloister.

   _____

3. when: You're going to enter the room called the Treasury.

   You're going to see many valuable religious objects.

   _____

4. until: You aren't going to be allowed to take photographs.

   We're going to go into the gardens outside the museum.

   _____

5. by the time: You're going to know much more about art in the Middle Ages.

   You're going to go home.

   _____

> *Middle Ages* = the period in European history from about 500 to about 1450.

 Go to the *Grammar Links* Website to learn more about the Cloisters.

7 Using *Will* and *Be Going To*: I'll Give You the Guided Tour

 A. Imagine that you are going to give a tour of a place that you know very well, for example, your school, your home, or your room. Write a one-paragraph introduction to tell the members of the tour group what they will see. Use *will*, and use at least three sentences with time clauses.

Example: Welcome to my house. After I tell you a little about it, I'll show you the living room. You'll see a couch and other furniture there. Before we go into the kitchen, I'll show you our new television. . . .

 See the *Grammar Links* Website for a complete model paragraph for this assignment.

 B. Work in small groups. The other students in your group are going to go on your tour. Tell them what they are going to see. You can base what you say on the paragraph that you wrote, but use *be going to* instead of *will*.

GRAMMAR BRIEFING 3

Expressing the Future with Present Progressive, Simple Present, and *Be About To*

FUNCTION

A. Present Progressive

The present progressive can be used to talk about planned future actions. A future time expression is stated or implied.	We're meeting her in Paris in a month. A: What **are** you **doing** tomorrow afternoon? B: I'm buying a bicycle.

(continued on next page)

B. Simple Present

1. The simple present can be used to talk about future actions or states that are scheduled. A future time expression is stated or implied.	The semester **ends** on December 17. Next week I**'m** on vacation. *A:* What time **does** our flight **leave** tomorrow? *B:* It **leaves** at 9:00 a.m.
2. The simple present is used in time clauses instead of the future. (See Grammar Briefing 2, page 86.)	After he **comes**, we'll visit many sites.

C. *Be About To*

Use *be about to* to talk about the immediate or very near future.	We**'re about to leave** for the airport. Our bags are in the car. That glass **is about to** fall.
Time expressions are not usually used in sentences with *be about to*.	The plane **is about to** leave. **NOT:** The plane is about to leave ~~in five minutes~~.

GRAMMAR **HOT**SPOT!

1. Often, several forms can express the future. Here are the best forms to use:

   - Predictions, expectations: *will, be going to.*

     Brazil **will win/is going to win** the World Cup this year.

     If about the immediate future: *be going to, be about to.*

     Be careful! You**'re going to knock over/'re about to knock over** that glass.

   - Plans: *be going to,* present progressive.

     He**'s going to start/'s starting** college in the fall.

     If about the immediate future: *be about to.*

     We**'re about to leave.**

   - Scheduled events: simple present; also, *will, be going to,* present progressive.

     School **starts/will start/is going to start/is starting** on September 3 this year.

2. Do **not** use the present progressive or simple present to talk about unplanned events in the future.

   It **will rain/is going to rain** tomorrow.
 NOT: It ~~is raining/rains~~ tomorrow.

Expressing the Future with Present Progressive, Simple Present, and *Be About To*

8 **Present Progressive Versus *Will*:** In Washington, D.C.

Decide whether each item is expressing a planned future action or a prediction. Complete the items with the words in parentheses and the present progressive or *will*. Use contractions with subject pronouns and with *not*.

1. Lisa: I've decided to go to Washington, D.C., with Mike and Theo next week.

   Mariah: That sounds great! You __'ll have_____ a good time there.
   (have)

2. Lisa: Did you listen to the weather forecast for Washington?

   Mike: Yes, I did. Bring your umbrella. It _____ tomorrow.
   (probably, rain)

3. Airline Ticket Agent: Good morning, sir. Do you have your tickets?

   Theo: Yes, I do. We _____ to Washington, D.C.
   (fly)

4. Theo: Has Lisa chosen a place for dinner tonight?

   Mike: Yes, she has. We _____ at an Indian restaurant near the White House.
   (eat)

5. Lisa: There's a special exhibition at the National Gallery of Art. Let's go see it.

   Mike: That exhibition is really big. I want to see it, but it _____ a lot of time.
   (take)

6. Mike: Let's go to the National Archives. I want to look at the Declaration of Independence.

   Theo: We don't have time to do everything. We _____ home tomorrow.
   (go)

7. Lisa: It's almost time to go. Where's Mike?

   Theo: I'm not sure. I hope he gets here soon. He _____ the plane.
   (miss)

8. Theo: Hey, Mike! We have to leave for the airport soon. Where's your bag?

   Mike: I _____ with you. I've decided to stay longer and see everything
   (not, leave)
   in Washington.

Go to the *Grammar Links* Website for information about the museums in Washington, D.C.

9 **Future Time with Present Progressive:** You're Going on Vacation Next Week!

 Imagine that next week you can spend a three-day vacation anywhere you want. Choose a place, and complete the chart with the activities you plan to do there. Then write a paragraph about your plans, using the present progressive.

Example: I'm going on vacation in San Francisco next week. On Thursday morning, I'm taking a tour of the city. In the afternoon, I'm visiting Golden Gate Park. Then I'm meeting a friend, and we're having dinner at a restaurant on Fisherman's Wharf in the evening. . . .

	Thursday	Friday	Saturday
Morning			
Afternoon			
Evening			

See the *Grammar Links* Website for a complete model paragraph for this assignment.

10 **Future Time with Simple Present:** An Outdoor Vacation—
Yellowstone National Park

Work in pairs. Student A looks at the information on this page. Student B looks at
the information on page A-2. Ask *wh-* questions to get information to complete both
schedules. Use simple present and these verbs: *start, begin, end, finish, open, close,
leave,* and *return.*

Example: Student A: When *does* the summer season begin?
Student B: It begins on April 15.

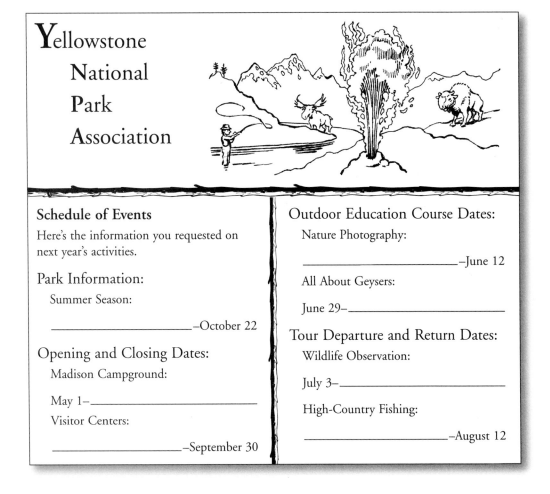

Y ellowstone
National
Park
Association

Schedule of Events

Here's the information you requested on
next year's activities.

Park Information:

Summer Season:

_____—October 22

Opening and Closing Dates:

Madison Campground:

May 1—_____

Visitor Centers:

_____—September 30

Outdoor Education Course Dates:

Nature Photography:

_____—June 12

All About Geysers:

June 29—_____

Tour Departure and Return Dates:

Wildlife Observation:

July 3—_____

High-Country Fishing:

_____—August 12

---

geyser = a natural hot spring that regularly erupts (sends a spray of steam and boiling water
up into the air). *wildlife* = animals living in nature. *high-country* = area in mountains.

11 Future Time with *Be About To*: Yellowstone Vacation

Work with a partner. Write a sentence about each of the pictures. Use *be about to*.

1. <u>They're about to go on a trip.</u>

2. _____

3. _____

4. _____

5. _____

6. _____

12 Expressing Future Time: Vacation Finales

Work with a partner. Three forms for the future are given in each item in the conversations. Two of the forms are appropriate for expressing the future in the sentence and one is not. Cross out the form that is not appropriate.

I. Museum Vacation:

A: The museum is closing / closes / is about to close in 15 minutes. I wish
   <u>   1</u>
   we didn't have to leave.

B: I read about the museum's plans for a special exhibition next month.

   Artists give / are giving / are going to give demonstrations.
   <u>   2</u>

A: That exhibition probably is including / will include / is going to include lots of
   <u>   3</u>
   interesting art. Let's come back for it!

II. Shopping Vacation:

A: Hurry up! The bus leaves / is leaving / is about to leave in a few minutes.
   <u>   4</u>
   You miss / 're going to miss / 're about to miss it. What have you been doing?
   <u>   5</u>

B: Did you know that the mall has a Fall Festival every year? I was buying a ticket because

   I 'll come back / 'm going to come back / 'm coming back for it. Come back with me.
   <u>   6</u>

III. Outdoor Vacation:

A: Why are you setting the alarm clock?

B: I 'm getting up / 'm going to get up / 'll get up in time to see the sun rise over the mountains
   <u>   7</u>
   tomorrow. It's the last day of our vacation and our last chance to watch the sun rise.

A: I heard the weather forecast. The colors in the sky are / will be / are going to be beautiful
   <u>   8</u>
   at sunrise tomorrow.

Early the next morning:

A: Look at the sky. It's really dark and cloudy. It'll rain / 's going to rain / 's raining soon.
   <u>   9</u>
   The weather forecast was wrong.

B: We don't see / won't see / aren't going to see the sun rise this morning, I'm afraid.
   <u>   10</u>
   We'll have to come back to Mesa Verde again.

**Check your progress! Go to the Self-Test for
Chapter 5 on the *Grammar Links* Website.**

6

Future Progressive, Future Perfect, and Future Perfect Progressive

Introductory Task: Predictions About Transportation and Travel in the Future

A. Work with a partner. Read the following statements. Some of the boldfaced verbs talk about actions that will be in progress at a time in the future. Circle them. Some of the boldfaced verbs talk about actions that will be completed at a time in the future. Underline them.

1. Twenty years from now, most international airlines (will be using) planes that fly faster than the speed of sound.

2. Twenty years from now, most students in the class **will have flown** faster than the speed of sound at least once.

3. Five years from now, most people **will be driving** cars that have computers connected to the Internet.

4. Ten years from now, at least one student in the class **is going to be driving** a car that steers itself.

5. By 2015, a spacecraft **will have brought** rocks from Mars back to Earth.

6. By 2015, scientists **are going to have proven** that life existed on Mars in the past.

B. 1. The circled verbs are in the future progressive. List them:

   will be using,

2. The underlined verbs are in the future perfect. List them:

   will have flown,

3. Compare the two forms. How are the future progressive and future perfect similar? How are they different?

C. Discuss the predictions in the sentences. Which ones do you think will prove to be accurate? Which ones do you think won't?

Future Progressive I

FORM

A. Affirmative Statements

WILL		
SUBJECT	WILL + BE + PRESENT PARTICIPLE*	
I	**will be working**	tomorrow.

BE GOING TO		
SUBJECT	BE GOING TO + BE + PRESENT PARTICIPLE*	
I	**am going to be working**	tomorrow.

(See Appendix 3 for spelling rules for the *-ing* form of the verb.)

B. Negative Statements

WILL		
SUBJECT	WILL + NOT + BE + PRESENT PARTICIPLE*	
We	**will not be working**	in July.

BE GOING TO		
SUBJECT	BE + NOT + GOING TO + BE + PRESENT PARTICIPLE*	
We	**are not going to be working**	in July.

C. *Yes/No* Questions and Short Answers

WILL	
QUESTIONS	SHORT ANSWERS
Will Jill **be working** this summer?	Yes, she **will** (**be**).
	No, she **won't** (**be**).

BE GOING TO	
QUESTIONS	SHORT ANSWERS
Is Jake **going to be working** this summer?	Yes, he **is** (**going to be**).
	No, he **isn't** (**going to be**).

D. *Wh-* Questions

Wh- Questions About the Subject

WILL	BE GOING TO*
Who will be traveling next year?	**Who is going to be traveling** next year?

Other Wh- *Questions*

WILL	BE GOING TO*
When will they **be traveling**?	**When are** they **going to be traveling**?

*For contractions with *will* and *be going to* (e.g., *will* + *not* → *won't*, *you* + *are* + *going to* → *you're going to*), see Chapter 5, Grammar Briefing 1, page 83.

GRAMMAR PRACTICE 1

Future Progressive I

1 **Future Progressive with *Will*—Form:
The Flight of the Future**

It's possible that airlines will be using High-Speed
Civil Transport (HSCT) planes in the future.
What will the flights be like? Use the words in
parentheses to complete the statements and
questions in the future progressive with *will*.
Complete the short answers. Use contractions
with subject pronouns and with *not*.

Announcement: Flight 101 from Los Angeles to Tokyo **will be boarding**_____ shortly.
1 (board)

A few minutes later:

Passenger: This is my first HCST flight, so I'm a little nervous. **Will the plane be taking off**_____
2 (the plane, take off)

soon?

Flight Attendant: Yes, **it will/it will be**_____. Please fasten your seat belt, sir.
3

Passenger: How fast _____? At what altitude
4 (we, fly)

_____?
5 (the plane, cruise)

Flight Attendant: The pilot _____ you that information soon.
6 (give)

Pilot: Welcome aboard. We _____ in a few minutes.
7 (take off)

Then we _____ to an altitude of 60,000 feet.
8 (climb)

The plane _____ the sound barrier until we
9 (not, break)

are over the ocean. After that, we _____ at
10 (cruise)

1,800 miles per hour—almost two and a half times the speed of sound. Sit back and

relax. The flight attendants _____ through the
11 (come)

cabin to make sure that you're comfortable.

Passenger: Excuse me. _____ dinner soon?
12 (you, serve)

Flight Attendant: No, _____. I _____
1314 (not, bring)

you dinner until the plane reaches its cruising altitude. Just relax until then.

Three and a half hours after takeoff:

Pilot: Please fasten your seatbelt. About ten minutes from now, we

_____ at Tokyo's Narita Airport.
15 (arrive)

2 Future Progressive with *Be Going To*—Form: The Car of the Future

Use the words in parentheses to complete the statements and questions in the future progressive with *be going to*. Complete the short answers. Use contractions with subject pronouns and with *not*.

Reporter: What kind of cars <u>are people going to be driving</u> in the future?
1 (people, drive)

Engineer: In the future, people _____ much
2 (not, do)

of the driving. Cars _____ computer
3 (use)

technology to drive themselves.

Reporter: What new technology _____ me today?
4 (you, show)

Engineer: I _____ a computer-based system
5 (demonstrate)

called Ralph. Ralph is short for Rapidly Adapting Lateral Position Handler.

We _____ an automated car for a
6 (take)

test drive. Let's go. . . .

Reporter: _____ itself all the time?
7 (the car, drive)

Engineer: No, _____. I _____ it
8   9 (steer)

at first. But after I switch to the automated system, I _____
10 (not, control)

its steering or speed. Ralph _____ its tiny video
11 (use)

cameras and sensors to "see" the road. . . . Okay, Ralph is in control now.

In a few seconds, it _____ lanes to avoid that
12 (change)

car ahead of us.

Reporter: You seem very relaxed. _____ soon?
13 (you, fall asleep)

Engineer: No, _____. Don't worry. Ralph is good, but it isn't
14

perfect yet. Until it is, I _____ my eyes on the road.
15 (keep)

Future Progressive II; Future Progressive Versus Future with *Will* or *Be Going To*

FUNCTION

A. Future Progressive

Use the future progressive to talk about actions that will be in progress in the future. The action may be in progress:

- At a moment in time.

> At this time tomorrow, **I'll be relaxing** on the beach.

- Over a period of time.

> She**'s going to be working** in Bangkok for the next few years.

Time Expressions

The time expressions used with the future progressive are the same as those used with *will* and *be going to* (see Chapter 5, Grammar Briefing 2, page 86). They include *tomorrow*, *next week* (*summer*, etc.), and *in a few months* (*a year*, etc.).

> He will be working **tonight.**
>
> We are going to be leaving **in three weeks.**

B. Future Progressive Versus Future with *Will* or *Be Going To*

1. To talk about actions over a **period of time** in the future, use the future progressive or the future with *will* or *be going to*. The sentences have the same basic meaning. The progressive emphasizes that the action will be ongoing.

> We**'ll be living** in a new place. = We**'ll live** in a new place.
>
> He**'s going to be studying** architecture. = He**'s going to study** architecture.

(continued on next page)

2. To talk about actions at a **moment of time** in the future:

    • Use the future progressive for actions in progress (i.e., actions that began before and continue through that moment).

    At ten o'clock tomorrow, I **will be flying** to Europe. (The plane will leave before ten o'clock.)

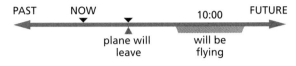

    • Use the future with *will* or *be going to* for actions that begin at that moment.

    At ten o'clock tomorrow, I **will fly** to Europe. (The plane will leave at ten o'clock.)

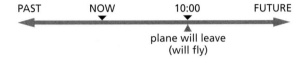

3. Remember, progressives are not used to talk about states. With verbs that have stative meaning, use the future with *will* or *be going to*.

    After this course, you**'ll know** all about computers.
    NOT: After this course, you'll be knowing all about computers.

GRAMMAR HOTSPOT!

The future progressive is often used in the main clause of sentences that have time clauses. Remember that the verb in the time clause is in the present.

She**'ll be flying** to London while we **are** at the meeting.
When we **arrive**, he**'s going to be waiting**.

Future Progressive II; Future Progressive Versus Future with *Will* or *Be Going To*

3 **Future Versus Future Progressive:** Coming and Going

Work with a partner. Choose the form or forms—future, future progressive, or both—that can be used.

1. We plan to drive to Denver tomorrow. We _a, b_____ for eight hours.

   a. 're going to drive
   b. 're going to be driving

2. My vacation starts tomorrow. At this time next week, I _____ a wonderful time in Hawaii.

   a. 'll have
   b. 'll be having

3. I haven't gotten my itinerary from the travel agent yet. I _____ it tomorrow.

   a. 'll have
   b. 'll be having

4. I don't want to go to the beach until you come. When you come, we _____ to the beach together.

   a. 'll go
   b. 'll be going

5. Lily's making plans for her vacation. She _____ in a youth hostel for a week.

   a. 's going to stay
   b. 's going to be staying

6. Casey is coming home late tonight, so we can't wait for him. When he comes,

   we _____.

   a. 're going to eat
   b. 're going to be eating

7. Vincent is coming home late tonight, but we'll wait for him. When he comes, we _____.

   a. 're going to eat
   b. 're going to be eating

8. My boyfriend promised to meet me at the airport. When I get there, he _____.

   a. 'll wait
   b. 'll be waiting

4 **Using Future Progressive:** Making Predictions About Transportation of the Future

A. How are people going to be traveling in the future? What kinds of transportation will we be using? Write six sentences about your predictions for the transportation of the future. Use the future progressive with both *will* and *be going to*. Use *not* in at least two sentences. Include at least three of these time expressions: *in a few years, in 20 years, in 2050,* and *at the end of this century*.

Example: In 20 years, buses will be traveling at very high speeds and will be floating above the road. OR People won't be using transportation much in 2050. Instead, they're going to be using their computers to take virtual reality trips.

B. Work in small groups. Discuss your predictions and decide on four predictions that everyone likes best. Tell these predictions to the class.

5 **Future Progressive in Sentences with Time Clauses:** "Smart" Cars

A. A car salesman is trying to persuade a customer to buy a "smart" car. Use the words in parentheses to complete the sentences. Use the future progressive with *will* and the simple present. Use contractions with subject pronouns.

1. Before you __begin_____ a trip, the car's computer
   (begin)

   __will be downloading_____ useful information from the Internet.
   (download)

2. While the driver _____ the car, the computer
   (steer)

   _____ traffic conditions.
   (monitor)

3. The computer _____ to your voice commands
   (respond)

   while you _____ your eyes on the road.
   (keep)

4. When the car _____ in motion, a satellite
   (be)

   _____ track of its position.
   (keep)

5. The car's computer _____ a new route before
   (search for)

   the car _____ stuck in a traffic jam.
   (get)

6. The computer _____ your e-mail and faxes while
   (send)

   it _____ your favorite music.
   (play)

7. _____ one of our "smart" cars as soon as
   (you, drive)

   they _____ available?
   (be)

---

monitor = keep track of something. *satellite* = a mechanical device in orbit around the earth. *route* = a road or way for traveling from one place to another.

 B. Think of some type of technology of the future, for example, a telephone or other communication device, a machine, a form of transportation, a computer program, or a robot. Write a paragraph that tries to persuade someone to buy it. Include at least four sentences with the future progressive and a time clause.

Example: Your Roboready will *do everything you want it to do. Before you wake up, Roboready will be making your breakfast. Roboready will be cleaning the kitchen while you get ready for school. . . .*

 See the *Grammar Links* Website for a complete model paragraph for this assignment.

GRAMMAR BRIEFING 3

Future Perfect and Future Perfect Progressive I

FORM

A. Affirmative Statements

FUTURE PERFECT			FUTURE PERFECT PROGRESSIVE		
SUBJECT	*WILL/BE GOING TO + HAVE + PAST PARTICIPLE**		SUBJECT	*WILL/BE GOING TO + HAVE + BEEN + PRESENT PARTICIPLE**	
I	**will have studied**	by then.	You	**will have been studying**	by then.
She	**is going to have eaten**	by then.	They	**are going to have been studying**	by then.

(See Appendix 7 for the past participles of irregular verbs.)

(See Appendix 3 for spelling rules for the *-ing* form of the verb.)

(continued on next page)

B. Negative Statements

FUTURE PERFECT			FUTURE PERFECT PROGRESSIVE		
SUBJECT	*WILL + NOT* (OR *BE + NOT + GOING TO*) + *HAVE* + PAST PARTICIPLE*		SUBJECT	*WILL + NOT* (OR *BE + NOT + GOING TO*) + *HAVE + BEEN* + PRESENT PARTICIPLE*	
We	**will not have worked**	together yet.	You	**will not have been working**	together yet.
They	**are not going to have worked**	together yet.	We	**are not going to have been working**	together yet.

C. *Yes/No* Questions and Short Answers

FUTURE PERFECT		FUTURE PERFECT PROGRESSIVE	
QUESTIONS	SHORT ANSWERS	QUESTIONS	SHORT ANSWERS
Will she **have studied** English by then?	Yes, she **will (have).**	**Will** he **have been studying** English by then?	Yes, he **will (have/have been).**
Are you **going to have studied** English by then?	No, I'm not **(going to have).**	**Are** they **going to have been studying** English by then?	No, they **aren't (going to have/ going to have been).**

D. *Wh-* Questions

Wh- *Questions About the Subject*

FUTURE PERFECT*	FUTURE PERFECT PROGRESSIVE*
Who will have visited Chicago by then?	**What will have been happening** by then?
What is going to have happened by then?	**Who is going to have been studying** English by then?

Other Wh- *Questions*

FUTURE PERFECT*	FUTURE PERFECT PROGRESSIVE*
Where will they **have traveled** by then?	**Where will** they **have been living**?
What are they **going to have finished** before Tuesday?	**How long are** they **going to have been traveling** by then?

*For contractions with *will* and *be going to* (e.g., *will* + *not* → *won't*, *you* + *are* + *going to* → *you're going to*), see Chapter 5, Grammar Briefing 1, page 83.

Future Perfect and Future Perfect Progressive I

6 **Future Perfect with *Will* and *Be Going To*—Form:** The Mars Exploration Program

A. Use the words in parentheses to complete the statements and questions in the future perfect with *will*. Complete the short answer. Use contractions with subject pronouns and with *not*.

NASA's Mars Exploration Program

Ask the Space Scientist:

Q: __Will NASA have brought__ rocks back to Earth from Mars by 2010?
    1 (NASA, bring)

A: No, __it won't/won't have__. But it's likely that by then NASA
         2

_____ a great deal of progress toward missions to bring
       3 (make)

rock samples back from Mars. For example, it _____ an
                                                      4 (launch)

orbiter to photograph Mars.

Q: _____ landers to explore Mars before these missions begin?
       5 (NASA, send)

A: Yes, _____. We _____
            6   7 (not, get)

enough information about Mars from orbiters alone. By the time the missions to bring back rocks

begin, scientists _____ a lot of knowledge about Mars's
                        8 (gain)

atmosphere and surface, and you _____ many interesting
                                        9 (see)

close-up photos of the planet.

Orbiter   Lander

B. Use the words in parentheses to complete the statements and questions in the future perfect with *be going to*. Complete the short answer. Use contractions with subject pronouns and with *not*.

Q: <u>Are humans going to have gone</u> _____ to Mars by 2020?
                1 (humans, go)

A: No, <u>they aren't/aren't going to have</u> _____. Space scientists
                  2

_____ a lot more about the history of Mars,
     3 (learn)

though. For example, it's possible that we _____ evidence
                                4 (find)

that life existed on Mars in the past. But we _____
                                5 (not, develop)

all the technology we need to send humans there by then.

Q: _____ a lot of progress toward a human
         6 (NASA, make)

mission to Mars by the time the Mars exploration program ends?

A: Yes, _____.
         7

Q: How much progress _____?
         8 (it, make)

A: The Mars exploration program _____
         9 (have)

successes and failures. I hope that it _____
                        10 (not, have)

more failures than successes.

NASA = National Aeronautics and Space Administration (the U.S. government's agency for air and space science and technology).

 Check out the *Grammar Links* Website to get updates on the exploration of Mars and other planets.

7   Future Perfect Progressive with *Will* and *Be Going To*—Form: Terraforming Mars

A. Use the words in parentheses to complete the statements with the future perfect progressive with *will*. Use contractions with subject pronouns and with *not*.

Some people believe that it will be possible to "terraform" Mars, that is, to change it into an Earth-like environment that people can live in.

    Terraforming Mars is a big challenge. But by the time we begin the project in the middle

of the twenty-first century, we <u>'ll have been preparing</u> _____
                               1 (prepare)

for more than 50 years and will have plenty of information. Small crews of astronauts

_____ to Mars regularly by then.
                    2 (travel)

Scientists _____ for evidence of present or
                          3 (search)

past life. This search _____ everywhere on
                                4 (not, take place)

Mars—only where life is most likely. By the time people begin to colonize the planet,

astronauts and scientists _____ on
                                      5 (stay)

Mars for long periods, and engineers _____
                                                6 (build)

bases. We _____ many supplies from
                  7 (not, send)

Earth to these crews. Such supplies won't be necessary because the crews

_____ how to live on Mars with the
                  8 (learn)

resources that are available there.

B. Use the words in parentheses to complete the statements with the future perfect
progressive with *be going to*. Use contractions with subject pronouns and with *not*.

   By the year 2150, the terraforming project _is going to have been going on_ for almost a
                                                          1 (go on)

hundred years. Mars _____
                              2 (not, change)

rapidly, but some gradual changes _____.
                                              3 (occur)

The colonists _____ the bases
                        4 (expand)

into towns. They _____ crops in
                          5 (raise)

greenhouses. Special equipment _____
                                          6 (pump)

water to the surface of the planet. Other equipment _____
                                                                7 (add)

nitrogen, oxygen, and water vapor to the planet's atmosphere.

> *colonize* = create a new settlement in a distant place. *base* = a starting point or central
> place for supplies and activities. *resource* = something that can be used to support life.
> *greenhouse* = a building, usually made of glass, used for growing plants.

 Check out the *Grammar Links* Website to find out more about the possibility of
terraforming Mars.

Future Perfect and Future Perfect Progressive II

FUNCTION

A. Future Perfect

Use the future perfect to talk about an action or state that will occur before a future action, state, or time.

> I **will have cooked** dinner before you come home.
>
> He**'ll have traveled** to Japan three times before the end of the month.

PAST   NOW   FUTURE

             I will have   you come
             cooked   home

Often, the later action, state, or time is expressed:

- In a time clause, usually beginning with *before*, *when*, or *by the time*.

> The movie is going to have started **by the time we get there**.

- With a time expression.

> We will have finished **by next week**.

Time Expressions

1. Time expressions with *by* (*by then, by 2020,* etc.) or *before* (*before then, before next week,* etc.) often indicate the later time.

> I'll have graduated from college **by then**.

2. *Already, just,* and *yet* (in questions and negatives) are also used with the future perfect.

> By Monday, Eva will **already** have left Tokyo.

B. Future Perfect Progressive

Use the future perfect progressive to talk about an action that will continue to a future action, state, or time.

> By the time we get to Chicago, we**'ll have been driving** for eight hours.
>
> By then, **I'm going to have been studying** Chinese.

That action, state, or time is often expressed in a time clause or time expression with *by* (*by the time . . . , by then,* etc.).

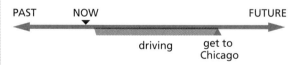

PAST   NOW   FUTURE

              driving   get to
                     Chicago

Time Expressions

In addition to time expressions with *by*, *already* and *yet* are used, and *for* indicates duration.

> **By the time** you get to the office, we'll **already** have been working **for several hours**.

(continued on next page)

C. Future Perfect Versus Future Perfect Progressive

1. The future perfect expresses actions and states that will be **completed** before some point in the future.	By then, we **will have studied** chemistry. (The study of chemistry will be completed.)
2. The future perfect progressive expresses actions that will **continue up to** some point in the future.	By then, we **will have been studying** chemistry. (The study of chemistry will be ongoing.)
3. Use the future perfect for states that continue. Progressives are not used with verbs with stative meaning.	By then, we **will have been** here for a year. **NOT:** By then, we ~~will have been being~~ here for a year.

GRAMMAR **HOT**SPOT!

1. Sometimes the future perfect is used with *for*. In these sentences, the future perfect expresses continuing actions. The sentences have the same meaning as sentences with the future perfect progressive.	By then, I'**ll have studied** chemistry for a year. (= By then, I'll have been studying chemistry for a year.)
2. The action or state expressed by a verb in the future perfect or future perfect progressive doesn't have to **begin** in the future. It may even have begun in the past.	We began driving on Monday. By the time we get to California, we'll have been driving three days. (The driving began in the past.)
3. Remember that in sentences about the future with a time clause, the verb in the time clause is in the simple present.	Before I **leave** the United States, I **will have graduated** from the university. **NOT:** Before I ~~will have left~~ the United States, I will have graduated from the university.

Future Perfect and Future Perfect Progressive II

8 Using Future Perfect: Future Accomplishments

A. Work in pairs. Use the cues and the future perfect with *will* and *be going to* to ask and answer questions about what each of you expects to do in the future. First, Student A asks Student B all the questions. Then Student B asks Student A all the questions.

Example: Student A: *What will you have done by ten o'clock tonight?*
Student B: *By ten o'clock tonight, I'll have finished my homework.*
Student A: *What are you going to have done by Saturday evening?*
Student B: *By Saturday evening, I'm going to have fixed my car.*

will	be going to
1. ten o'clock tonight	2. Saturday evening
3. a week from today	4. the time this semester ends
5. a year from now	6. five years from now
7. 10 years from now	8. the time you are 60 years old

B. Which one of your partner's expectations seems to be the most ambitious, that is, like it will take the most effort to achieve? Report this expectation to the class.

Example: *By five years from now, Mae is going to have gotten a Ph.D. in civil engineering.*

9 **Future Perfect Progressive in Sentences with Time Clauses:** A Future Astronaut

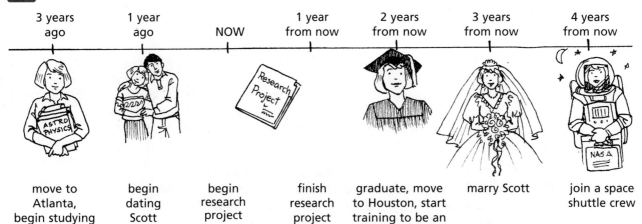

3 years ago	1 year ago	NOW	1 year from now	2 years from now	3 years from now	4 years from now
move to Atlanta, begin studying astrophysics	begin dating Scott	begin research project	finish research project	graduate, move to Houston, start training to be an astronaut	marry Scott	join a space shuttle crew

A. Courtney is a student and a future astronaut. Use the information given to complete sentences in the future perfect progressive. Use the future perfect progressive with *will*.

1. Courtney has been living in Atlanta for three years. She'll move to Houston two years from now. By the time she <u>moves to Houston</u>, she <u>'ll have been living in Atlanta</u> for five years.

2. She's been studying astrophysics for two years. She'll graduate two years from now. By the time she _____, she _____ for four years.

3. She and Scott have been dating for a year. They'll get married three years from now. By the time they _____, they _____ for four years.

4. She's working on her research project starting this year. She'll finish it a year from now. By the time she _____, she _____ for one year.

5. She'll train to be an astronaut starting two years from now. She'll join a space shuttle crew four years from now. By the time she _____, she _____ for two years.

 B. Draw a timeline like the one in Part A on a separate piece of paper. Fill it in with information and predictions about your life. Include activities beginning in the past, present, and future. Then write three groups of three sentences, using the items in Part A as a model. Use the future perfect progressive with *will* and a time clause in the third sentence of each group.

Example: I've been studying English for a year. I'll graduate from the English program in one year. By the time I graduate, I'll have been studying English for two years.

10 Future Perfect Versus Future Perfect Progressive: E-mail from an Astronaut

Circle the correct form or forms to complete the sentences.

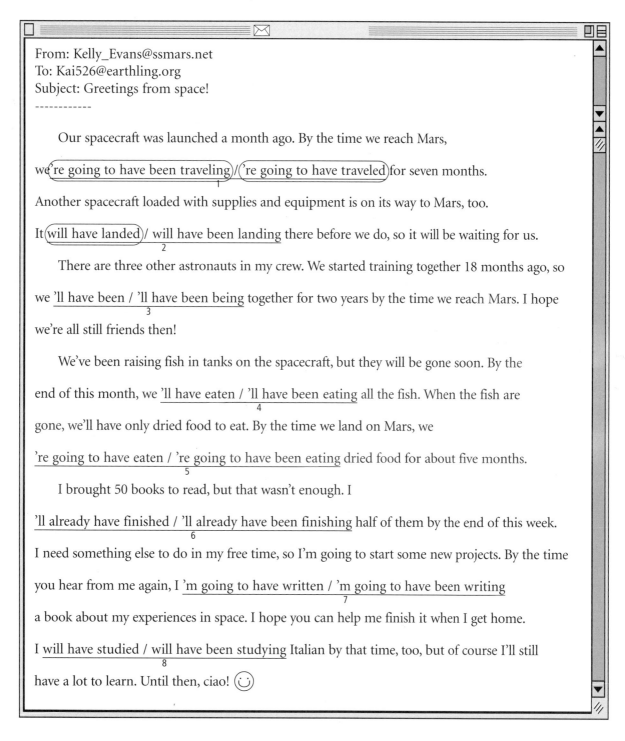

From: Kelly_Evans@ssmars.net
To: Kai526@earthling.org
Subject: Greetings from space!

Our spacecraft was launched a month ago. By the time we reach Mars,

we 're going to have been traveling / 're going to have traveled for seven months.

1

Another spacecraft loaded with supplies and equipment is on its way to Mars, too.

It will have landed / will have been landing there before we do, so it will be waiting for us.

2

There are three other astronauts in my crew. We started training together 18 months ago, so

we 'll have been / 'll have been being together for two years by the time we reach Mars. I hope

3

we're all still friends then!

We've been raising fish in tanks on the spacecraft, but they will be gone soon. By the

end of this month, we 'll have eaten / 'll have been eating all the fish. When the fish are

4

gone, we'll have only dried food to eat. By the time we land on Mars, we

're going to have eaten / 're going to have been eating dried food for about five months.

5

I brought 50 books to read, but that wasn't enough. I

'll already have finished / 'll already have been finishing half of them by the end of this week.

6

I need something else to do in my free time, so I'm going to start some new projects. By the time

you hear from me again, I 'm going to have written / 'm going to have been writing

7

a book about my experiences in space. I hope you can help me finish it when I get home.

I will have studied / will have been studying Italian by that time, too, but of course I'll still

8

have a lot to learn. Until then, ciao! ☺

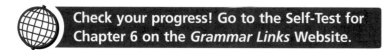

Check your progress! Go to the Self-Test for
Chapter 6 on the *Grammar Links* Website.

Chapter 7

Phrasal Verbs; Tag Questions

Introductory Task: Why Do Explorers Take On the Challenges?

A. Read these paragraphs.

Many people believe that it's necessary to **put off** a human mission to Mars until we have developed more advanced technology. But some space scientists think that better technology isn't necessary and that explorers will be able to **set off** soon on a mission to Mars.

Why will explorers **take on** the challenges of traveling to a cold, distant planet? They'll have the same motives that past explorers had: knowledge, fame, and profit. Profit might be the strongest motive. It will cost a lot to reach Mars, but explorers will **put up** the money to be the first to get there. Then they will have many possibilities for making even more money: They may be able to **take over** new territory; they'll **set up** bases and perhaps even colonies; they'll **bring back** valuable resources; and they'll **bring out** books, movies, and television programs for fascinated audiences on Earth.

B. Work with a partner. The boldfaced verbs in the paragraphs are phrasal verbs. Phrasal verbs have two words: a verb and a particle.

1. Look at the phrasal verbs in the paragraphs. Write the verbs next to their meanings.

   a. _bring back_____ : return with

   b. _____ : produce or publish

   c. _____ : delay

   d. _____ : invest or pay in advance

   e. _____ : accept responsibility for

   f. _____ : get control or ownership of

   g. _____ : start on a journey

   h. _____ : build or establish

2. Are phrasal verbs with the same verb similar to each other in meaning? _____

3. What happens to the meaning of a verb when the verb combines with a particle to form a phrasal verb?

_____

4. Can you predict the meaning of a phrasal verb from the meanings of its two words? _____

motive = the cause for a person's doing something.

Phrasal Verbs I

FORM

A. Overview

1. Phrasal verbs consist of a verb + an adverb. (The adverb is called a particle; phrasal verbs are sometimes called two-word verbs.) The most common particles are _up, out, down, off, on,_ and _over_. Others include _along, back, behind, in, through,_ and _together_.	The receptionist **set up** the appointment. He **found out** the truth. Our car **broke down**.
2. Phrasal verbs can occur in any tense.	The plane **takes off** at 7:37 every day. The plane **took off** on time. The plane **will take off** at 6:10 tomorrow.

B. Phrasal Verbs Without Objects

Some phrasal verbs do not have objects. (See Appendix 8 for a list of common phrasal verbs without objects.)	**Watch out!** They **are coming over** soon. My friends **didn't show up**.

C. Phrasal Verbs with Objects

Some phrasal verbs have objects: • If the object is a noun, it can come before or after the particle.	She **took** the book **back**. OR She **took back** the book. **Turn** the light **off**. OR **Turn off** the light.

• If the object is a pronoun, it must come before the particle.
(See Appendix 8 for a list of common phrasal verbs with objects.)
	She **called** him **up**.
	  NOT: She ~~called up him~~.
	I **will be picking** her **up** soon.
	  NOT: I ~~will be picking up her~~ soon.

Phrasal Verbs I

1 Identifying Phrasal Verbs: A Success I

Underline the phrasal verbs. If the verb has an object, circle the object. Including the examples, there are 10 phrasal verbs. Compare answers with a partner.

In the early twentieth century, the earth's polar regions seemed almost as far away and dangerous as Mars does today. The conditions were difficult, but a few polar explorers figured out (ways) to reach the poles and come back safely. One of these men was Roald Amundsen.

Amundsen was born in Norway in 1872. While he was growing up, he wanted to be a polar explorer. He therefore built up his strength in extremely cold and difficult conditions. He worked out by skiing long distances. As a result of this training, he got along well in very cold climates. Amundsen's strength and adaptability paid off later on. He understood the dangers of polar expeditions, especially freezing, hunger, and exhaustion. So before an expedition, he always prepared carefully.

In 1910, Amundsen decided to try to be the first to reach the South Pole. He planned an expedition and set off with a small crew. Then he found something out: A British expedition led by Robert Falcon Scott was also trying to reach the South Pole. Amundsen and Scott were in a race. How did this race turn out?

polar regions = areas around the North and South poles. expedition = a trip made by a group of people with a definite purpose. adaptability = ability to deal with changing conditions. exhaustion = the state of being extremely tired.

2 Phrasal Verbs: A Success II

Work with a partner. Use the appropriate form of the phrasal verbs in the box above each paragraph to complete the paragraph. (If necessary, look in Appendix 8 for help.)

let up	push on	~~set in~~	set up

Amundsen's ship landed in Antarctica in February 1911. Then he and his crew worked hard and fast before the dark, icy winter _set in _____1_____. They stored supplies and _____2_____ trail markers along the first part of their route. In October, after the Antarctic winter finally _____3_____, Amundsen and four men started south, traveling on skis and sleds pulled by dogs. There were some terrible snowstorms at first, but Amundsen and his men _____4_____.

Antarctica

+ South Pole

← Amundsen's route

get through	head back	keep up	set back

The bad weather didn't _____5_____ their progress _____ for long, so they _____6_____ their spirits _____. On December 14, they reached the South Pole and realized that they had beaten the British! Amundsen placed Norwegian flags around the area. After three days, he and his crew _____7_____ north. They returned on January 25, 1912, having traveled 1,860 miles in 99 days. Amundsen's adaptability, determination, and careful preparations had _____8_____ them _____.

> *store* = put away for future use. *trail markers* = signs that show the way.
> *determination* = unwillingness to quit.

3 **Phrasal Verbs; Placement of Noun and Pronoun Objects:** A Successful Failure

Use the words under the blanks to complete the sentences. Use appropriate verb
forms. Place the objects after the particles where possible.

Ernest Shackleton, from
England, failed to reach the
South Pole in 1908 but then
became a hero and became
rich by telling stories about
his experiences.

When Amundsen's expedition succeeded in 1911, Shackleton could

no longer become the first to reach the South Pole, but this didn't

<u>keep him back</u>_____. He decided to

          1 (keep back / him)

become the first explorer to travel across Antarctica. In 1915, he

<u>put together an expedition</u>_____. However, the

          2 (put together / an expedition)

expedition's ship became trapped in thick ice. The pressure of the ice

_____. After their ship sank,

          3 (break up / the ship)

Shackleton and the crew were left floating on a huge sheet of ice with very few

supplies. Shackleton _____

          4 (think over / their situation)

and made a plan to reach safety. They still had a couple of small boats, and

they _____ as they walked

          5 (pull along / them)

across the ice. After weeks of walking and sailing in the small boats, they reached

Elephant Island, a desolate ice-covered place. Many of the men were too weak to

go on. So Shackleton _____ and went to get help.

          6 (leave behind / them)

He sailed 800 miles in a small open boat. After he got to the Falkland Islands, near South America,

he tried to rescue his men several times, but problems

_____

          7 (drive back / him)

each time. Finally, 18 weeks later, he reached Elephant Island.

Miraculously the men were all still alive! After Shackleton

_____,

          8 (pick up / the men)

he _____ to England.

          9 (bring back / them)

And he _____, too.

          10 (bring back / another exciting story)

South Georgia	**Antarctica**
Elephant Island	+ South Pole
	Ross Sea

desolate = empty, without people or plants. *miraculously* = amazingly.

 To find out more about Shackleton, Amundsen, and other polar explorers, see the
Grammar Links Website.

Phrasal Verbs II

FUNCTION

Meaning of Phrasal Verbs

1. The meaning of a phrasal verb is different from the meaning of the verb + the meaning of the particle. Phrasal verbs with the same verb but different particles are different in meaning.

   For example, *put* = place, set, or lay, but:

• *Put up* = pay.	He **put up** the money for the tickets.
• *Put off* = postpone.	We **will put off** the trip until April.
• *Put on* = host.	They **are putting on** a great party.
• *Put down* = insult.	He **was** constantly **putting** her **down**.

2. A phrasal verb may have more than one meaning. The phrasal verb may have an object in one meaning and not in another.

   For example:

• *Set off* = start a journey.	We **will set off** tomorrow.
• *Set off* + object = make different from others.	Her red hair **sets** her **off** from the rest of the family.
• *Set off* + object = cause to explode.	The town **has set off** fireworks on Independence Day for many years.
• *Set off* + object = make angry.	His lateness **set** her **off**.

1. The words used as particles in phrasal verbs can also occur in prepositional phrases. In this case, they are prepositions that indicate location or direction. The verb + preposition is not a phrasal verb; it has the meaning of the verb + the meaning of the preposition.

   > prepositional phrase
   > He climbed up the tree. (preposition *up* tells direction)

2. Sometimes the same words can be a phrasal verb + object or a verb followed by a prepositional phrase.* There are two ways to tell the difference:

   - The meaning of a phrasal verb is different from the meaning of its two words.

     > phrasal verb + object
     > They **looked up** a word. (*look up* = search for in a dictionary)
     >
     > verb + prepositional phrase
     > They **looked up** the mountain. (*look up* = look in an upward direction)

   - A phrasal verb object can come before the particle, and if it's a pronoun, it must come before the particle.

     > phrasal verb + object
     > They **looked** a word **up**.
     >
     > They **looked** it **up**.
     >   NOT: They ~~looked up it.~~
     >
     > verb + prepositional phrase
     > They **looked** up a mountain.
     >   NOT: They ~~looked a mountain up.~~
     >
     > They **looked** up it.
     >   NOT: They ~~looked it up.~~

*A verb + prepositional phrase is also different from a verb + preposition combination followed by an object (see Grammar Briefing 3, page 125).

Phrasal Verbs II

4 Phrasal Verbs—Meaning: Check This Out

A. Use the appropriate form of the phrasal verbs in the box to complete the sentences.

> bring down: cause something or somebody to lose power
> bring in: earn profits or income
> ~~bring on: cause something to appear~~
> bring out: produce of publish something
> bring up: take care of and educate

1. I have a terrible cold. I think that staying outside in cold, wet weather
   __brought__ it _on_ .

2. My grandmother knows a lot about raising children. She _____
   eight of them.

3. He's written an adventure travel book. A publisher is going to _____
   it _____ later this year.

4. That movie was very popular. It _____ a lot of money.

5. The president of the country committed crimes. His actions _____
   his government _____ .

B. Write the letter of the correct meaning before each sentence.

> Phrasal verb: *blow up*
>   Meanings: a. ~~come into being, happen suddenly~~
>   b. express anger suddenly and forcefully
>   c. explode
>   d. fill with air
>   e. make (a photograph) larger

_____a_____ 1. When we were hiking in the mountains, a storm suddenly *blew up*, so we got cold
          and wet.

_____ 2. My bicycle tire has lost all its air. Can I use your pump to *blow it up* again?

_____ 3. This photo is too small. Let's take it to Custom Camerawork. They'll *blow it up* for
          us.

_____ 4. My sister has a tendency to get angry quickly. Whenever we get into an argument, she
          just *blows up*.

_____ 5. Someone dropped a lighted match into the gas tank, and the car *blew up*.

5 **Particle Versus Preposition:** Look This Over

In one sentence of each pair, the underlined word is a particle (i.e., part of a phrasal verb); in the other, it is a preposition. Circle the letter of the sentence that contains the particle, and rewrite the sentence with the object before the particle.

1. (a.) When Carla and Bill left the house, they turned <u>off</u> the light.

   b. When Eugene got to the hotel, he turned <u>off</u> the road.

   When Carla and Bill left the house, they turned the light off.

2. a. When the car skidded on ice, it ran <u>off</u> the road.

   b. Everyone in the group needed a map, so Paula ran <u>off</u> some photocopies.

   _____

3. a. Judy checked <u>in</u> her purse to make sure that her plane ticket was still there.

   b. Ethan checked <u>in</u> his luggage at the airline counter.

   _____

4. a. When Mark and Terry talked long distance for hours, they ran <u>up</u> a huge bill.

   b. When the children got out of school, they ran <u>up</u> the street.

   _____

5. a. The committee passed <u>over</u> two other people and chose Tim for the job.

   b. You passed <u>over</u> the Hudson River when you drove across the bridge.

   _____

6. a. As soon as I looked <u>over</u> the top of the hill, I saw the valley below it.

   b. As soon as I looked <u>over</u> the exam, I saw that it wasn't difficult.

   _____

6 **Using Phrasal Verbs:** Turn This In

Write a one-paragraph story about a travel experience. The experience can be a real one or one that you make up. Include at least five phrasal verbs from the following list. You may include other phrasal verbs, too (see Appendix 8).

break down	go back	think over	put off
come along	find out	pick up	set off
come up	take off	point out	turn out

Example: Last year, my brother and I went back home for a vacation. The trip was a disaster. After we got to the airport, we found something out. The airline had put off our flight. It finally took off eight hours late. . . .

 See the *Grammar Links* Website for a complete model story for this assignment.

Verb–Preposition Combinations; Phrasal Verbs with Prepositions

FORM and FUNCTION

A. Form of Verb–Preposition Combinations

1. Verbs and prepositions sometimes combine as a fixed unit. (Like phrasal verbs, these combinations are sometimes called two-word verbs.)

   Prepositions used in these combinations include *about, at, for, from, in, of, on, to,* and *with.*

   Verb–preposition combinations are always followed by an object.

   Think about your decision.

   They **confide in** us.

   We **lived on** pasta.

2. In some verb–preposition combinations, the verb can also have an object.

   (See Appendix 9 for a list of common verb–preposition combinations.)

               verb   obj   prep   obj
   His coat **protected** him **from** the cold.

B. Meaning of Verb–Preposition Combinations

1. Verbs of attitude, sense, speech, and thought are common in verb–preposition combinations. The meaning of a combination can often be figured out from the meaning of the verb.

   I **agree with** you. (attitude)

   We **listened to** some music. (sense)

   Let's **talk to** him about it. (speech)

   I **didn't think of** the answer. (thought)

2. A verb–preposition combination + object is a verb + prepositional phrase, like those in the Grammar Hotspot on page 122. However, the combinations are fixed units, and, often, the preposition does not have its usual meaning.

          verb prep obj
   We **lived on** pasta. (survived by eating pasta—i.e., ate a lot of pasta)
              verb prep obj
   Compare: We **lived on** a hill. (lived in a location)

C. Phrasal Verbs with Prepositions

Phrasal verbs, too, can be combined with prepositions. (These combinations are sometimes called three-word verbs.)

(See Appendix 10 for a list of common phrasal verbs with prepositions.)

     phrasal verb   prep
We**'re running out of** money this month.

He **hasn't caught up with** the group yet.

They **got back from** the hike.

Watch out for falling rocks!

Here are some ways to tell the difference between verb–preposition combinations and phrasal verbs: In verb–preposition combinations:

- The verb has its usual meaning.

- The object can't come between the two words.

- *Up, out, off,* and *down* are **not** used (they are common in phrasal verbs).

He **played with** the children. (*Play* has its usual meaning.)
NOT: He ~~played the children with~~.
Compare the phrasal verb play down: He **played down** the problems. (*Play down* means "make seem less important.") OR He **played** the problems **down**.

GRAMMAR PRACTICE 3

Verb–Preposition Combinations; Phrasal Verbs with Prepositions

7 **Verb–Preposition Combinations:** Preparing for the Unexpected

A. Use the appropriate form of the verb–preposition combinations in the boxes to complete the sentences.

~~dream of~~	plan for

Both Roald Amundsen and Robert Falcon Scott were experienced explorers who

__dreamed of_____ reaching the South Pole. But their personalities
           1

were very different, and they _____ their expeditions in
                2

different ways.

talk to	rely on	prepare for	concentrate on

Amundsen _____ practical experience and careful
           3

preparation. Before he explored an area, he _____
                4

experienced people and got useful information from them. In addition, Amundsen

_____ the details of an expedition. He always
         5

_____ the worst possible conditions, so he was ready for
         6

the unexpected.

worry about	believe in	agree with	prevent from

Scott was an officer in the British navy. He _____ 7

tradition and determination, and he didn't _____ 8 details.

Unfortunately, Scott's personal feelings often _____ 9 him

_____ making wise decisions. For example, he felt that using dogs to

pull his sleds was cruel. He _____ 10 people who believed that

the men should pull the sleds, although this was exhausting.

B. When you travel to a new place, how do you prepare for the trip? Write a paragraph describing your typical preparations. Use four verb–preposition combinations from Part A and Appendix 9.

Example: *Before I travel to a new place, I always read about it. I like to be well organized, so I worry about details. . . .*

See the *Grammar Links* Website for a complete model paragraph for this assignment.

8 Verb–Preposition Combinations Versus Phrasal Verbs: Do You Know About the Antarctic Region?

An explorer is questioning a person who wants to join an expedition. Complete the answers, changing the noun objects in the questions to pronouns. Be careful to put the pronoun in the correct position.

1. Q: I need someone who is knowledgeable. Do you know about the Antarctic region?

   A: Yes, I <u>know about it</u>.

2. Q: My plans are summarized in these papers. Have you looked over these papers?

   A: Yes, I <u>'ve looked them over</u>.

3. Q: These are the maps of the route I plan to follow. Have you looked at these maps?

   A: Yes, I _____.

4. Q: The members of the group must be adaptable. Do you learn from your mistakes?

   A: Yes, I _____.

5. Q: Our equipment must be tested in advance. Will you try out the equipment?

   A: Yes, I _____.

6. Q: The trip will be very dangerous. Have you thought about the dangers?

   A: Yes, I _____.

7. Q: You seem to be determined to come along. Have you thought over your decision?

   A: Yes, I _____.

9 Phrasal Verbs with Prepositions: Running Up Against Difficulties

Use the appropriate form of the phrasal verb–preposition combinations in the box above each paragraph to complete the paragraph. (If necessary, look in Appendix 10 for help.)

catch up + with	~~run up + against~~	stand up + to	start out + for

Scott's expedition __ran up against__ ₁ difficulties from the beginning. Scott _____₂ the South Pole two weeks after Amundsen because of problems with his equipment. He had planned to use motorized sleds, but they didn't _____₃ Antarctic conditions. Scott never _____₄ Amundsen.

close in + on	face up + to	keep on + at

Scott and his men began their journey south on November 1, 1911, but bad weather soon _____₅ them. Although the conditions were terrible, they _____₆ the tiring job of pulling their sleds to the pole. They finally reached it on January 17, 1912—only to see the Norwegian flags that Amundsen had left there. They _____₇ the fact that they had been beaten.

cut down + on	gave up + on	run out + of

On the return journey, Scott's group _____₈ supplies and luck. Because they _____₉ food, they became weak and confused. They struggled on to a point only 11 miles from a place where they had stored food. Each day they tried to start for it, but snowstorms drove them back. Finally, they _____₁₀ their attempts. By the end of March, Scott and his men had died from hunger, cold, and exhaustion.

10 Using Verb–Preposition Combinations and Phrasal Verbs with Prepositions: Your Expedition Diary

We know the story of Scott's expedition because he kept a diary, which was found later. In his final message, he wrote:

> *We took risks—we knew we took them; things have come out against us. . . . I do not think we can hope for any better things now. We shall stick it out to the end but we are getting weaker of course and the end cannot be far. . . . For God's sake, look after our people.*

Imagine that you are on an expedition in a distant and dangerous place, for example, Antarctica or a desert, jungle,or mountain. Write a two-paragraph diary entry. Use at least four verb–preposition combinations (see Appendix 9) and four phrasal verbs with prepositions (see Appendix 10). Here are some suggestions:

Verb–preposition combinations: *come from, depend on, happen to, hope for, learn from, live on, look for, prepare for, prevent (someone or something) from, recover from, search for, think about, wait for*

Phrasal verbs with prepositions: *catch up with, close in on, come up with, get back from, give up on, keep up with, put up with, run out of, run up against, start out for, watch out for*

Example:

Before we started out for the mountaintop, we had prepared for bad conditions. Then we ran up against difficulties. First, we met up with a bear. . . .

Now, we're living on crackers and juice. We haven't given up on getting to the top of the mountain. We've come up with a plan. . . .

 See the *Grammar Links* Website for a complete model diary entry for this assignment.

GRAMMAR BRIEFING 4

Tag Questions I

FORM

A. Forming Tag Questions and Their Answers

TAG QUESTIONS			ANSWERS
STATEMENT	TAG		
	BE/DO/HAVE/ MODAL (+ *NOT*)	PRONOUN	
You're hungry now,	**aren't**	**you?**	Yes, I am./No, I'm not.
The bus didn't come,	**did**	**it?**	Yes, it did./No, it didn't.
They've already left,	**haven't**	**they?**	Yes, thcy have./No, they haven't.
Bob can drive us,	**can't**	**he?**	Yes, he can./No, he can't.

(continued on next page)

A. Forming Tag Questions and Their Answers (continued)

1. To form tag questions, add to a statement: *be*/*do*/*have*/modal (+ *not*) + pronoun.

You haven't seen my pen, **have you**?

2. The tag can be affirmative or negative:

   • With an affirmative statement, use a negative tag, contracting the *not*.

   It**'s going to rain**, **isn't** it?

   • With a negative statement, use an affirmative tag.

   It **isn't going to rain**, **is** it?

3. The pronoun in the tag corresponds to the subject in the statement.

   Bob and John are leaving tomorrow, aren't **they**?

B. Verb Forms in Tags

1. If the statement has a modal auxiliary (*can*, *should*, etc.) or other auxiliary verb (*be*, *do*, *have*), use the auxiliary. If it has more than one auxiliary, use the first.

   We **can** get tickets, **can't** we?
   We **are** leaving now, **aren't** we?
   Pete **didn't** go, **did** he?
   He **hasn't been** practicing, **has** he?
   They **won't have** returned by June, **will** they?

2. If the statement doesn't have an auxiliary but has main verb *be*, use *be*.

   She **was** in the Bahamas last year, **wasn't** she?

3. It the statement doesn't have an auxiliary or main verb *be*, use *do*.

   You **go** to the beach every year, **don't** you?
   I **arrived** late, **didn't** I?

4. The verb usually agrees with the subject of the statement.

   It**'s** leaving at 8:00, **isn't** it?
   They**'re** leaving at 8:00, **aren't** they?

   Exceptions to this are:

   • With *I am*, the tag is *aren't I*.

   I**'m** leaving at 8:00, **aren't I**?

   • With indefinite pronouns that stand for people (*everyone*, *someone*, *nobody*, etc.), use plural verbs in the tag instead of singular verbs.

   Everyone is ready, **aren't** they?
   No one knows the answer, **do** they?

(continued on next page)

C. Other Subjects in Tags

1. If the subject in the statement is:

   - *This* or *that*, use *it* in the tag.

     This isn't right, is **it**?

   - *These* or *those*, use *they* in the tag.

     Those aren't heavy, are **they**?

2. If the subject is an indefinite pronoun:

   - With pronouns that stand for people (*everyone, someone, nobody*, etc.), use *they* in the tag.

     Everyone is going to be here tomorrow, aren't **they**?

   - With pronouns that stand for things (*everything, something, nothing*, etc.), use *it* in the tag.

     Something is wrong, isn't **it**?

3. If *there* is in subject position, use *there* in the tag.

   There's some pizza in the refrigerator, isn't **there**?

GRAMMAR **HOT**SPOT!

1. When the statement includes *never* (= *not ever*), use an affirmative tag.

   The bus **never comes** on time, **does it**? (= The bus doesn't ever come on time, does it?)

2. When the subject of the statement is an indefinite pronoun with *no-* (*nobody, nothing*), use an affirmative tag.

   Nobody is still hungry, **are** they?

   Nothing happened, **did** it?

TALKING THE TALK

The tag of tag questions can be an expression such as *right, isn't that right, isn't that so,* or *correct.* These tags can be used with affirmative and negative statements and all tenses. The questions can be answered like other tag questions.

A: He won't be in today, **right**?
B: No, he won't.

A: She'll be back from her trip by then, **isn't that right**?
B: Yes, she will.

Tag Questions I

11 **Tag Questions—Form:** Test Anxiety—I'll Be Ready, Won't I?

A. For each statement, underline the subject and circle the first verb, auxiliary or main. Then complete the tag question.

1. Tests (cause) anxiety, _don't they_____?

2. Ms. Moore doesn't give difficult tests, _____?

3. The first test is going to cover Columbus's voyages to America, _____?

4. Christopher Columbus wasn't from Portugal, _____?

5. The other students already know a lot about the topic, _____?

6. You weren't absent from class, _____?

7. Kim and Oliver hadn't studied before this week, _____?

8. We can study together, _____?

B. Complete the tag questions.

1. Those weren't the right answers, _____?

2. There is a lot to learn, _____?

3. Someone will fail the test, _____?

4. Victoria was taking notes, _____?

5. That could be a question on the test, _____?

6. The library has all the information we need, _____?

7. Everything is going to be okay, _____?

8. This isn't taking too much time, _____?

9. You and I will have learned everything by tomorrow, _____?

10. I'm driving you crazy with all these questions, _____?

11. I've never failed an exam before, _____?

12. Nobody's perfect, _____?

Tag Questions II

FUNCTION

A. Uses of Tag Questions

1. Speakers use tag questions when they have some sense of the answer. (Otherwise, they use *yes/no* questions.)

Speaker thinks there might be a bus stop nearby: There's a bus stop nearby, isn't there?
Compare: speaker has no idea if a bus stop is nearby: Is there a bus stop nearby?

2. Speakers may use a tag question just to make conversation. (They know the answer.)

It's hot today, isn't it? (You're standing at a bus stop on a very hot day.)

Or they may use a tag question to confirm an answer. (They have a strong sense of the answer.)

This is Mr. Lee's class, isn't it? (You're quite sure it's his class.)

In these uses:

- The tag is spoken with falling intonation.

It's hot today, **isn't it?**

- The listener often just nods or responds with some expression of agreement.

Um. OR Uh-huh.

3. Speakers may use a tag question to get information. (They don't have a strong sense of the answer.)

It'll be hot today, won't it? (Yesterday was hot, but you haven't been out yet.)

This is Mr. Lee's class, isn't it? (You think it might be here or in some other room.)

In this use:

- The tag is spoken with rising intonation like a *yes/no* question.

It'll be hot today, **won't it?**

- The listener is likely to answer yes or no or otherwise give information.

Yes, it will. OR No, the forecast is for cooler weather today.

B. Speaker Expectations

The statement part of the tag question expresses the speaker's expectation about the answer:

- When speakers think the answer is yes, they usually use an affirmative statement.

We **have** a test tomorrow, don't we? (The speaker thinks there's a test.)

- When speakers think the answer is no, they usually use a negative statement.

We **don't have** a test tomorrow, do we? (The speaker thinks there isn't a test.)

(continued on next page)

C. Answering Tag Questions

1. Answer the question the same way regardless of whether the statement is affirmative or negative.

   A: You borrowed my book, didn't you?
   B: Yes, I did. (if B borrowed the book)

   A: You didn't borrow my book, did you?
   B: Yes, I did. (if B borrowed the book)
   NOT: ~~No,~~ I did. OR ~~No,~~ I borrowed your book.

2. Especially, if your answer doesn't agree with the speaker's expectations, you probably should give an explanation for your answer.

   A: We have a test on Friday, don't we?
   B: No, we don't. The teacher postponed it until next week.

   A: We don't have a test on Friday, do we?
   B: Yes, we do. The teacher told us about it yesterday at the end of class.

GRAMMAR PRACTICE 5

Tag Questions II

12 **Listening to Tag Questions; Answering Tag Questions:** Christopher Columbus

A. Listen to the questions once, paying attention to the speaker's intonation. Then listen again and decide whether the speaker wants confirmation or information. Check the correct choice.

	The speaker is sure and wants confirmation.	The speaker is not sure and wants information.
1.	☑	❏
2.	❏	❏
3.	❏	❏
4.	❏	❏
5.	❏	❏
6.	❏	❏
7.	❏	❏
8.	❏	❏
9.	❏	❏
10.	❏	❏
11.	❏	❏

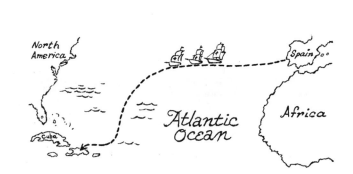

B. Read the information about Columbus on page A-2. Listen to the questions again and answer each one orally as a class.

Example: "Columbus set out on his first voyage in 1492, didn't he?" **Yes, he did.**

 Visit the *Grammar Links* Website to learn more about Columbus and his voyages.

13 **Asking and Answering Tag Questions:** Test Anxiety Again

Work in pairs. Take turns asking and answering the questions in Exercise 11. Try to use falling intonation in asking the questions. Give the answer that agrees with the speaker's expectation.

Example: Student A: Tests cause anxiety, don't they?
Student B: Yes, they do.
Student B: Ms. Moore doesn't give difficult tests, does she?
Student A: No, she doesn't.

14 **Using Tag Questions:** You're from Spain, Aren't You?

A. How well do you know your classmates? Write five statements with information about your classmates that you're quite sure is true.

Example: Luis isn't from Spain.

Write five statements with information that you aren't so sure about.

Example: Amy has four sisters.

B. 1. Go around the classroom, checking the information in your statements by using tag questions. Use falling intonation for the information you're quite sure about:

Luis, you aren't from Spain, are you?

Use rising intonation for the information you aren't so sure about:

Amy, you have four sisters, don't you?

2. When answering your classmates' questions, give an explanation when your answer isn't the one your classmate expects or when you think an explanation is useful.

Example: A: Luis, you aren't from Spain, are you?
B: No, I'm not. (I'm from Argentina.) (expected answer) OR Yes, I am. I was born there, but I've lived in this country for five years.
A: Amy, you have four sisters, don't you?
B: Yes, I do. (expected answer) OR No, I don't. You're almost right, though, because I have three sisters.

Check your progress! Go to the Self-Test for Chapter 7 on the *Grammar Links* Website.

Wrap-up Activities

1 Radio Talk Time: EDITING

Correct the 13 errors in the transcript of a radio show. There are errors in verb forms and tenses and in tag questions. Some errors can be corrected in more than one way. The first error is corrected for you.

Host:　　This is Radio Talk Time. If you have an interesting
　　　　　opinion, call ~~up me~~ *me up* and tell me.

Caller: What do you think about NASA's space program? I've
　　　　　thought it about. It's all a lie. Nothing is real,
　　　　　isn't it?

Host:　　You're joking, don't you?

Caller: No, I'm serious. NASA says that it's going to send a
　　　　　spacecraft to Mars next October. But they don't really
　　　　　send it to Mars in October. We'll believe that it's on
　　　　　Mars, but they'll be fooling us.

Host:　　How they'll do that? After the spacecraft reaches Mars,
　　　　　its cameras will take photos and send back them to
　　　　　Earth. We'll see those photos of Mars.

Caller: It's going to be seeming to us that a spacecraft is on
　　　　　Mars. Antarctica looks a lot like Mars, isn't it? By
　　　　　the time they'll launch the fake spacecraft next
　　　　　October, they'll have sent people to Antarctica with
　　　　　video cameras and a fake lander. After they set the
　　　　　cameras up there, they'll be able to send back pictures
　　　　　of the lander. While we're going to be watching the
　　　　　videos on television, we're going to be looking at
　　　　　Antarctica, not Mars. But we won't be knowing that,
　　　　　will we?

Host:　　I'm sorry, sir. We've run out of time. It's time for
　　　　　the weather forecast. It's snowing tomorrow.

Caller: Wait! Don't hang up on me! I'm right, aren't I?

2 Your Island Vacation: SPEAKING/WRITING

Work with a partner. Imagine that you are going to Getaway Island for a three-day vacation.

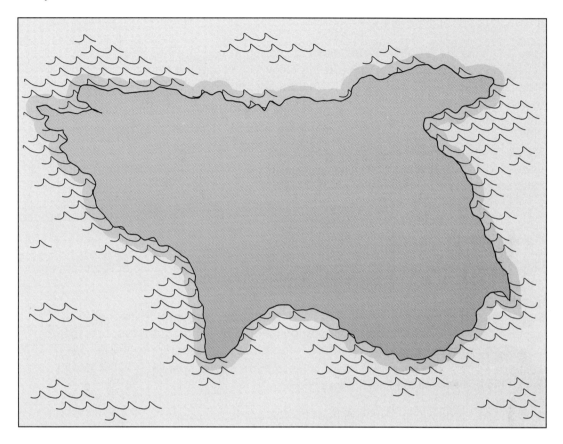

Getaway Island

Step 1 Use your imagination to fill in the map with the features of the island, for example, towns, beaches and other natural attractions, hotels and stores, amusement parks and other entertainment places—anything you want to include.

Step 2 Discuss what you are going to do when you visit the island, and make a plan for your vacation there.

Step 3 Write two paragraphs about your plans. In the first paragraph, describe what you'll be doing day by day. Use *will*, *be going to*, and the future progressive.

Example: On the first morning of our vacation, we're going to go to the beach. After we have lunch at an outdoor café, we'll rent motorbikes. We're going to be riding them to the waterfall in the center of the island in the afternoon. . . .

In the second paragraph, summarize what you'll have done by the end of the vacation. Use the future perfect.

Example: By the time our vacation ends, we're going to have had a lot of fun. We will have ridden our motorbikes all over the island. . . .

 See the *Grammar Links* Website for complete model paragraphs for this activity.

3 Your Outdoor Vacation: SPEAKING

Work in small groups to plan a trip to a national park in the United States.

Step 1 Find information about various national parks at a library or on the Internet. (If you look on the Internet, use "National Park Service" as the term for your search.)

Step 2 Discuss the possibilities and make plans: Which park are you going to visit? When will you go? How long will you stay? How are you going to get there? What activities are you going to do? What equipment and supplies will you need to take? What responsibilities will each member of the group have? Write notes about your plans.

Step 3 Give oral reports about your plans to the class, referring to your notes as needed. Which trip sounds the most adventurous? Which one sounds the most educational?

4 Game: Ask the Oracle: SPEAKING

Step 1 One member of the class should play the part of the oracle. He or she looks at page A-3 and follows the instructions there.

Step 2 The other members of the class each write three questions about their future travels to ask the oracle. Two of the questions should be *yes/no* questions; one should be a tag question. Use a different future form in each question. For example: Am I going to go on a trip soon? Will I have gone to Mars by the time I'm 50? I'm going to spend my honeymoon in Hawaii, aren't I?

Step 3 Take turns asking your questions for the oracle to answer.

> *oracle* = someone thought to have knowledge about the future.

5 Acting Out the Verbs: WRITING/SPEAKING

Work in small groups to write and then perform a skit.

Step 1 Each group chooses one of the lists of phrasal verbs on page A-3.

Step 2 Work together to write your skit. The story is up to you, but it should use all the phrasal verbs in your list and should include actions that will show the meanings of these verbs. Everyone in the group should have a role.

Step 3 Present your skit to the rest of the class.

 See the *Grammar Links* Website for a model skit for this activity.

Noun Phrases

TOPIC FOCUS
Food

UNIT OBJECTIVES

▧ **proper and common nouns**
(*Emily Custer* just opened a *restaurant*.)

▧ **count and noncount nouns**
(I can make some *suggestions* if you want *advice* about what to order.)

▧ **uses of definite and indefinite articles**
(*The* cake looks too sweet. I'll have *a* cookie instead.)

▧ **general quantifiers**
(I had *a lot of* coffee and *several* cookies.)

▧ **adjectives and other noun modifiers**
(I crave *delicious*, *fresh*, *home-grown* tomatoes.)

▧ **reflexive, reciprocal, and indefinite pronouns**
(Andrew made the cake *himself*. Liz and Val helped *each other* make the appetizers. *Everything* is ready now.)

▧ **possessives—determiners, nouns, pronouns, and phrases**
(This is *my* office. It isn't *Ms. Baca's* office. *Hers* is down the hall in the corner *of the building*.)

Grammar in Action

Reading and Listening: Food Choices

Read and listen to this passage from a guidebook for international visitors to the United States.

Food Choices

People from many countries have become familiar with one type of American food—fast food. So you may consider fast food to be the typical American food. And you'll find that **lots of Americans** do eat fast food, often because we want to save time. But as you travel through the country, you will also discover many interesting differences among places and people. Our regional, cultural, and individual differences influence our food choices and our eating habits. These choices and habits are always changing, and often the changes seem to go in different directions at the same time.

For example, recently Americans have been going out to eat at restaurants more than ever before. Does this mean that we don't have much interest in home cooking? Not at all. **Quite a few people** are taking up cooking as a hobby. They've been buying **lots of new cookbooks** and spending hours reading recipes on **the Internet**. Cooking programs on television have become popular; one TV channel has just cooking programs. In fact, **some professional chefs** have become **big celebrities**.

Some Americans don't worry much about **their diets**. But many of us are concerned about our diets and our health. We have questions about what's in **our food** and how safe it is. And we worry about eating too much fat. This doesn't mean that we can resist fatty foods, though. One person can't resist a chocolate bar; another can't resist an ice cream cone or **a delicious hot cheese pizza**.

At the end of your visit to **the United States**, you might not be able to make many general statements about our food except for this one: There's plenty of it!

---

celebrity = a famous person.

Think About Grammar

A phrase is a group of related words. One type of phrase is the noun phrase. Some of the noun phrases in the passage are boldfaced. Work with a partner. Look at the boldfaced noun phrases. Complete the sentences about the parts of noun phrases.

1. There are two types of nouns, proper nouns and common nouns. Proper nouns start with a capital letter. Examples of proper nouns are __Americans_____,

    _____, and _____.

2. Common nouns do not start with a capital letter unless they begin a sentence. Examples of common nouns are __countries_____, _____, and

    _____.

3. Quantifiers tell the amount or number of a noun. Examples of quantifiers are

    __lots of_____, _____, and

    _____.

4. Possessives indicate a noun as belonging to someone or something. Examples of possessives are

    __their_____ and _____.

5. Adjectives and other modifiers describe and give more information about nouns. Examples of modifiers are __new_____, _____, and

    _____.

Chapter 8

Nouns, Articles, and Quantifiers

Introductory Task: Survey on the Cooking and Eating Habits of Your Class

A. Work with a partner. Take turns asking each other the questions. Mark each of your partner's answers with a check (✔) in the appropriate box.

Survey Questionnaire

1. How much time do you spend cooking each day?

   ❑ 0 to 30 minutes   ❑ 30 to 60 minutes   ❑ 60 minutes or more

2. How many times do you go to fast-food restaurants each week?

   ❑ 0 times   ❑ one or two times   ❑ three to five times   ❑ six or more times

3. How much ice cream do you eat each week?

   ❑ no ice cream   ❑ not much ice cream   ❑ some ice cream   ❑ a lot of ice cream

4. How much fruit do you eat each day?

   ❑ no fruit   ❑ hardly any fruit   ❑ some fruit   ❑ a lot of fruit

5. How many vegetables do you eat each day?

   ❑ no vegetables   ❑ not many vegetables   ❑ some vegetables   ❑ a lot of vegetables

6. How much coffee do you drink each day?

   ❑ no coffee   ❑ one or two cups of coffee   ❑ three or more cups of coffee

---

B. Find out about your class. Write the questions on the blackboard and add up the answers in each category. As a class discuss the results. What can you conclude about the group's habits?

Example: *We don't spend much time cooking.*

Nouns; Proper Nouns and Common Nouns

FORM and FUNCTION

A. Overview

1. Nouns name people, places, and things.

   > teachers, children, Robert, city, Venezuela, school, food, trouble

2. There are various types of nouns:

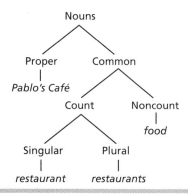

B. Proper Nouns

Proper nouns name particular people, places, and things.

They always start with a capital letter.

> *Names of people*: **Mrs. Fields, Alex Dean**
>
> *Names of places*: **South America, China, New Orleans, Lake Placid, Comfort Inn**
>
> *Titles*: ***Good News Cookbook, Time, USA Today***
>
> *Days, months, holidays*: **Friday, June, Thanksgiving**
>
> *Nationalities, languages, religions*: **Mexican, Japanese, Islam**

(continued on next page)

Article Use with Proper Nouns

1. With most proper nouns, the articles *the* and *a/an* are not used.

> They climbed **Mount Everest.**
> **NOT:** They climbed ~~the Mount Everest~~.

2. With certain proper nouns, however, *the* must be used. These include some names of countries, regions, geographical features, buildings, and vehicles, as well as newspapers and magazines.

   (See Appendix 11 for more proper nouns with *the*.)

> **The United States** is in North America.
>
> **The Middle East** produces dates.
>
> We went to **the Rocky Mountains.**
>
> My favorite restaurant is **the New York Deli.**
>
> In 1620, some colonists sailed from England on **the *Mayflower*.**
>
> I usually read **the *Washington Post*.**

3. *The* is used with family names in the plural form.

> **The Smiths** are our neighbors. (the Smith family)

4. In some special uses, a proper noun does **not** refer to one particular person, place, or thing. When this happens, the proper noun can be used with an article or a number.

> Can I have an appointment on **a Saturday**? (not a particular Saturday)
>
> There are **three Jasons** in my class. (three students named Jason)

C. Common Nouns

Common nouns are not names of particular people, places, or things.

They do not start with a capital letter unless they begin a sentence.

(For more on common nouns, see Grammar Briefing 2, page 147.)

> The **teacher** is talking to a **student** now. (people)
>
> That **restaurant** is in the **city**. (places)
>
> **Computers** are important in many **jobs**. (things)

Nouns; Proper Nouns and Common Nouns

1 **Identifying Proper and Common Nouns:** Celebrating with Food

Read the following passage. Capitalize the proper nouns. Underline the common nouns.

Celebrating with Food

When are you planning to be in the ~~u~~nited ~~s~~tates? If you are here in
the <u>fall</u>, you might be here at the right time to have a special meal on
thanksgiving. This national holiday is on the fourth thursday in
november. In big cities, restaurants stay open and offer meals. In
chicago, the oak leaf restaurant at the westlake hotel is a good place
to go. The chef there is henry lee. Although mr. lee is vietnamese, he
speaks both french and english, and americans love his food,
especially the turkey. If you are in a small town, maybe you can cook
the special dinner. Look for recipes in newspapers like the *new york
times*. Or try a cookbook like *the thanksgiving table* by diane morgan.
Wherever you are, have a happy celebration!

2 Article Use with Proper Nouns: Regional Specialties I

Different regions of the United States have different food specialties. Work with a partner. Insert *the* where needed with proper nouns in the following sentences. (If necessary, look in Appendix 11 for help.)

1. When English colonists sailed across *the* ^ Atlantic Ocean to North America on *Mayflower*,

   they landed in New England, an area that's known for its maple syrup, blueberries,

   lobster, and clams.

2. New Orleans, a city in Louisiana, where Mississippi River flows into Gulf of Mexico,

   has its own typical style of cooking, which shows influences from France and Africa.

3. After they settled in Midwest, immigrants from Germany, Sweden, Norway, and

   Netherlands continued to prepare the traditional foods of their native countries.

4. Cattle are raised on ranches in Rocky Mountains, so visitors often have steaks when

   they're staying at Brown Palace Hotel in Denver, the capital of Colorado.

5. The food of West Coast, like that of Hawaiian Islands in Pacific, has been influenced

   by Asia.

3 Articles and Numbers with Proper Nouns: Regional Specialties II

Use the article or number in parentheses or, if it is not appropriate, write *NA*.

A: Let's have a potluck dinner soon. We'll ask everyone to bring a special food from the

   region where they grew up.

B: That sounds like fun. We can have it on *a* _____ Sunday next month.
                                              1 (a, NA)

A: I think it would be better to have it on _____ Saturday next month.
                                              2 (a, NA)

B: Okay. Let's invite _____ Callahans. They're from Boston, and they make great
                        3 (the, NA)

   clam chowder.

A: Let's invite _____ Tom, too. I talked to him on _____
                  4 (the, NA)   5 (a, NA)

   Tuesday, and I know he'd like to come.

B: I know _____ Toms. Which one do you mean?
            6 (two, NA)

A: The one from Georgia. He makes delicious pecan pies!

Count Nouns and Noncount Nouns

FORM and FUNCTION

A. Overview

There are two types of common nouns:	
• Count nouns—nouns that can be counted.	**idea: one idea, three ideas**
• Noncount nouns—nouns that cannot be counted.	**advice** NOT: ~~one advice, three advices~~
Be careful! Some nouns that are noncount nouns in English are count nouns in other languages.	

B. Count Nouns

1. Count nouns generally have singular and plural forms.	**banana, bananas**
2. When the subject of a sentence is:	
• A singular count noun, the verb is singular.	A **banana was** in the bowl.
• A plural count noun, the verb is plural.	Two **bananas were** in the bowl.
3. However, some count nouns have only a plural form. When they are the subject, the verb is plural.	I need **glasses** for reading. These **jeans are** too small for me.
4. Regular plural count nouns add -s/-es to the singular form.	school → **schools** tomato → **tomatoes**
(See Appendix 12 for spelling rules for regular plural count nouns and Appendix 13 for pronunciation rules.)	
Irregular plural count nouns:	
• Differ from the singular form in some other way.	man → **men** mouse → **mice**
• Are the same as the singular form.	sheep → **sheep** deer → **deer**
• Come from another language and have kept their original plural form.	bacterium → **bacteria** analysis → **analyses**
(See Appendix 14 for more irregular plural count nouns.)	

(continued on next page)

C. Noncount Nouns

1. Because noncount nouns are not countable, they cannot be plural. They always take a singular verb.

> Her **advice was** good.
> **NOT**: Her ~~advices were~~ good.

2. Many noncount nouns belong to certain categories:

NAMES OF GROUPS OF SIMILAR ITEMS	NATURAL PHENOMENA	ABSTRACT CONCEPTS
clothing, equipment, food, fruit, furniture, garbage, homework, jewelry, money, traffic	cold, electricity, fire, heat, humidity, rain, scenery, weather	advice, beauty, confidence, education, energy, freedom, fun, health, information, luck, progress, time

SOLIDS	LIQUIDS	GASES
glass, gold, ice, paper, silver, wood	coffee, milk, soup, tea, water	air, oxygen, smoke, steam

FOODS	ACTIVITIES	FIELDS OF STUDY
bread, butter, cheese, chicken, flour, rice, salt, spinach, sugar	chess, cooking, driving, soccer, traveling	business, chemistry, engineering, history

(See Appendix 15 for more noncount nouns.)

3. Certain noncount nouns can be made "countable" with measure phrases, which put them into units (e.g., *a slice of, a box of, two pounds of*).

> I'd like **a cup of coffee**, please.
>
> We need **a quart of milk** and **two loaves of bread**.

D. Noncount Nouns Used as Count Nouns

1. Some noncount nouns that refer to solids, liquids, foods, and other substances can be used as count nouns. In this use they refer to a type or serving of the substance. (Examples: *aspirin, cake, cheese, chocolate, coffee, food, tea.*)

> I like many different **foods**. (types)
> *Compare*: All living things need food. (substance)
>
> I'd like **two coffees** to go, please. (servings)
> *Compare*: I like coffee in the morning. (substance)

2. Some noncount nouns that refer to abstract things can be used as count nouns. In this use they refer to individual examples of the abstract thing. (Examples: *art, business, crime, education, freedom, law, life, truth.*)

> He committed three **crimes**. (three individual examples of crime)
> *Compare*: Crime is a serious issue. (crime in general)
>
> My grandparents' **lives** were difficult. (the life of particular people)
> *Compare*: Life is sometimes difficult. (life in general)

1. Some noncount nouns end in *-s* (e.g., *news*, *physics*). These nouns are not plural. They take a singular verb.

   Bad **news** travels quickly.

2. Collective nouns, which are usually count nouns, are nouns that refer to groups (e.g., *group, team, audience, committee*). Singular collective nouns are usually used with singular verbs and pronouns.

   The **team** of experts **has** finished **its** work.

GRAMMAR PRACTICE 2

Count Nouns and Noncount Nouns

4 **Identifying Count and Noncount Nouns:** Food for Sightseeing

Read the following passage. Circle the count nouns. Underline the noncount nouns. Including the examples, there are 12 count nouns and 13 noncount nouns.

Food for Sightseeing

Will you be traveling through the United States in the warm months? If so, we have some advice for you: Have picnics often, especially when the weather is good. You'll be able to avoid crowded restaurants, save money, and have a lot of fun, too. You don't have to do any cooking—

just stop at a supermarket and pick up some food to take with you. You can get bread and cheese for sandwiches. Get some fruit, too, and fresh vegetables such as carrots or celery. You'll want to have a drink, so don't forget to buy bottled water or juice. Then put your purchases into your backpack and take off. When you find the perfect place, enjoy the beautiful scenery and your meal!

5 Count Nouns Versus Noncount Nouns; Plural Count Nouns: A Good Career Choice

Write the correct form of the noun in parentheses. Each noun is either a noncount noun or a plural count noun. (If necessary, look in Appendix 12, 14, or 15 for help.)

Allison: I wanted to get some __information__ about career choices, so I went to see
                                1 (information)

my advisor. It's always hard for me to make important __decisions__ .
                                                        2 (decision)

Magda: Did she have any _____ for you?
                          3 (advice)

Allison: She gave me a lot of helpful _____ . Now I'm thinking about
                                       4 (suggestion)

becoming a professional cook.

Magda: That's an interesting possibility. Have you had any restaurant _____ ?
                                                                        5 (experience)

Allison: I've had plenty of restaurant _____ . But so far I haven't had any
                                        6 (job)

_____ . The advisor said that cooking has become an excellent
7 (training)

profession for _____ . They've made a lot of _____
                8 (woman)   9 (progress)

in the profession, and they're even getting jobs as executive chefs.

Magda: It will be exciting, but I think you can expect to do a lot of hard _____ ,
                                                                            10 (work)

even when you become an executive chef. Before you go to cooking school, you'll need

to buy some really good _____ for peeling and chopping.
                          11 (knife)

Allison: Professional kitchens have lots of _____ to do things like that.
                                            12 (machinery)

Magda: But really good restaurants don't use many _____ . The chefs
                                                    13 (machine)

prepare almost everything by hand, so they're on their _____ most
                                                        14 (foot)

of the day.

Allison: Yeah, but some of them are real _____ !
                                          15 (celebrity)

> *executive chef* = the chef in charge of a restaurant kitchen.

Go to the *Grammar Links* Website to find out more about cooking careers and celebrity chefs.

6 Singular and Plural Count Nouns; Subject–Verb Agreement:
Culinary Education

Circle the correct form of the verb or noun.

1. The news (is) / are good if you want to be a professional chef: There are lots of jobs available.

2. A committee choose / chooses the students to admit to cooking school.

3. Mathematics is / are important for chefs and restaurant managers.

4. Bacteria / Bacterias are becoming more dangerous, so it's important to keep kitchens clean.

5. Please be sure that your clothes is / are clean.

6. The professor's food-cost analysis / analyses have helped restaurants save money.

7. There were a lot of students in cooking school last year, and this year the group is / are even larger.

8. We've learned how to choose the freshest grocery / groceries.

9. "Venison" is meat from deer / deers, and "mutton" is meat from sheep / sheeps.

7 Nouns Used as Count and Noncount Nouns: Good Food and Good Fortune

A. Use the appropriate noun phrases from the boxes to complete each dialogue.

> food/foods

Dustin: I'm hungry. Let's get some _food___ . What do you like to eat?
        ___1___

Joel: Well, I like many different ethnic _____, but my favorite is Chinese.
        ___2___

> tea/teas

Waitress: What would you like to drink?

Dustin: Do you have _____?
        ___3___

Waitress: Yes, of course we do.

Dustin: We'd like two _____.
        ___4___

> business/a business

Joel: Naomi told me that you've gone back to school. What are you studying?

Dustin: I'm studying _____. I'd like to own _____ in the future.
        ___5___   ___6___

cake/a cake

Waitress: Are you ready for dessert? The chef made _____ . It has almonds in it.
                                                                      7

Joel: No, thanks. I don't really like _____ . But I do want fortune cookies.
                                                         8

experience/experiences

Dustin: I like this fortune. It says, "You will have exciting _____ ."
                                                                        9

Joel: Some of the fortunes aren't really fortunes. They're proverbs like "There's no better

           teacher than _____ ."
                              10

life/lives

Joel: Here's another one: "Learn to treasure even the difficulties of _____ ."
                                                                                  11

Dustin: This one's better: "You and your loved ones will find more happiness than sadness in

           your _____ ."
                      12

beauty/a beauty

Dustin: This is the last one: "You will find _____ everywhere you go."
                                                        13

Joel: I'd prefer one that says "You will meet _____ , and she will love
                                                           14

           you forever."

 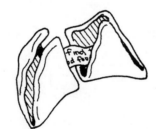 

 B. Work with a partner. Write your own one-sentence fortunes or proverbs. Use each
of these noncount/count pairs: *education/an education, friendship/a friendship,
love/loves, opportunity/opportunities.* Read your sentences to the class.

 See the *Grammar Links* Website for model sentences for this assignment.

Articles

FORM and FUNCTION

A. Articles as Determiners

The articles (*the*, *a*/*an*, and [0]) are a type of determiner. Determiners come before common nouns. The other determiners are quantifiers (see Grammar Briefing 4, page 161), demonstratives (*this*, *that*, *these*, *those*), and possessive determiners (see Chapter 9, Grammar Briefing 4, page 182).

det	noun
The children went home. (article)	
Some children went home. (quantifier)	
Those children went home. (demonstrative)	
My children went home. (possessive)	

B. The Definite Article (*The*)

1. The definite article, *the*, is used with all common nouns—noncount, singular count, and plural count.

   The electricity is off. (noncount)

   I fed **the cat**. (singular count)

   The cookies were good. (plural count)

2. *The* is used when the noun refers to something specific and the speaker and listener know what it is. This can happen when:

   - The noun has already been mentioned.

     I made some cookies and a cake. **The cookies** were delicious, but **the cake** was horrible.

   - The noun is part of or clearly related to something that has already been mentioned.

     I baked a cake. **The frosting** was too sweet. (The frosting is part of the cake.)

   - The noun is made clear by other words in the sentence.

     The bread on the table is delicious. (*On the table* tells which bread.)

   - The noun is unique—there is only one.

     The sun is shining now.

   - The noun is part of everyday life for the speaker and the listener.

     Mom, I'll feed **the dog**. (The speaker and listener know this refers to their dog.)

   - The noun is part of the larger social context of the speaker and the listener.

     The president was on TV. (The speaker refers to the president of their country—part of their social context.)

   - The noun is part of the immediate situation—speaker and listener can see or hear it.

     Could you pass **the butter**? (The speaker and listener can see it.)

(continued on next page)

C. The Indefinite Article (*A/An*)

1. The indefinite article, *a/an*, is used only with singular count nouns.

    I need **a pen**.
    He ate **an apple**.

2. The indefinite article occurs as:

    - *A* before consonant sounds.

      a kitchen, **a** hospital, **a** uniform

    - *An* before vowel sounds.

      an orange, **an** honor, **an** umbrella

3. *A/an* is used when:

    - The noun doesn't refer to something specific.

      Jack needs to find **a job**. (any job, not a specific job)
      Can I take **an apple**? (any apple from a group, not a specific apple)

    - The noun refers to something specific but the speaker and listener don't **both** know what it is. That is, the noun hasn't been mentioned yet and the other reasons for using *the* don't apply (see section B, 2). *A/an* introduces the noun.

      A man is here to see you.
      I just started **a new job**.

4. *A/an* is also used in a subject complement (i.e., after *be* and similar verbs). *A/an* + noun describes the subject but doesn't refer to a specific person, place, or thing.

    My brother is **an electrician**. (*An electrician* is just a description of the brother; it doesn't refer to a particular person.)
    Compare: An electrician is here to fix the lights. (a particular person)

(continued on next page)

D. The [0] Article

1. The [0] article is used instead of *a/an* with plural count nouns and noncount nouns.

   I put **[0] nuts** in the pie. (plural count noun)

   I put **[0] fruit** in the pie. (noncount noun)
   Compare: I put an egg in the pie.

2. The [0] article + plural subject noun is often used in statements about categories of people, places, or things. The subject noun does **not** refer to specific members of the category.

   Oranges are a good source of vitamin C.
   (*Oranges* doesn't refer to specific oranges; the sentence is about oranges in general.)

3. Some words commonly occur with the [0] article, especially in certain phrases with prepositions; for example:

   - *Breakfast, lunch, dinner.*

     We ate **[0] dinner** but didn't have a snack.

   - *Go to/be in bed, school, class, college.*

     The children haven't **gone to [0] bed** yet.

     He's **in [0] college** now.

   - *Come by/go by train, bus,* etc.

     She **came by [0] car.**

   - *At night, before morning,* etc.

     He eats a lot **at [0] night** but not in the morning.

4. *Some* can be used instead of the [0] article to talk about an indefinite quantity of the noun.

   After dinner, I'd like **[0]/some dessert.** (an indefinite quantity of dessert)

   However, it **cannot** be used to talk about the noun in general.

   I like **[0] dessert.** (*Some* can't be used; this is about dessert in general—not about a quantity of a dessert.)

Articles

8 Definite and Indefinite Articles: The Eating Patterns of a North American Family

The conversations in Column I took place during a typical week in the life of Mona and Doug and their daughter, Erin. Listen once for the main ideas. Listen again and circle the correct choice. Then read the statements in Column II and circle the letter of the statement that fits the conversation.

Column I	Column II
1. Erin: Mom, I've got to hurry! The school bus is coming, and I can't find my lunch box. Mona: I haven't seen it. Did you leave it on (a)/ the chair in the living room?	1. a. There's more than one chair in the family's living room. b. There's one chair in the family's living room.
2. Erin: Mom, I hope you had time to stop for groceries on your way home from work. Mona: They're in the car. You could help me by carrying in a / the bag.	2. a. There's more than one bag of groceries in the car. b. There's one bag of groceries in the car.
3. Doug: Erin, please don't turn on the television yet. You haven't finished your dinner. Erin: Do I have to? I don't really like [0] / the vegetables.	3. a. Erin doesn't like vegetables in general. b. Erin doesn't like tonight's vegetables.
4. Mona: Erin, if you want a snack, have a piece of fruit. Erin: I want a snack but fruit doesn't sound good. Could we go to a / the bakery?	4. a. Neither Mona nor Erin knows which bakery it is. b. Both Mona and Erin know which bakery it is.
5. Mona: I can't leave work until six tonight. Do you think you could cook dinner? Doug: Mona, you know I can't cook. Let's get fast food and then watch a / the movie.	5. a. This is the first time the movie has been mentioned. b. Doug and Mona have talked about the movie before.
6. Mona: Erin, try to eat more politely. You've got ketchup all over your face. Erin: I can't help it, Mom. I like [0] / the french fries a lot.	6. a. Erin likes french fries in general. b. Erin likes these particular french fries.
7. Erin: Are you and Mom going out to dinner alone tonight? Doug: Yes, we are. A / The babysitter is coming to take care of you.	7. a. Doug knows who the babysitter is, but Erin doesn't. b. Both Doug and Erin know who the babysitter is.
8. Doug: Can I have a taste of your dessert? It looks like it has a lot of good things in it. Mona: It does. I really like [0] / the chocolate.	8. a. Mona likes chocolate in general. b. Mona likes the chocolate in this dessert.

9 The Definite Article: The Story of Their Lives

Work with a partner. Read the dialogue between Stuart and his wife, Melissa. Above each boldfaced noun, write the letter of the reason why the speaker used *the*.

> **A.** The noun has already been mentioned.
>
> **B.** The noun is part of or is related to something that has already been mentioned.
>
> **C.** The noun is made definite by other words in the sentence.
>
> **D.** The noun is unique.
>
> **E.** The noun is part of Stuart and Melissa's everyday lives or larger social context.

Stuart: Melissa, I'm glad you're finally home. What's kept you so long?

Melissa: I had to work late, so I missed ^C ¹**the bus** near my office. Then I took a different bus, but ²**the engine** broke down. By the time another bus came, it was already dark and ³**the moon** had come up. Have you started cooking dinner?

Stuart: Not yet. I had a busy day, too. First, I went to a meeting. ⁴**The meeting** went on for hours. Then I spent the whole afternoon learning how to use a new computer. I had some trouble getting used to ⁵**the keyboard**. After I got home, I wanted to read ⁶**the newspaper**. There's an interesting article about a new scandal.

Melissa: What does ⁷**the article** say?

Stuart: ⁸**The mayor** might be involved in ⁹**the scandal**. She may have to resign.

Melissa: Let's not worry about that now. We need to think about dinner. We could make sandwiches, but ¹⁰**the bread** in the cupboard is really old.

Stuart: That's because it's been days since either one of us has had time to go to ¹¹**the store**.

Melissa: This is ¹²**the story** of our lives, Stuart. Hand me ¹³**the phone**, please. I'm going to order a pizza.

> *scandal* = something that shocks or offends the community. *mayor* = the highest official of a city or town.

10 Definite and Indefinite Articles: Food Here and There

A. Complete the conversations with *a, an, the,* or [0].

I. *In a university dormitory dining hall:*

Cindy: Good morning, Angela. Have you already had __[0]__ breakfast?
                                                                    1

Angela: Yeah. I had __an__ omelet and __a__ doughnut. I hated
                       2   3

__the__ omelet because _____ filling tasted strange.
    4   5

_____ F/food in this dormitory is disgusting.
    6

Cindy: I think I'll have _____ doughnut.
                              7

Angela: I don't want to go to _____ school today. Look at _____ sky.
                                  8   9

_____ W/weather is going to be terrible. I want to go back to
    10

_____ bed.
    11

Cindy: Stop complaining. We can go by _____ bus. Do you have plans
                                            12

for tonight?

Angela: Yeah, I do. I'm going to _____ party. Do you want to come along?
                                      13

Cindy: What time does _____ party start?
                           14

Angela: I'm not sure, but I'll look at _____ invitation.
                                           15

II. *At the party:*

Cindy: Noah, I didn't expect to see you here. I heard that you went on _____
                                                                            1

trip. I'd like to hear about it. We could have _____ lunch together
                                                  2

sometime.

Noah: What about tomorrow? We could meet at _____ restaurant, if you're free.
                                                  3

Cindy: Okay. Let's think of _____ interesting place to eat. Do you like
                                 4

_____ salads?
    5

Noah: Not really. But _____ salads are good for you, so I eat them sometimes.
                            6

Cindy: Let's go to Café Viva. You'll love _____ salads at Café Viva. My friend Liz
                                               7

works there part-time. Do you know her? She's _____ great cook, and
                                                  8

she's _____ honor student, too.
         9

Noah: I don't know Liz, but I've seen that café. It's close to _____₁₀ university, isn't it?

Cindy: Right. It's across from _____₁₁ library. I'm going to be in _____₁₂ class all morning. If _____₁₃ teacher lets us out on time, I can meet you at _____₁₄ café at noon.

III. *At lunch the next day:*

Noah: When I was traveling, I found out that this isn't _____₁ only country with lots of fast food. There are _____₂ American fast-food restaurants everywhere now.

Cindy: Do they serve exactly _____₃ same things as they do here?

Noah: Sometimes they do. For example, I went into _____₄ fast-food restaurant in Beijing. I ordered _____₅ hamburger. After I took off _____₆ wrapper, I lifted up _____₇ bun and looked at _____₈ meat. It looked exactly like _____₉ hamburger from _____₁₀ fast-food restaurant in Miami or Omaha. It tasted exactly like one, too.

Cindy: Was that _____₁₁ most interesting experience you had while you were traveling?

Noah: I was interested in _____₁₂ hamburgers at that restaurant in Beijing because I'm _____₁₃ international business major, and I'm interested in working abroad. Someday I may be selling _____₁₄ hamburgers in China.

B. Listen to the conversations. Check your answers.

11 *The, A, Some,* **[0]:** Old and New Recipes

A. Use *a, the,* or *some* to complete the paragraphs.

I have my great-grandmother's recipes, but they're hard to use. For example, her

recipe for pancakes starts: "Make __a_____ thick batter by mixing
                                     1

_____ flour with _____ milk." _____
         2   3   4

recipe doesn't tell you how much flour or milk to use or how to cook

_____ batter.
         5

This is her recipe for soup: "Catch and kill _____ chicken, cut it
                                                          6

up, and put it into _____ boiling·water. When _____
                              7   8

chicken is nearly done, add _____ chopped onions and
                                       9

_____ spices. If you have _____ fresh carrot, add it to
         10   11

_____ soup."
         12

B. For each pair, decide which sentence can be completed with *some* or [0] article and
which should be completed with [0]. Write *some*/[0] or [0].

1. a. My hobby is finding __[0]_____ new recipes on the Internet.

   b. I've found __some/[0]_____ interesting recipes on the Internet.

2. a. One of the recipes was for _____ pancakes.

   b. I immediately used it to make _____ pancakes.

3. a. I thought about making _____ chicken soup for dinner.

   b. Everyone in my family likes _____ chicken soup.

4. a. I bought _____ fresh spinach at the farmers' market.

   b. I didn't know how to cook _____ spinach, so I found a recipe on the Internet.

C. Write a one-paragraph recipe like the ones in Part A. Pay attention to your use of
the, a(n), some, and [0].

Example: *To make stewed apples, first peel and cut up some apples. Put the*
apples in a pan and add water. Put the pan on the stove and cook the
apples. When they are very soft, stir in some sugar. Add lemon juice
and cinnamon.

For links to thousands of recipes on the Internet, go to the *Grammar Links* Website.

12 Using *The, A, Some,* [0]: Two Memorable Meals

1. Work with a partner. Ask your partner to tell you about a very bad and a very good meal she or he has eaten. Your partner should tell you what dishes were included in the meals and describe each dish. Ask questions to get all the details. Both partners should pay attention to their use of the, a, some, and [0].

Example: Student A: Tell me about a very bad meal that you've had.
Student B: I had a terrible lunch at school once. The lunch was soup, some noodles, and a sweet dessert. Everything was awful.
Student A: What was the soup like?
Student B: It was just hot water with some meat in it. The meat was gray and slimy. The sauce on the noodles was gray, too. . . .

2. Tell the class about the worst and best parts of your partner's meals.

GRAMMAR BRIEFING 4

General Quantifiers

FORM and FUNCTION

A. Quantifiers

Like other determiners, quantifiers are used before nouns. Quantifiers include:	
• Numbers and measure phrases, which indicate a specific amount.	Can I borrow **two eggs**? Can I borrow **two cups of flour**?
• General quantifiers, which indicate a nonspecific amount.	Can I borrow **some eggs/some flour**?

B. General Quantifiers with Singular Count Nouns

Each and *every* are used with singular count nouns. Both mean "the total number."	I read **each paper** carefully. I read **every paper**.

(continued on next page)

C. General Quantifiers with Plural Count Nouns and Noncount Nouns

Other quantifiers are used with plural count nouns, noncount nouns, or both.

> I need **a few quarters**.
>
> I have **a little money**.
>
> I have **some quarters/some money**.

QUANTIFIERS USED		
WITH PLURAL COUNT NOUNS	WITH NONCOUNT NOUNS	WITH BOTH
		all
		most
a great many	a great deal of	a lot of/lots of
many	much	plenty of
a (large) number of	a/an (large) amount of	
quite a few		
several		some/any
		enough
a few	a little	
not many	not much	
few	little	
		hardly any
		not any/no/none of

D. Notes on General Quantifiers Used with Plural Count Nouns and Noncount Nouns

Many and Much; A Lot

1. *Many* and *much* are used mainly:

   - To ask questions about quantity.
   - In negative statements.
   - After *so* or *too* in affirmative statements.

   > **How many** people were at the party?
   >
   > We **don't** have **much** milk left.
   >
   > The teacher gives **so/too much** homework.

2. In other affirmative statements, *a lot of* is more common. *Many* is considered formal. *Much* is even more formal and is usually avoided.

   > They had **a lot of** fun.

(continued on next page)

Some and Any

1. In affirmative statements, *some* is used.	I'd like **some** dessert.
2. In questions, *any* is often used instead of *some*.	Would you like **any/some** dessert?
3. In negatives, *any* is usually used.	I **don't** want **any** dessert now.

A Few, A Little; Few, Little

1. *A few* and *a little* express the positive idea that there is some.	Let's go to that restaurant. It has **a few** really healthy dishes. I have **a little** free time, because I finished my work.
2. *Few* and *little* express the negative idea that there is hardly any or not enough.	Let's not go to that restaurant. It has **few** really healthy dishes. I have **little** free time, because I have so much work.

E. Notes on All General Quantifiers

1. *Of* is always part of certain general quantifiers (e.g., *a lot of*). It can also be part of all other general quantifiers (except for *no* and *every*) when the quantifier occurs with:

   - A pronoun.
   - *The*
     Demonstrative } + noun.
     Possessive

   Each of them came.

   Most of the students came.

   Most of those students came.

   Most of my students came.
     NOT: ~~Each/Most of students~~ came.

2. All of the quantifiers except *no* and *every* can be used without nouns if the meaning is clear.

   Each is good.

   I learned **a lot**.

GRAMMAR **HOT**SPOT!

In negative statements, do not use *no*, *none of*, or *hardly any*. This is often referred to as avoiding double negatives.	I don't want **any** dessert now.
	  NOT: I don't want ~~no~~ dessert now.
	
	He doesn't have **much** money.
	  NOT: He doesn't have ~~hardly any~~ money.

General Quantifiers

13 General Quantifiers: A "Big" Trend

A. Complete the passage with the correct quantifiers.

There is a "big" trend in food in the United States—it seems that __many__
1 (much / many)

food portions and packages have become enormous. _____
2 (Not much / Not many)

Americans notice this trend anymore, but _____
3 (quite a few / a large amount of)

international visitors do. A first-time visitor from Europe commented, "They serve

_____ food in _____ restaurants here.
4 (a great many / a lot of)   5 (every / most)

_____ meal that I've had has been big." An Asian visitor added,
6 (Each / All)

"The meals are huge. How do you eat so _____ food?"
7 (much / many)

Marketing experts say that the "big" trend began in fast-food restaurants. It

takes only _____ money to "up-size" a fast-food meal, and
8 (a little / a few)

_____ customers pass up the chance to do it. After they
9 (hardly any / not much)

noticed the popularity of oversize portions in restaurants, food manufacturers began

to make _____ products in "grand," "jumbo," or
10 (a large number of / a large amount of)

"mammoth" sizes. They have had ____ _____ success with
11 (a great many / a great deal of)

these packages. A new-products consultant says this success is natural.

"_____ years ago, health experts started warning us of the dangers of
12 (Several / Little)

eating such large portions. But _____ people seem to be able to resist
13 (few / little)

them. They just want to have _____ food."
14 (plenty of / a large number of)

> *marketing* = the business activity that involves selling, advertising, and packaging
> products. *consultant* = a person who gives expert or professional advice.

B. As a class, compare the portions discussed in Part A to portions in other
places you know about. What is your opinion of this trend toward big
packages and portions?

14 General Quantifiers: Market Research I

Circle the correct choice. Where both choices are correct, circle both.

Interviewer: Do you mind answering (a few)/ a little questions about your purchases
<u>1</u>

today? It won't take (much)/ (a lot of) time.
<u>2</u>

Shopper: I don't mind. I have <u>some / any</u> time.
<u>3</u>

Interviewer: Did you spend <u>much / a lot of</u> money shopping today?
<u>4</u>

Shopper: Yeah. I got <u>much / lots of</u> things. I bought ice cream because we don't have
<u>5</u>

<u>some / any</u> at home. I got three packages of hot dogs. I always like to have
<u>6</u>

<u>plenty of / quite a few</u> hot dogs.
<u>7</u>

Interviewer: It looks like you bought <u>a great deal of / a lot of</u> potato chips, too.
<u>8</u>

Shopper: Yes. We didn't have <u>many / hardly any</u> at home, and I wanted to be sure we
<u>9</u>

had <u>any / enough</u>.
<u>10</u>

Interviewer: Did you buy <u>any / some</u> fresh vegetables?
<u>11</u>

Shopper: No, as a matter of fact, I got <u>none / no</u> at all.
<u>12</u>

Interviewer: Did you buy <u>many / some</u> sweets?
<u>13</u>

Shopper: I don't usually buy <u>any / no</u> sweets, but I bought <u>any / some</u> today.
<u>14</u>   <u>15</u>

Interviewer: Do you have <u>much / a lot of</u> experience with shopping?
<u>16</u>

Shopper: I don't have <u>much / a lot</u>, but I know what I like.
<u>17</u>

15 *Few, A Few; Little, A Little:* Shopping Behavior

Complete each sentence with *few, a few, little,* or *a little*.

I.   Marketing Expert: Let me give you <u>a little</u> advice. Don't put important

items just inside the entrance of the store, because <u>few</u>
₂

shoppers notice anything in that area. Also, shoppers, especially women

shoppers, don't like to be crowded. They don't like stores with

_____ space in the aisles.
₃

Supermarket Manager: How many men do the food shopping for their families?

Marketing Expert: Not many. _____ men do the shopping because usually
₄

women do the food shopping for their families.

II. Wife: I've got a lot to do today and _____ time to do it. Would you mind
₅

going to the grocery store?

Husband: We don't need to go to the store yet. We have _____ cheese and
₆

_____ pickles. We can make _____ sandwiches.
₇   ₈

Wife: Never mind. I'll go. Do you have any money?

Husband: Sure, I have _____. How much do you need?
₉

III. Marketing Expert: Women are usually more patient than men. Men seem to have

_____ patience for shopping. Also, children can talk their
₁₀

fathers into buying almost anything. _____ fathers can refuse
₁₁

their children's requests.

IV. Child: Look, Daddy, they have chocolate chip cookies in the bakery! Could we please get

some cookies?

Father: Okay, you can get _____, but let's not tell your mother.
₁₂

16 Quantifiers with and Without *Of*: Focus Groups

Complete the sentences by writing *of* or 0 in the blanks.

1. Many __0__ companies want to know what products appeal to people.

2. A lot __of__ food manufacturers use focus groups to get information.

3. Each _____ the members of a focus group tries the new product.

4. Each _____ member of the group gives an opinion about the product.

5. Several _____ my friends participated in a focus group recently.

6. Did any _____ these flavors appeal to you?

7. I haven't tried any _____ new flavors yet.

8. Plenty _____ products are introduced in this country every year.

9. Most _____ people in the group don't like this product.

10. Most _____ them don't think it will be successful.

17 Using Quantifiers: Market Research II

You have just gone to the supermarket to buy groceries. After you finished shopping, a market researcher gave you the list below and asked you to write a paragraph about your purchases. In your paragraph, tell about five items that you bought—three items on the list and two not on the list. Tell how much of each item you bought and why. In addition, mention three items on the list that you didn't buy and tell why you didn't buy them. Try to use a different general quantifier in each sentence about the items you bought. Use *not . . . any* in the sentences about the items you didn't buy.

Example: When I was shopping today, I bought a little coffee. I don't have coffee at home every day, so I didn't buy a lot. I bought several lobsters because I'm going to give a dinner party for my friends. All of my friends love lobsters. . . . I didn't get any peanut butter because I never eat it. . . .

Food Products List			
bananas	coffee	ice cream	peanut butter
candy	cookies	oranges	rice
carrots	frozen dinners	lobsters	spinach
cheese	fruit juice	potato chips	steaks

 See the *Grammar Links* Website for a complete model paragraph for this assignment.

Check your progress! Go to the Self-Test for Chapter 8 on the *Grammar Links* Website.

Chapter 9

Modifiers, Pronouns, and Possessives

Introductory Task: What's Your Reaction?

A. Check the box before the sentence that describes your reaction to the particular food. If your reaction is somewhere in between, check the middle box.

1. ❏ Broccoli is a vitamin-filled green vegetable. It has a pleasant flavor.

   ❏

   ❏ Broccoli is an unpleasant vegetable. It has a very strong, bitter flavor.

2. ❏ Chocolate is my favorite candy. I can't resist eating lots of rich, wonderful chocolate.

   ❏

   ❏ Chocolate isn't an exciting food. I don't eat much chocolate.

3. ❏ I love to eat lobsters. I really enjoy their delicious, juicy white meat.

   ❏

   ❏ I refuse to eat lobsters. I have no desire to put a frightened lobster into boiling water.

4. ❏ Snails make a wonderful meal. I like them cooked with melted butter and fresh garlic.

   ❏

   ❏ I would never eat snails. They're slimy, disgusting animals.

B. Work in small groups. First, compare your reactions to the foods in the pictures. Were they similar or different? Then discuss other foods that you like or dislike very much. Why do you like or dislike these foods? Find two foods that everyone in the group likes and two foods that everyone in the group dislikes. As a class, compare likes and dislikes. Are there any foods that all the groups agree on?

Modifiers
■ Adjectives and Other Modifiers of Nouns

FORM and FUNCTION

A. Modifiers of Nouns

Modifiers of nouns describe and give more information about nouns. (The modifiers in this grammar briefing come before nouns. Adjective clauses, modifiers that follow nouns, are discussed in Unit Five.)	modifier modifier noun Fernando is the **tall, good-looking** boy modifier (adjective clause) **who always comes to class late.**

B. Adjectives

Adjectives are the most common modifiers of nouns. They describe nouns by telling their appearance and other qualities.	**strong, black** Colombian coffee **long wooden** spoon **polite, well-behaved** children

-Ing and -ed Adjectives

Adjectives that end in -*ing* and -*ed* often describe feelings.* If the adjective ends in:	
• -*ing*, the noun that it modifies causes the feeling.	What a **boring** woman! No one wants to talk to her.
• -*ed*, the noun that it modifies experiences the feeling.	What a **bored** woman! She doesn't have anything to do.
*These adjectives have the same form as present and past participles. If the past participle doesn't end in -*ed*, the adjective doesn't either (e.g., *broken, upset*).	

Use of Intensifiers with Adjectives

Adjectives can be strengthened by intensifiers—words like *really* and *very*.	She's a **really/very** good teacher.

(continued on next page)

C. Nouns as Modifiers

A noun can modify another noun. The noun modifier is singular.	There are several **steak restaurants** near our house.
	Let's go on the **bike path**.

D. Compound Modifiers

Compound modifiers have two words joined by a hyphen. Often the words are:

- Number + singular noun.

  three-pound chicken
  NOT: ~~three-pounds~~ chicken

- Noun
  Adjective } + -*ed* adjective,
  Adverb   -*ing* adjective

  sun-filled room, **time-wasting** activity
  best-liked student, **good-looking** boy
  well-known actor, **slow-moving** traffic

■ Order of Modifiers Before Nouns

MODIFIERS								NOUN MODIFIED
ADJECTIVES							NOUN	
OPINION/ QUALITY	APPEARANCE (INCLUDING SIZE, HEIGHT, LENGTH)	AGE	SHAPE	COLOR	NATIONALITY/ ORIGIN	MATERIAL	NOUN	
lovely		new				silk		blouse
	big		round				fruit	bowl
good					French			food
ugly				gray			rain	clouds

1. When two or three adjectives modify a noun, they tend to occur in a certain order.

   He was a **mean old** man.
   NOT: He was an ~~old mean~~ man.

2. Use a comma between adjectives that seem to modify the noun equally. (Hint: These adjectives can be separated by *and*.)

   good, nutritious food (food that is good and nutritious)

   Do not use a comma if the last adjective + noun makes a combination, and the first adjective modifies that combination.

   good Italian food (Italian food that is good)

Modifiers

1 **Identifying Modifiers:** Another Look

Work with a partner. Go back to the introductory task on page 168. Find the modifiers in the sentences, underline them, and circle the noun that they modify.

Example: Broccoli is a <u>vitamin-filled</u> <u>green</u> (vegetable.) It has a <u>pleasant</u> (flavor.)

2 **-Ing and -ed Adjectives:** Food and Feelings

A. Use the adjectives to complete the sentences.

Satisfied

Satisfying

satisfied/~~satisfying~~

Waiter: Did you enjoy your dinners?

Customer: Yes, we did. Please give our compliments to the chef. That was a really

      <u>satisfying</u> meal.
         1

Waiter: I will. The chef likes to have _____ diners.
                                    2

> comforted/comforting

Psychologist: When adults feel stressed, they want _____ foods, often the foods
                                                             3

they loved as children. When they eat these foods, they feel less stressed. They feel

like _____ children again.
       4

> relaxed/relaxing

Fitness Instructor: For relaxation, it's better to exercise than to eat. Sports and workouts at the

gym are _____ activities. And a _____
            5   6

person may be able to handle stress without frequent visits to the refrigerator.

> bored/boring

Vicky: I was thinking about boredom and food. Do you think that _____
                                                                        7

people sometimes eat just because they need stimulation?

Jennie: Yes, I do. Whenever I'm doing a _____ assignment, I have a hard time
                                              8

concentrating until I eat chocolate.

> tempted/tempting

Meg: This bakery has the most _____ pastries I've ever seen. Don't they
                                     9

look delicious?

Terry: My feeling is that a _____ person shouldn't resist temptation. Let's
                                10

try them!

> *stimulation* = an increase in physical or mental activity.

B. Work with a partner. Write two sentences about each kind of person.

1. amusing people; amused people

   Amusing people tell jokes and funny stories. They're fun to be with.
   Amused people smile and laugh. They're having a good time.

2. annoying people; annoyed people

3. boring people; bored people

4. interesting people; interested people

5. shocking people; shocked people

3 Noun Modifiers: Food Safety

Change the words in parentheses to noun modifier + noun and complete the sentence.

1. Handle __steak knives_____ carefully. They're very sharp.
   (knives for steaks)

2. There might be dirt or germs on fresh vegetables. Wash them before you cut them up for

   _____.
   (soup made of vegetables)

3. Don't let the _____ stay open too long. Warm food can spoil.
   (door to the refrigerator)

4. Don't let small children play with _____. The children could suffocate.
   (bags made of plastic)

5. Never try to dry a wet newspaper in the _____. It could catch fire.
   (oven powered by microwaves)

6. Accidents can happen. Keep a _____ in the kitchen.
   (extinguisher for fires)

7. Keep your fingers out of the _____. The blades are dangerous.
   (processor for food)

8. Do you think that we really need all this _____?
   (advice about safety)

4 Compound Modifiers: Long-Lasting Memories

Complete the sentences with a compound modifier formed by using the appropriate words from the sentence in parentheses.

1. Childhood memories stay with you. (They last a long time.) They're

   __long-lasting_____ memories.

2. I used to visit my grandmother during vacations. (One vacation was two months.)

   Once I stayed with her for a _____ vacation.

3. My grandmother cooked on an old stove. (That kind of stove burns wood.) It was a

   _____ stove.

4. When I was young, we ate cookies on holidays. (They were baked at home.)

   They were _____ cookies.

5. My mother made all our meals. (They were cooked well.)

   They were _____ meals.

6. Every Thanksgiving my mother roasted a big turkey. (One weighed thirty pounds.)

   She once roasted a _____ turkey.

7. My mother doesn't do much cooking anymore. (The activity consumes time.)

   Cooking is a _____ activity.

8. But I still have memories of our kitchen. (It smells sweet.)

   I remember a _____ kitchen.

5 Order of Modifiers: What Are Your Food Cravings?

A. Write the modifiers under the blanks in an appropriate order. Include commas when they are indicated.

Hank: What am I craving right now? I'd like a <u>really big, thick</u> hamburger. But I

1 (big / , / really / thick)

don't crave the _____ hamburgers from fast-food restaurants.

2 (boring / little)

Greta: I crave ice cream constantly. At the moment, I want a _____

3 (round / big / very)

scoop of triple-fudge ice cream.

Rolf: I've been thinking about pizza. I'm going to have a _____ pizza

4 (mushroom / delicious)

as soon as I can. I'm going to get it at a(n) _____

5 (charming / Italian / old / ,)

restaurant in my neighborhood.

Patty: My favorite snack is _____ chips. I get the ones that

6 (corn / crunchy / very)

come in a _____ bag. And I dip them in a

7 (plastic / large / blue)

_____ sauce.

8 (chili / red / tasty)

Tanya: I'm trying to lose weight, so I've stopped eating butter. But I dream about the kind of

butter in the _____ box.

9 (cardboard / , / rectangular / yellow)

It has a picture of a _____ woman on it.

10 (Native American / young / beautiful)

> *food craving* = a very strong desire for a certain food.

B. 1. Write five sentences about foods that you crave or like best. In each sentence, use two or three modifiers to describe a noun. Use an intensifier in at least two sentences.

> Example: I crave delicious, smooth milk chocolate. I like very strong, black Colombian coffee.

2. Read your sentences to the class. As a class discuss your cravings. Are people's cravings similar or different? What are some cravings that seem surprising or unusual?

6 Using Modifiers: Memories of the Past

 Read the following story about Dino, who wanted to open a restaurant that would serve people's favorite foods—the ones they loved eating in their childhood. Use your imagination to rewrite the story, adding modifiers before nouns. It isn't necessary to add modifiers before all the nouns. Pay attention to modifier order. Include at least one of each of the following: *-ing* adjective, *-ed* adjective, noun modifier, and compound modifier. Change *a* to *an* where necessary.

Example: First, he talked to an amusing young Greek woman named Helen.... OR
First, he talked to a very short, good-looking woman named Helen....

Dino asked various people to tell him about their memories. First, he talked to a woman named Helen. She told him stories about the meals her grandmother cooked. She described the fish, the vegetables, and the desserts. Then Dino talked to a teacher named Vinnie, who remembered some meals. Vinnie also talked a lot about the house and the garden where he lived and played as a child. After that, Dino heard from Evan, a man who loved music and art. But Evan didn't want to be reminded of his childhood. Finally, Dino met a woman named Cora. Cora had grown up in a family that lived in a city. She had memories of hot dogs and candy. Cora told Dino about the boyfriend she had just broken up with. In the end, Dino realized that his idea wouldn't work—people's feelings about food are too complicated. He decided to write stories instead. He married Cora and wrote her story first.

 See the *Grammar Links* Website for a complete model story for this assignment.

GRAMMAR BRIEFING 2

Reflexive Pronouns; Reciprocal Pronouns; *Other*

FORM and FUNCTION

A. Pronouns

Pronouns replace noun phrases that have already been mentioned or that are clear from the context. (For a summary chart of pronouns, see Appendix 16.)	**Bob** isn't here now. But **he**'ll be back in a minute.

(continued on next page)

B. Reflexive Pronouns

1. The reflexive pronouns are *myself, yourself, himself, herself, itself, ourselves, yourselves,* and *themselves.*

   Use a reflexive pronoun instead of an object pronoun (*me, her,* etc.) when an object refers to the same person or thing as the sentence subject.

   The cook burned **herself**. (herself = the cook)

   They have confidence in **themselves**. (themselves = they)
   Compare: They have confidence in them. (*Them* and *they* refer to different people.)

2. Reflexive pronouns are also used to emphasize a noun. In this use, they often come right after the noun.

   Go if you want. **I myself** wouldn't go. (emphasis to show the speaker feels strongly)

   The **principal herself** taught our class today. (emphasis because it's unexpected for a principal to teach a class)

3. Use *by* + reflexive pronoun to mean "alone" or "without help."

   I was eating **by myself**.

   The children went to the store **by themselves**.

C. Reciprocal Pronouns

Each other and *one another* are reciprocal pronouns. They are used as objects when two or more people or things, mentioned in the subject, give and receive the same feelings or actions. The reciprocal pronouns refer to these people or things.

Tom and Paula don't really trust **each other**. (Tom doesn't trust Paula, and Paula doesn't trust Tom.)

The children cooperate well with **one another**. (Each child cooperates with the other children.)

D. *Other*

Other and *another* refer to an additional one or more of a noun that has been mentioned.

A: Look! There's a baby robin. And there's **another**.
B: And there are **others** under that tree.

The other and *the others* refer to all other instances of that noun.

One of the boys in the class is my best student; **the other** is having a lot of problems. (There are only two boys in the class.)

Another and *others* refer to only some other instances of that noun.

One of the boys in the class is my best student; **another** is having a lot of problems. (There are boys in addition to these two.)

Reflexive Pronouns; Reciprocal Pronouns; *Other*

7 Reflexive and Reciprocal Pronouns—Meaning: Seeing Differences

Work with a partner. Explain the difference in meaning or emphasis between the sentences in each pair.

1. a. Lewis saw himself in the mirror.
   b. Lewis saw him in the mirror.

   In (a), <u>himself</u> refers to Lewis. Lewis saw Lewis in the mirror. In (b), <u>him</u> doesn't refer to Lewis; it refers to some other man or boy. Lewis saw someone else in the mirror.

2. a. Lucy and Trevor ordered dinner for themselves.
   b. Lucy and Trevor ordered dinner for each other.

3. a. Monica and Howard were writing letters to them.
   b. Monica and Howard were writing letters to each other.

4. a. Eva was talking to her.
   b. Eva was talking to herself.

5. a. Dora served herself dinner.
   b. Dora herself served dinner.

6. a. I myself have gone to Paris.
   b. I've gone to Paris by myself.

7. a. I talked to the president himself.
   b. I talked to the president myself.

8 Reflexive and Reciprocal Pronouns: Movable Feasts

Circle the correct pronoun.

1. Today one out of 10 meals in the United States is eaten in a car, but when I was growing up, my family always ate at home. My mother put the food on the dining room table, but she didn't serve us / ourselves the food. We served us / ourselves.

2. Whenever I was sick, my father myself / himself served me / myself breakfast in bed. This was unusual, though.

3. My sister has five-month-old twins, Yolanda and Yvonne. Right now she's busy feeding them / themselves. When the twins are old enough to feed them / themselves, my sister won't be so busy.

4. Yesterday my children ate in the car. They took turns feeding themselves / each other. First, Toby put a chicken nugget into Sam's mouth. Then Sam put a chicken nugget into Toby's mouth.

5. A: After we pick up our food, let's all sit in the car and listen to the radio while we eat.

   B: Let's talk to ourselves / one another instead. I want to hear what everyone's been doing.

6. Sometimes I like to be myself / by myself in my car, because then I can sing to me / myself and no one else can hear.

9 Forms of *Other*: Sharing

Complete the sentences by using *another, others, the other,* or *the others.*

1. A: Thanks for the cookie. It was delicious.

   B: There are plenty more. Do you want _another_____?

2. I have two cookies. I'm going to eat one. Do you want to eat _____?

3. A: I'm like a lot of young single people. I like living by myself. I don't want to share my food or space.

   B: I'm used to sharing everything with _____. I grew up in a big family.

   A: So did I. That's why I'm so happy being alone now. I got tired of sharing with all _____ in my family.

4. A: I brought back the CD you loaned me. Can I trade it for _____?

   B: Sure, but why just borrow one? I have a lot of CDs. If you want to borrow _____, you can pick out as many as you'd like.

5. A: Would you like something to eat or drink? I know how to make exactly five things. Tea and coffee are two of them; instant noodles and scrambled eggs are _____; and, believe it or not, lobster Newburg is _____.

   B: I'm sorry. I heard tea and coffee, but I didn't hear _____. Could you repeat them?

6. A: I like Irene because she has so many fine qualities. One is kindness. _____ is honesty.

   B: And _____ is generosity. She gave me her last piece of chocolate this morning.

GRAMMAR BRIEFING 3

Indefinite Pronouns

FORM and FUNCTION

A. Forming Indefinite Pronouns

	SOME-	ANY-	NO-	EVERY-
+ -ONE	someone	anyone	no one	everyone
+ -BODY	somebody	anybody	nobody	everybody
+ -THING	something	anything	nothing	everything

B. The Meaning of the Indefinite Pronouns

1. To say none (not any), use indefinite pronouns with *no-*.	There's **nothing** in the house to eat. **Nobody** told me.
However, following a negative, use indefinite pronouns with *any-*.	There isn't **anything** in the house to eat. I didn't tell **anybody**.
2. To say all of a group, use indefinite pronouns with *every-*.	It was a good party. **Everyone** had fun. The guests loved the food. They ate **everything**.

(continued on next page)

B. The Meaning of the Indefinite Pronouns (continued)

3. To talk about people and things in general, use indefinite pronouns with *any-* or *every-*.	**Anyone/Everybody** can learn to cook. When you're hungry, **anything/everything** tastes good.
4. To talk about particular unspecified people and things, use indefinite pronouns with *some-*.	**Someone/Somebody** called for you. I know I'm forgetting **something**.
In questions, pronouns with *any-* often have the same meaning as pronouns with *some-*.	Is **anyone** at the door? = Is **someone** at the door?
5. To talk about unspecified people or things but not particular ones, use indefinite pronouns with *any-*.	*A:* What do you want to do tonight? *B:* You choose. I'll do **anything**.

GRAMMAR **HOT**SPOT!

When used as subjects, indefinite pronouns take singular verbs.	Everyone **is** hungry. Nobody **was** home.

TALKING THE TALK

1. *They, them,* and *their* are often used with indefinite pronouns.	Anyone can do this if **they** really try. Everyone needs to bring **their** book with **them**.
In formal writing, *he or she, him or her,* and *his or her* are usually used instead.	Everyone can improve **his or her** life.
2. In conversation, *you* is often used as an indefinite pronoun meaning "people in general."	**You** can't always believe the newspapers. (*you* = people in general)

Indefinite Pronouns

10 **Indefinite Pronouns:** Something for Everyone

Use combinations of the words in the box to complete the sentences. More than one answer may be possible.

some-		-one
any-	+	-body
no-		-thing
every-		

1. I need to answer all my e-mail messages. I haven't written back to _anyone/anybody_ for ages.

2. The drawer was empty. _____ was in it.

3. Harriet goes running with _____, but I don't know his name.

4. A: We can ask one more person to dinner. Who do you want to invite?

   B: You decide. I'll be happy with _____.

5. A: Is Otis a vegetarian?

   B: Yes, he is. He doesn't eat _____ with meat in it.

6. A: Do you know Cedric Lawton?

   B: No, I don't know _____ named Cedric.

7. A: When you go to the store, please get me _____ to eat.

   B: What do you want?

   A: I don't care. I just feel like having a snack. _____ will be fine.

8. A: Do you have all the ingredients for the soup?

   B: Yes, I do. I have _____ I need.

9. Finding recipes on the Internet is easy. _____ can do it.

10. A: You look worried. Is _____ wrong?

    B: No, _____ is wrong. I don't have any problems.

    _____ is okay.

11. A: _____ is knocking at the door. Are you expecting

    _____ to visit?

    B: No, _____ is supposed to be coming now.

12. You get to try a lot of different dishes at a potluck dinner because _____ brings a dish to share.

Possessives

FUNCTION

Use of Possessives

1. Possessives show ownership.	**his** restaurant **the Smiths'** house
2. Possessives also show:	
• Amount (e.g., of time or money).	**10 dollars'** worth of gas **two months'** salary
• Origin.	the cheeses **of France** **Shakespeare's** plays
• That something is part of another thing.	**the restaurant's** kitchen **my** leg

FORM

A. Possessive Determiners

1. The possessive determiners are *my, your, his, her, its, our,* and *their.*	**my** parents, **its** purpose, **our** party
2. Like articles and other determiners, these words come before the noun and any modifiers. They cannot be used with articles, since a noun has only one determiner.	**My** favorite movie is on TV tonight. I gave him **my** sandwich. **NOT:** I gave him ~~the~~ my sandwich.

B. Possessive Nouns

1. A possessive noun can be made from any noun, by:	
• Adding an apostrophe to a plural noun that ends in *s.*	The **boys'** names are Paul and Jeremy. The **Smiths'** party was fun.
• Adding apostrophe + *-s* to all other nouns. (Names ending in an *s* are sometimes followed with just an apostrophe, e.g., *Charles', Mr. Jones'.*)	The **boy's** name is Michael. *Sesame Street* is a popular **children's** show. **Mr. Jones's** job pays well.
2. Possessive nouns are used with an article or another determiner.	**The/My boss's** office is large.

(continued on next page)

C. Possessive Pronouns

The possessive pronouns are *mine, yours, his, its, hers, ours,* and *theirs.* They take the place of a noun phrase.	She gave away her banana, but I ate **mine**. (= *my banana*)

D. Possessive Phrases

1. Possessive phrases are formed with *of* + a noun phrase. They follow the noun.

   The seat **of the chair** needs to be fixed. (*of the chair = the chair's*)

2. Possessive phrases are usually used:

   - For things, rather than people. (For people, use possessive nouns instead.)

     What's the color **of the walls**? (walls are things)
     NOT USUALLY: What's ~~the walls~~' color?

     Myra's office is over there.

   - To avoid a long string of words before the noun.

     She's a friend **of a roommate from college**. (avoids "a roommate from college's friend")

GRAMMAR PRACTICE 4

Possessives

11 **Possessives—Form and Uses:** Biology + Engineering = Bioengineering

Work with a partner. Underline the possessive forms in the sentences and mark each one with the letter of the meaning it indicates.

a. ownership   **b.** amount   **c.** part   **d.** origin

1. The scientist's microscope is on a table in the laboratory.
   a

2. The top of the table is covered with equipment.

3. A: How much new equipment did she buy for this experiment?

   B: She bought ten thousand dollars' worth.

4. The exports of the United States include bioengineered food products.

5. Have you seen bioengineered vegetables on the shelves of a grocery store?

6. The researcher made the discovery after four years' work.

7. Quite a few farmers have tried growing bioengineered potatoes in their fields.

8. I was interested in the researcher's ideas about how to increase food production.

> *bioengineering* = the combination of biology and engineering used to study, experiment with, and try to improve living things.

12 Forming Possessive Determiners, Possessive Pronouns, and Possessive Nouns: Technology and Food I

Complete the sentences with the correct possessive form of the pronoun or noun in parentheses.

1. Wait a minute, Richard. You put on __my__ (I)

   lab coat by mistake. __Yours__ (You) is over there.

2. This laboratory has one director. The __director's__ (director)

   job is to plan the experiments. The company has nine

   directors. The _____ (directors) job is to decide what

   policies the company will follow. Our _____ (company) goal is to develop foods that are easier

   to grow and process. Several companies are doing this kind of research. The _____ (companies)

   technology has created new types of plants.

3. A: Can you help me? I'm looking for the _____ (boss) office.

   B: I'm sorry, this office isn't _____ (she). You want the office with

   _____ (Ms. Tanaka) name on the door. This is _____ (Ms. Harris) office.

   A: It isn't easy to find a _____ (person) office in this building.

   B: You can find _____ (people) office numbers in _____ (we) directory.

4. In this laboratory, the _____ (scientists) work involves changing the characteristics of plants by

   changing _____ (they) genes. That _____ (scientist) experiment involved changing the

   characteristics of a plant by putting genes from an animal into _____ (it) cells.

5. A: Where are Bella and Charles? Are these salads _____ (they)?

   B: Yes, they are. This is _____ (she) salad, and that one is _____ (he).

6. A: _____ (you) salads look all right, but you should try some of _____ (I).

   It has a bioengineered tomato in it.

   B: That's okay. We don't really want _____ (you). _____ (we) are more natural.

   C: Actually, I'm interested in that tomato. What's _____ (it) flavor like? Does it taste
   like chicken?

> *cell* = the basic unit of living matter in plants and animals. *gene* = a cell part that
> determines a feature or characteristic of a plant or animal.

13 **Possessive Nouns Versus Possessive Phrases:** Food and Technology II

Complete the sentences by forming possessive nouns and possessive phrases from the words in parentheses. In each, use the preferred possessive form. Add *the* where necessary.

1. <u>Richard's laboratory</u> is using biotechnology to change plants and animals.
    (Richard / laboratory)

2. To find his lab, go through the door at the <u>end of the hall</u> and up the stairs.
    (hall / end)

3. The lab is at the _____.
    (stairs / top)

4. I have some questions about the new foods. Will they affect _____?
    (people / health)

5. I talked to the _____,
    (well-known biotechnology laboratory / director)

    and he explained his opinion.

6. Through bioengineering, _____ will be able to resist diseases and
    (farmers / crops)

    insects, and people everywhere will have more food.

7. Now Richard is looking into _____.
    (another scientist in the laboratory / microscope)

8. There's a problem with an experiment. They're looking for the _____.
    (problem / cause)

9. I'm still worried. Could bioengineers accidentally create something like

    _____?
    (Dr. Frankenstein / monster)

 To learn more about the pros and cons of bioengineering, go to the *Grammar Links* Website.

 **Check your progress! Go to the Self-Test for Chapter 9 on the *Grammar Links* Website.**

Wrap-up Activities

1 **A Restaurant Review:** EDITING

Correct the 20 errors in the restaurant review. There are errors in articles, quantifiers, modifiers, possessives, nouns, and pronouns. The first error is corrected for you.

Taste of the Town—
A Review of Magnificent Food

Last week, I had dinner at Magnificent Food, ~~a~~ *the* newest restaurant in town. I invited the friend to come with me. The owner of Magnificent Food is the famous chef. His name is Charles whitney. My friend and I were looking forward to eating delicious specialties prepared by Mr. Whitney hisself.

When we arrived at the restaurant, we had to wait, so we sat down and began to look at the four-pages menu. When our table was finally ready, we asked our waiter for some advice about what to order. Although he didn't seem to have a lot of knowledges about the menu, he made any suggestions. We ordered two appetizers; one was smoked fish, and another was vegetable soup. The smoked fish looked beautiful, but it's flavor was strange. A vegetable soup had too many salt in it. The other people in the restaurant got their main courses right away, but we had a long wait for our because of a problem in the kitchen. When our plates finally came, there was plenty food on them. I had ordered a regional specialty from South. It shouldn't have been a bored dish, but it was— every of the bites was tasteless. My friends' steak looked very good, but everything on her plate was cold. We decided to go to an excellent small European café across the street for coffee and dessert.

New restaurants often have few problems, so I wasn't expecting Magnificent Food to be perfect. But I wasn't expecting to be such a disappointing customer. I hope that this restaurant improves and becomes truly magnificent.

2 A Very Special Dinner Party—Who's Invited? SPEAKING/WRITING

Step 1 Work in small groups. Imagine that your group is going to give a very special dinner party. You can invite any seven famous people, living or dead—no one will refuse to come to your party. You can invite people like Elvis Presley, Bill Gates, Hillary Clinton, Michael Jordan, John F. Kennedy, Jennifer Lopez, Tiger Woods, Princess Diana, or anyone you choose. Think of people you would like to invite and discuss them. Decide on seven guests that you would all like to invite.

Step 2 Write two or more sentences about each person and the reasons the group wants to invite him or her. Pay attention to your use of articles, modifiers, and pronouns.

Example: Tiger Woods is a well-known, talented golfer. We hope that he will talk about himself and tell us the secrets of his success. OR Princess Diana was a beautiful young woman. She had an interesting life.

Step 3 Read your sentences to the class. Which group's dinner party will be the most interesting? Why?

3 Review a Restaurant: WRITING

Step 1 Work with a partner. Imagine that the two of you are restaurant reviewers for a newspaper. Decide what restaurant you want to review. The restaurant can be a real one or one that you make up, and it can be any kind of restaurant—ethnic, fast food, casual, or elegant. Talk about the food (how it looks and tastes), the service (what the waiters or waitresses are like, how well they do their job), and the décor (what the restaurant and its furniture look like).

Step 2 Make notes about the food, service, and décor of the restaurant.

Step 3 Write a three-paragraph review of the restaurant. Use at least one of each of the following: an *-ing* and *-ed* adjective, a noun modifier, a compound modifier, a possessive noun, a possessive determiner, and a possessive phrase. Pay attention to your use of articles and pronouns.

 See the *Grammar Links* Website for a model review for this activity.

4 | **Create a Culture:** SPEAKING

Step 1 Work in groups of three. The three of you are members of an imaginary culture. Discuss the answers to these questions: What does your culture consider to be appropriate food for each meal? How much of each food do people eat at each meal? Are there separate courses, or do people eat all the food at the same time? Who does the cooking in families? Are there any prohibited foods (foods that people aren't allowed to eat)? What do people eat when they celebrate special occasions?

Step 2 Make notes on your answers to the questions.

Step 3 Describe your culture's food and food habits to the class. Refer to your notes if necessary. Pay attention to your use of count and noncount nouns, articles, quantifiers, and modifiers.

Example: In our culture, most people eat one small meal, one large meal, and several snacks each day. We eat the small meal as soon as we wake up in the morning. We usually have a few dill pickles, some apple pie or a little ice cream, and a lot of hot tea. . . . Our most important holiday is on June 21. On that day, everyone eats young green onions and hard-boiled eggs.

Adjective Clauses

TOPIC FOCUS
Personality

UNIT OBJECTIVES

▪ **adjective clauses with subject relative pronouns (*that, who, which*)**

(Psychologists are scientists *who study thoughts, feelings, and behavior*. Psychology is a subject *that interests me*.)

▪ **adjective clauses with object relative pronouns (*that, who[m], which, [0]*)**

(The work *that they do* is interesting. Are you shy with people *who you don't know well*?)

▪ **adjective clauses with relative pronouns that are objects of prepositions**

(Personality is a topic *that we are learning about*. The professor is someone *for whom I have a lot of respect*.)

▪ **adjective clauses with possessive relative pronouns**

(That's the teacher *whose class I want to take*.)

▪ **adjective clauses with *where* and *when***

(Tell me about the place *where you grew up*. I remember the day *when we met*.)

Grammar in Action

🎧 Reading and Listening: Alive in Our Times

Read and listen to this radio interview.

Host: Lorrie Kress
Guest: Professor Bruno Schiller

A: Hello, everyone. I'm Lorrie Kress, and this is "Alive in Our Times." My guest today is a (psychologist) **who does research on personality**. He's someone **whom I admire very much**. I'd like to welcome a man **whose ideas are always interesting**, Professor Bruno Schiller.

B: Thank you, Lorrie.

A: Professor Schiller, personality is something **that many of us want to know more about**. Can you tell us how we get our personalities?

B: Well, Lorrie, psychologists have developed many theories about this. Basically, there are two factors **which work together in childhood to form people's personalities**. The first is biology. Biology is responsible for the characteristics **that you are born with**. And the second is environment. Your environment includes your surroundings, your family and friends, and your experiences.

A: My sisters and I had the same parents and the same environment as children, but we have really different personalities now. Do you know why?

B: Actually, there is a theory **which might explain the differences among children in the same family**. According to this theory, your personality differences are a result of your birth order, in other words, your position as the oldest, a middle, or the youngest child in your family. A firstborn child experiences things differently than a laterborn child does. Only children, that is, children who have no brothers or sisters, are in many ways similar to firstborn children.

A: So, Professor Schiller, what are some characteristics **that birth order might be responsible for**?

B: Well, birth order might determine whether you are creative or practical. It could also determine whether you are the kind of person **that usually follows rules** or the kind of person **that sometimes breaks the rules**.

A: Can you guess my birth order?

B: Perhaps. Let me give you a test **whose results could tell me about your personality**.

---

factor = something that helps cause a certain result. *characteristic* = a feature or quality.
firstborn = the oldest child in a family. *laterborn* = a child born second, third, etc., in a family.

Think About Grammar

Work on your own to complete the task.

1. The boldfaced clauses in the radio interview are adjective clauses. Adjective clauses modify nouns and indefinite pronouns (e.g., *someone*). They give information about the noun or pronoun. An adjective clause comes after the noun or pronoun it modifies. Look at the boldfaced adjective clauses in the radio interview. Circle the noun or pronoun that each one modifies. The first one is circled for you.

2. Adjective clauses begin with relative pronouns. Look at the boldfaced adjective clauses.

   The relative pronouns are _who_____, _____,

   _____, _____, and _____.

3. Nouns and pronouns can refer to people (e.g., *man* and *someone*) or things, including abstract things and ideas (e.g., *factors* and *something*). The relative pronoun in an adjective clause refers to the same person or thing as the noun that it modifies. Look at the nouns and pronouns you circled and at the relative pronouns in the adjective clauses that modify them.

   a. The relative pronouns _who_____, _____,

      _____, and _____ can refer to people.

   b. The relative pronouns _____, _____, and

      _____ can refer to things.

Chapter 10

Adjective Clauses

Introductory Task: The Birth-Order Theory of Personality Development—A Test

A. Complete the sentences by circling the letter, **a** or **b**, of the choice that describes you better.

1. I am someone who _____.
   a. doesn't like much change
   b. likes new experiences

2. Other people see me as somebody who _____.
   a. is self-confident
   b. is a little insecure

3. I am the type of person who _____.
   a. tries to dress and act as others do
   b. tries to dress and act differently

4. In my work or studies, I'm the kind of person that _____.
   a. likes to be practical and realistic
   b. likes to be imaginative and creative

5. I am a person who _____.
   a. enjoys being a leader
   b. isn't interested in being a leader

6. Politically, I see myself as someone that _____.
   a. wants to keep things the same
   b. wants to change things

7. I am the type of person that _____.
   a. usually follows rules
   b. is sometimes willing to bend or break rules

B. Turn to page A-3 to find out what your answers mean. Then circle the appropriate choices:

According to the theory, I have the personality characteristics of [a firstborn child / a laterborn child]. In fact, I am [a firstborn child / a laterborn child] in my family.

C. Work as a class. Count the number of people who are firstborns **and** according to the theory have the personality characteristics of firstborns. Count the number of people who are laterborns **and** according to the theory have the personality characteristics of laterborns. Add these two groups to find out how many people the theory works for. Then count the number of people the theory does **not** work for. Does the theory work for most of the class members? Discuss your opinions of the theory.

For more information about birth order and personality, go to the *Grammar Links* Website.

Adjective Clauses

FORM and FUNCTION

A. Uses of Adjective Clauses

1. Adjective clauses modify nouns. They give information about the nouns. An adjective clause can modify any noun in a sentence. Put the adjective clause right after the noun it modifies.

   subject noun
   The **man who was at the party** seemed really nice.

   object noun
   I'm looking for an English **class that meets in the evening**.

2. Adjective clauses can also modify indefinite pronouns (*someone, anything*, etc.).

   I know **someone who can help you**.

   Anything that is worth doing is worth doing well.

3. Adjective clauses make it possible to combine two sentences. The sentences must have noun phrases referring to the same person or thing.

   Sentence 1: **A man** just moved next door to me.
   Sentence 2: **The man** is a professional tennis player.

   Combined sentence: A **man who is a professional tennis player** just moved next door to me.
   OR The **man who just moved next door to me** is a professional tennis player. (*a man* in Sentence 1 must = *the man* in Sentence 2; *the man/a man* → *who*)

B. Sentences with Adjective Clauses; Structure of Adjective Clauses

MAIN CLAUSE	ADJECTIVE CLAUSE		
	RELATIVE PRONOUN (= SUBJECT)	VERB	
I'm reading a book	**that**	is	interesting.

MAIN CLAUSE	ADJECTIVE CLAUSE		
	RELATIVE PRONOUN (= OBJECT)	SUBJECT	VERB	
I'm reading a book	**that**	Lee	liked	a lot.

Adjective clauses are a kind of subordinate clause. That is, they cannot stand alone but must be used with a main clause.

main clause   adj clause   main clause
The man **who fixed the sink** is coming back tomorrow.

(continued on next page)

Relative Pronouns

1. An adjective clause begins with a relative pronoun.

> Paula is someone **that/who/whom** you would really like.
>
> The course **which/that** meets at eight in the morning is too early for me.

2. The relative pronouns presented in this chapter are *that*, *which*, *who*, and *whom*.*

   **Whose*, also a relative pronoun, is discussed in Chapter 11.

> She's the teacher **that/who/whom** I like.
>
> The notebook **that/which** I need has a blue cover.

3. The relative pronoun and the noun modified refer to the same person or thing.

> The **teacher that/who/whom** I really liked isn't there this year. (*that/who/whom = the teacher*)

4. The relative pronouns do not change. They do not have masculine or feminine or singular or plural forms.

> I know { a boy / a girl / some people } **who** went to school there.
>
> (*who = a boy, a girl, some people*)

Subject and Verb

Like all clauses, adjective clauses must have a subject and a verb.

>   subj V
> I didn't see any people **that I knew**.

The subject of the clause:

- May be the relative pronoun. (See Grammar Briefing 2, page 196.)

>   subj V obj
> He's the guy **who** likes Joan.

- May be another noun or pronoun in the clause. (See Grammar Briefing 3, page 199.)

>   obj   subj V
> He's the guy **who/whom** Joan likes.

GRAMMAR **HOT**SPOT!

What is not a relative pronoun.

> Everything **that/which** he said is true.
> **NOT:** Everything ~~what~~ he said is true.

Adjective Clauses

1 Identifying Adjective Clauses: Psychologists and Mothers

In the following passage, underline each adjective clause and circle the noun or pronoun it modifies. Put a second line under the relative pronoun in the clause.

A re you a (person) who is shy? Or are you a person who is outgoing? And why are you shy or outgoing? Are these characteristics which you had at birth? Or are they characteristics which came from your life experiences? These are questions that psychologists have been trying to answer for a long time. According to modern psychologists, a combination of biological factors and experience shaped your personality. This is something that mothers know, too. Each child that a mother has seems different from the others, even as a newborn. And as her children grow, the mother can see differences in their experiences. She can see how the experiences that her children have help to shape their personalities. Sometimes the theories that psychologists develop express what mothers have always known!

2 Adjective Clauses: Same Family, Different Personalities

A. David is telling Julie about the people in the photo. Listen once for the main idea. Listen again and fill in the name of each person.

Alan   ~~Barbara~~   Cathy   Dennis   Jack   Joan   Kyle   Mary

Barbara

practical

B. Now listen again and fill in the characteristic that's used to describe each person.

adventurous   insecure   ~~practical~~   shy   creative   outgoing   self-confident   timid

3 **Position of Adjective Clauses:** Telling More

Complete the sentences with the adjective clauses in parentheses.
Write the adjective clauses after the nouns that they modify.

1. The people *who are in the photo* are older now. (who are in the photo)

2. The aunt lives in New Mexico now. (who likes to paint)

3. I've had some great vacations with the uncle. (who's a mountain climber)

4. My aunts and uncles have telephone conversations. (that last for hours)

5. The bird-watching book is very popular. (which my uncle wrote)

6. My aunt is someone. (whom you would really like)

7. My outgoing uncle has become a talk show host, so now he has a job.

   (that's perfect for his personality)

8. People often comment on the differences in their personalities and interests.

   (that know my mother and her brothers and sisters)

GRAMMAR BRIEFING 2

Adjective Clauses with Subject Relative Pronouns

FORM

A. Structure of Adjective Clauses with Subject Relative Pronouns

MAIN CLAUSE	ADJECTIVE CLAUSE		
	SUBJECT RELATIVE PRONOUN	VERB	OBJECT
I have a friend	**who**	**is studying**	**psychology**.
= I have a friend. + **The friend/She** is studying psychology.			

MAIN CLAUSE	ADJECTIVE CLAUSE			MAIN CLAUSE CONTINUED
	SUBJECT RELATIVE PRONOUN	VERB	OBJECT	
My friend	**who**	**studies**	**psychology**	is interested in personality.
= My friend is interested in personality. + **My friend/She** studies psychology.				

1. In these adjective clauses, the relative pronoun is the subject of the adjective clause.

                         subj   V
   Psychology is a topic **that** really interests her.
                       subj
   = Psychology is a topic. + **The topic** really interests her. (*The topic → that*)

(continued on next page)

A. Structure of Adjective Clauses with Subject Relative Pronouns (continued)

2. The verb of the clause agrees with the noun that is modified. (Remember: This noun and the relative pronoun refer to the same person or thing.)	subj V She reads lots of **books that relate to psychology**. (*relate* agrees with *books*; *that = books*) **NOT:** She reads lots of books that ~~relates~~ to psychology.

B. Subject Relative Pronouns: *Who, That, Which*

1. For people, use *who* or *that*.	A **scientist who/that** studies personality has developed a new theory.
2. For things, ideas, and animals,* use *that* or *which*. *For pets, *who* can also be used (e.g., *I have a cat who's really affectionate*).	The scientist has developed a **theory that/which** explains personality. Recently, there was a **conference that/which** was just about his theory.

GRAMMAR **HOT**SPOT!

Remember! The relative pronoun is the subject of the adjective clause. Do not include another subject pronoun.	Children who are the youngest are often creative. **NOT:** Children who ~~they~~ are the youngest are often creative.

TALKING THE TALK

Who and *that* are often contracted in speech and informal writing.	She's someone **who's** creative. She teaches a course **that's** really interesting.

GRAMMAR PRACTICE 2

Adjective Clauses with Subject Relative Pronouns

4 **Adjective Clauses with Subject Relative Pronouns; Combining Sentences: Relationships and Personalities I**

Combine the sentences. Use the second sentence to make an adjective clause. Use any appropriate relative pronoun.

1. a. A big family lives in the house. The house is next door to mine.

   <u>A big family lives in the house that/which is next door to mine.</u>

b. The little girls are very talkative. They are outgoing.

_____

c. The little girl takes longer to make new friends. She is shy.

_____

d. Have you met the people? They live next door.

_____

2. a. I talked to a person. The person knows my sisters.

_____

b. Sleeping until noon is an activity. The activity appeals to my lazy sister.

_____

c. An activity is going running at 6 a.m. The activity appeals to my energetic sister.

_____

3. a. Elvira's two brothers have very different personalities. Her brothers are interested in Africa.

_____

b. The timid brother collects stamps. The stamps come from countries in Africa.

_____

c. The adventurous brother wrestles with crocodiles. The crocodiles live in rivers in Africa.

_____

5 Forming Adjective Clauses with Subject Relative Pronouns: Defining Terms

Use the words given to complete the definitions with adjective clauses. Use *who* or *which* and the correct form of the verb.

1. refer / to a person's way of thinking, feeling, and acting

   Personality is a term _which refers to a person's way of thinking, feeling, and acting_____.

2. study / people's thoughts, feelings, and behavior

   Psychologists are scientists _____.

3. make / a careful study of a certain subject or problem

   A *researcher* is a person _____.

4. try / to explain situations or events

   Theories are statements _____.

5. be / part of your personality

   Traits are characteristics _____.

6. be / the oldest child in a family

   A *firstborn* is someone _____.

7. be / born second, third, and so on, in a family

   Laterborns are children _____.

8. help / cause a certain result

   A *factor* is something _____.

6 Using *Someone* + *Who*: Who Does It Better?

Work with a partner. Take turns asking and answering questions about people and their characteristics. Follow the example. Use *someone who* as in the example.

1. Hair stylist: creative or practical?

   Example: Student A: Should a hair stylist be someone who's creative or someone who's practical?
   Student B: I think a hair stylist should be someone who's creative.
   Student A: Why?
   Student B: I want to have a hair style that's new and unusual.

   OR: Student B: A hair stylist should be someone who's practical.
   Student A: Why?
   Student B: Hair stylists should think of hair styles that are easy to take care of.

2. Car mechanic: creative or practical?
3. Scientist: realistic or imaginative?
4. Soccer player: calm or excitable?
5. Mountain climber: adventurous or careful?
6. The leader of a country: optimistic or pessimistic?

> *optimistic* = tending to expect good things to happen. *pessimistic* = tending to expect bad things to happen.

GRAMMAR BRIEFING 3

Adjective Clauses with Object Relative Pronouns

FORM

A. Structure of Adjective Clauses with Object Relative Pronouns

MAIN CLAUSE	ADJECTIVE CLAUSE		
	OBJECT RELATIVE PRONOUN	SUBJECT	VERB
I've met lots of people	who	I	like.
= I've met lots of people. + I like **the people/them.**			

MAIN CLAUSE	ADJECTIVE CLAUSE			MAIN CLAUSE CONTINUED
	OBJECT RELATIVE PRONOUN	SUBJECT	VERB	
The students	that	he	teaches	are very hard working.
= The students are very hard-working. + He teaches **the students/them.**				

In these clauses, the relative pronoun is the object of the verb. (Notice that it is the object of the sentence that becomes the adjective clause.) The subject of the adjective clause follows the relative pronoun.

> obj subj V
> The work **that** he does is interesting. = The work is
> obj
> interesting. + He does **the work**. (*the work → that*)

(continued on next page)

B. Object Relative Pronouns: *Who, That, Which, Whom,* [0]

1. For people, use *who, whom,* or *that.*

   It's important to have **friends who/whom/ that** you trust.

2. For things, ideas, and animals,* use *that* or *which.*

   *For pets, *who* can also be used (e.g., *My brother has a dog who he takes everywhere*).

   I can talk to my friends about any **problem that/which** I have.

   My brother has a **dog that/which** he takes everywhere.

3. The object relative pronoun is often omitted ([0] = no relative pronoun).

   It's important to have friends **[0]** you trust.

   I can talk to my friends about any problem **[0]** I have.

GRAMMAR **HOT**SPOT!

1. The object relative pronoun is the object of the verb. Do not include another object pronoun.

   I have a friend **who** I often visit.
   NOT: I have a friend who I often visit ~~her~~.

2. Remember that [0] is only an object pronoun. Do not omit a **subject** relative pronoun.

   He's someone **who/[0]** my father knows.

   But: He's someone **who** knows my father.
   NOT: He's someone ~~[0]~~ knows my father.

TALKING THE TALK

In speech, [0], *that,* and *who* are usually used. *Whom* is used mainly in formal speech and in writing.

In writing, use *whom* or *that* or [0] as object relative pronouns. *Who* is generally considered incorrect.

She's a teacher **[0]/that/who** students admire. (more informal)

She's a teacher **whom** students admire. (more formal)

Adjective Clauses with Object Relative Pronouns

7 **Adjective Clauses with Object Relative Pronouns;
Combining Sentences:** Relationships and Personalities II

Combine the sentences. Use the second sentence to make an adjective clause.
Use any appropriate relative pronoun (*who, whom, which, that,* [0]).

1. a. The woman is creative. Jerry dates the woman.

   The woman who/whom/that/[0] Jerry dates is creative.

   b. The pickle ice cream was delicious. She made the ice cream.

   _____

2. a. The story was true. I heard it.

   _____

   b. I heard the story from a person. I trust the person.

   _____

3. a. Arthur isn't shy when he's around people. He knows them well.

   _____

   b. The discussion was very serious. Arthur and I had the discussion recently.

   _____

4. a. The most fun-loving person is Tony. I know the person.

   _____

   b. The jokes are really funny. He tells them.

   _____

5. a. The man is generous. Tiffany plans to marry him.

   _____

   b. Tiffany's boyfriend gave her a kitten. She loves the kitten.

   _____

8 Object Relative Pronouns; Combining Sentences: Tell Me About It

Combine the sentences. Use the second sentence to make an adjective clause. Show all the relative pronouns (*who, whom, which, that,* [0]) that are possible.

1. Tell me about the psychology course. You're taking it.

   Tell me about the psychology course which you're taking.
   Tell me about the psychology course that you're taking.
   Tell me about the psychology course you're taking.

2. We have a teacher. Everyone admires her.

3. The students work very hard. She teaches them.

4. The topic is personality. We're discussing the topic.

5. Have you passed all the tests? The teacher has given the tests.

9 Subject and Object Relative Pronouns: Birth Order and Personality

Fill in the blanks with all the choices (*who, whom, which, that,* [0]) that are possible.

Are you someone __who/that__ was a firstborn child? Or were you
₁
a laterborn in your family? Some psychologists believe that your birth order and the

relationships _____ you had with the others in your family had
₂

a lot to do with the personality _____ you have now.
₃

   Children _____ are born first enjoy having all of their parents'
₄

attention. This attention is something _____ they want to keep.
₅

Children _____ are born later also want to get attention. Each
₆

laterborn wants to create a situation _____ is new and different
₇

and hopes to be the child _____ the parents notice most.
₈

   As a result of their early experiences, firstborns may become adults

_____ prefer to keep things as they are. Firstborns also tend to be
₉

natural leaders _____ have a great deal of self-confidence. Because
₁₀

of their place in the family, laterborns may become adults _____
₁₁

like to have new experiences. They tend to be imaginative and adventurous. Of course,

you may know laterborns _____ you consider to be self-
₁₂

confident leaders. And you probably know firstborns _____
₁₃

you regard as creative adventurers. This is because there are many factors

_____ can be important in forming personality.
₁₄

10 Subject and Object Relative Pronouns; Combining Sentences: Another Theory

Use the second sentence to form an adjective clause modifying the appropriate noun in the first sentence. Use any appropriate relative pronoun (*who, whom, which, that,* [0]).

1. Last week I read a book. It was about birth order and personality.

   Last week I read a book which was about birth order and personality.

   OR

   Last week I read a book that was about birth order and personality.

2. I talked to a scientist about it. She is a friend of mine.

   _____

3. My friend disagrees with the theory in the book. I read the book.

   _____

4. Other researchers have developed a more scientific theory. My friend respects them.

   _____

5. According to this theory, some personality characteristics have a source. The source is biological.

   _____

6. Chemicals can influence our personalities. The chemicals are in our brains and bodies.

   _____

7. These chemicals can affect our response to events. We experience the events.

   _____

8. What do you think of the theory? My friend believes it.

   _____

11 Completing Sentences with Adjective Clauses: An Alien Invasion?

Last night you had a terrifying experience. Afterward, you weren't able to do your homework or even speak. As a result, you need to write a letter to your teacher explaining what happened. Complete the sentences with adjective clauses.

Dear _____ ,

I'm very sorry that I haven't done my homework, but I hope you will excuse me. Last night I was kidnapped by aliens, that is, people from another planet. There were three different types of strange-looking people on the spaceship. The first type were people who had huge dark eyes and bald heads _____ .
                                                                    1
The second type were people _____ .
                                            2
The third type were people _____ .
                                          3
They all wore clothes _____ .
                                      4

The aliens spoke English to me, but among themselves they spoke a language _____ . They took
                                5
me onto a spaceship _____ .
                                  6
On the spaceship, they told me they were interested in talking to humans

_____
                                7

While I was on their spaceship, I could hear music

_____ . The aliens were eating
            8
kinds of food _____ .
                                9
They didn't give me any of the food, but they gave me a drink

_____ . Early this
            10
morning the aliens finally brought me back home. I know I have a creative imagination, but this is not science fiction!

        Your student,

        _____

12 **Using Adjective Clauses:** Describing Personalities

 A. Work with a partner. Choose one of the people in the photos. (Keep your choice a secret from other class members.) Discuss the person you have chosen: What do you think her personality is like? What are her likes and dislikes? What are her talents and interests? In your discussion, include sentences with adjective clauses.

Example: Student A: *She looks like someone who's outgoing and friendly.*
  Student B: *I agree. I think she's a woman who likes sports and is very athletic. . . .*
  OR
  Student A: *I think she's the type of person that's very creative.*
  Student B: *She also seems to be someone who's quiet and serious. Some things that she doesn't like are noisy, crowded parties and . . .*

 B. Write a one-paragraph description of the person you chose, but **don't** include anything about her appearance. Use at least five adjective clauses.

C. Read your description to the class. Can the class guess which person you are describing?

See the *Grammar Links* Website for a model paragraph for this activity.

Check your progress! Go to the Self-Test for Chapter 10 on the *Grammar Links* Website.

More About Adjective Clauses

Introductory Task: Do You Agree or Disagree?

A. Read the statements about personality and circle your response, *a* or *b*, to each one.

1. Personality comes from a combination of two factors: the characteristics that you are born with and the environment you grow up in.

   a. I agree.   b. I disagree.

2. The other children with whom a child plays or goes to school are important influences on the child's personality.

   a. I agree.   b. I disagree.

3. The way that parents treat a child is an important influence on the type of personality the child will have. For example, children whose parents treat them with kindness and patience will grow up to be kind and patient adults.

   a. I agree.   b. I disagree.

4. Personality develops in childhood and doesn't change after that. That is, adulthood is a time when personality does not change.

   a. I agree.   b. I disagree.

5. In order to choose a job in which you will be happy and successful, you need to know your personality type. People whose personalities aren't good matches for their jobs can't find happiness or be effective in their work.

   a. I agree.   b. I disagree.

B. Work in small groups. Compare your responses to the statements. Tell why you agree or disagree with each statement.

environment = surroundings, family and friends, experiences, etc.

Adjective Clauses with Relative Pronouns That Are Objects of Prepositions

FORM

A. Structure of Adjective Clauses with Relative Pronouns That Are Objects of Prepositions

MAIN CLAUSE	ADJECTIVE CLAUSE			
	OBJECT RELATIVE PRONOUN	SUBJECT	VERB	PREPOSITION
Personality is a topic	**that**	**we**	**are learning**	**about**.

= Personality is a topic. + We are learning about **personality/it**.

MAIN CLAUSE	ADJECTIVE CLAUSE				MAIN CLAUSE CONTINUED
	OBJECT RELATIVE PRONOUN	SUBJECT	VERB	PREPOSITION	
The friend	**who**	**I**	**went**	**with**	is here.

= The friend is here. + I went with **the friend/him**.

1. In these relative clauses, the relative pronoun is the object of a preposition. (Prepositions include *about, for, in, on, with*, etc.)

   obj of
   prep subj V
   She's someone **who** we have a lot of confidence

   prep
   in. = She is someone. + We have a lot of

   obj of
   prep
   confidence in her. (*her* → *who*)

2. The preposition can be put at the beginning of the adjective clause, before the relative pronoun.

   obj of
   prep prep subj V
   She's someone **in whom** we have a lot of confidence.

B. Relative Pronouns That Are Objects of Prepositions: *Who, That, Which, Whom,* [0]

1. The same relative pronouns are used as for the objects of verbs:

   • *Who, whom, that,* and [0] for people.

   She's **someone who/whom/that/[0]** I don't like to argue with.

   • *Which, that,* and [0] for things and ideas.

   My children have some **ideas which/that/[0]** I don't fully agree with.

   That's a **class which/that/[0]** he does well in.

(continued on next page)

B. Relative Pronouns That Are Objects of Prepositions (continued)

2. If the preposition is at the beginning of the adjective clause, use only *whom* or *which*.	He's someone **for whom** I have a lot of respect. Your company has several positions **for which** I'd like to apply.

TALKING THE TALK

In speech, the preposition usually occurs at the end of the adjective clause. Prepositions at the beginning of the adjective clause are considered formal and used mainly in writing.	The school offers some scholarships **which** I might qualify **for**. (more informal) I am writing to ask about scholarships **for which** I might qualify. (more formal)

GRAMMAR PRACTICE 1

Adjective Clauses with Relative Pronouns That Are Objects of Prepositions

1 Adjective Clauses with Relative Pronouns That Are Objects of Prepositions; Combining Sentences: Finding the Right Job I

Combine the pairs of sentences. Use the second sentence to make an adjective clause. Show all possible patterns.

1. The teacher explained personality types. We met with her.

   The teacher with whom we met explained personality types.
   The teacher whom we met with explained personality types.
   The teacher who we met with explained personality types.
   The teacher that we met with explained personality types.
   The teacher [0] we met with explained personality types.

2. The counselor discussed careers. We listened to him.

3. I learned about some jobs. I am suited for them.

2 Informal and Formal Versions of Adjective Clauses with Relative Pronouns That Are Objects of Prepositions: Writing About Jobs

Rewrite the sentences so that they are formal.

1. The counselor I talked to gave me some advice.

   The counselor to whom I talked gave me some advice.

2. We want to find jobs we will succeed in.

3. She is helpful to the students she works with.

4. The project they are working on will be finished soon.

5. The position he is applying for is in the sales department.

6. I am grateful to the person I got the information from.

3 Relative Pronouns as Objects of Prepositions: Your Preferences and Your Personality

Fill in the blanks with all the choices (*who, whom, which, that,* [0]) that are possible.

Psychology is a subject _which, that, [0]_ _____ many people are
                              1

interested in. And there are many people for _____
                                                          2

psychology can be useful. They include people who want to choose a job

_____ they are well suited for. By using psychology
         3

to understand their personality types, thes people can make choices with

_____ they will be satisfied.
         4

Psychologists often use a test to determine a person's personality type.

A personality test determines your type by asking you about your preferences.

For example, a personality test may ask you about the kinds of people

_____ you feel comfortable with. Do you like to
         5

be with a few people with _____ you have close
                                        6

friendships or with many people to _____ you aren't
                                                  7

so close?

When you are trying to understand your type, there are some important points

_____ you should be aware of. One is that there are
         8

no "good" or "bad" preferences. People are different, and these differences are useful.

You can get along well with the people _____ you study
                                                    9

or work with when you try to understand and accept their different personality types.

If your future career is something about _____
                                                      10

you've been thinking, you may want to take a personality test. It could help you

understand your preferences and find a job _____ you
                                                      11

will be excited about.

 Check out the *Grammar Links* Website for links to an online personality test.

4 **Adjective Clauses with Relative Pronouns That Are Objects of Prepositions:** What Are Your Interests?

A. You have just been hired by a large corporation. They want to know more about your interests so they can decide which department to place you in. Answer the questions, using the cues in parentheses.

MYMIX Corporation
Human Resources Department

1. Which corporation are you most enthusiastic about? ([0] . . . about)

The corporation [0] I am most enthusiastic about is MYMIX.

2. What kind of work are you most interested in? (which . . . in)

3. What free-time activities are you involved in? ([0] . . . in)

4. Which school subject have you excelled in? (that . . . in)

5. Which person are you most grateful to? (to whom . . .)

6. Which world problem are you most concerned about? (about which . . .)

B. 1. Imagine that you work in the Human Resources Department at MYMIX Corporation. Use the cues to write more questions like those on the form in Part A.

1. (music / like to listen to)

   What kind of _____?

2. (sports / be interested in)

   Which _____?

3. (people / like to work with)

   What kind of _____?

4. (job / be best suited for)

   What kind of _____?

B. 2. Work with a partner. Student A: Interview Student B, asking the questions in Part A and the questions you wrote. Student B: Answer the questions, omitting the relative pronoun in each answer. Then reverse roles.

Example:
Student A: Which corporation are you most enthusiastic about?
Student B: The corporation I'm most enthusiastic about is MYMIX.

Adjective Clauses with Possessive Relative Pronouns

FORM

A. Structure of Adjective Clauses with Possessive Relative Pronouns

MAIN CLAUSE	ADJECTIVE CLAUSE		
	POSSESSIVE RELATIVE PRONOUN	NOUN	
I spoke to the teacher	**whose**	**class**	**is so popular**.

= I spoke to the teacher. + **The teacher's/Her** class is so popular.

MAIN CLAUSE	ADJECTIVE CLAUSE			MAIN CLAUSE CONTINUED
	POSSESSIVE RELATIVE PRONOUN	NOUN		
The teacher	**whose**	**class**	**I want to get into**	is going to help me.

= The teacher is going to help me. + I want to get into **the teacher's/her** class.

1. These adjective clauses begin with the possessive relative pronoun *whose* + noun.

   I need to find the person **whose umbrella** I took. = I need to find a person. + I took the person's umbrella. (*the person's* → *whose*)

2. *Whose* + noun may be:

   • The subject of the adjective clause.

   I heard the scientist **whose work** is attracting so much interest. (subj V ... obj)

   • The object of the adjective clause.

   I met the scientist **whose work** I admire. (obj subj V)

   • The object of a preposition that is in the adjective clause.

   She is the scientist **whose work** I told you about. (obj of prep subj V prep)

B. The Relative Pronoun *Whose*

1. *Whose* is a possessive like *my*, *his*, etc. Like those words, it must be followed by a noun.

   That's the woman **whose husband** I was talking to.
   Compare: I was talking to **her husband**.

2. *Whose* is usually used to modify people. However, it can be used to modify things.

   That's the **teacher whose class** I'm interested in.

   That's the **school whose programs** I'm interested in.

Adjective Clauses with Possessive Relative Pronouns

5 **Adjective Clauses with Possessive Relative Pronouns; Combining Sentences:** Finding the Right Job II

A. Combine the pairs of sentences. Use the second sentence to make an adjective clause with *whose*.

1. The teacher explained personality types. We heard her lecture.

   The teacher whose lecture we heard explained personality types.

2. She talked about people. Their personalities are well suited for the work they do.

3. People are usually happy. Their work gives them a lot of satisfaction.

4. There are several authors. We may read their books.

5. I found out about some job counselors. Their specialty is personality testing.

6. The teachers have all been helpful. We've taken their courses.

7. The counselor gave me a personality test. I went to his office.

8. I am an outgoing person. My personality is practical.

9. The counselor recommended a book. Its title is *What Color Is Your Parachute?*

10. Now I'm planning to visit the departments. I'm interested in their programs.

11. There are organizations. Their websites have online personality tests and career guidance.

B. Complete the sentences with adjective clauses with *whose*.

1. I enjoy being around people _whose backgrounds are different from mine_____.

2. I get along well with students _____.

3. I prefer to work with people _____.

4. People _____

   are interesting to me.

5. I'm the kind of person _____.

6. I read a book _____.

7. I'd like to work for a company _____.

 To find out more about personality and careers, visit the *Grammar Links* Website.

Adjective Clauses with *Where* and *When*

FORM

A. Adjective Clauses with *Where*

1. *Where* can begin an adjective clause that modifies the noun *place* or a noun referring to a place—*country, city, building, house, room, street*, and so on.

> For our anniversary, we're going to go back to the **place where** we met.
>
> This is the **building where** I have my English class.

2. Instead of *where*, you can use an adjective clause with a relative pronoun that's an object of a preposition (see Grammar Briefing 1, page 207).

   Remember: Use only *which* if the preposition is at the beginning of the adjective clause.

> I really liked the **place that/which/[0]** Tom moved **to**.
>
> This is the **building that/which/[0]** I have my English class **in**.

> This is the building **in which** I have my English class.

B. Adjective Clauses with *When*

1. *When* can begin an adjective clause that modifies the noun *time* or a noun referring to a period of time—*century, year, day, night*, and so on.

> I remember a **time when** I didn't have so much homework.
>
> That was the **year when** we started college.
>
> I'm looking forward to the **day when** I graduate.

2. Instead of *when*, you can use an adjective clause with a relative pronoun that's an object of a preposition such as *in* or *on*.

   • With *that* and [0], the preposition is often omitted.

   • With *which*, the preposition must be included.

> That was the **year that/which/[0]** we started **college in**.

> That was the year **that/[0]** we started college.

> That was the year **which** we started college **in**. OR That was the year **in which** we started college.

1. Do not use a preposition with *where* or *when*.	This is the place where Nina lives. **NOT**: This is the place where Nina lives ~~at~~.
2. Do not use question word order if *where* or *when* introduces an adjective clause.	Wh- *question*: Where is your house? *Adjective clause*: Please describe the place where **your house is**. **NOT**: Please describe the place where ~~is your house~~.

GRAMMAR PRACTICE 3

Adjective Clauses with *Where* and *When*

6 **Adjective Clauses with *Where*; Combining Sentences:** Memories of Places

A. Combine the sentences. Use the second sentence to make a clause with *where*, omitting the unnecessary words.

1. These photos show the places. I spent my childhood in the places.
   These photos show the places where I spent my childhood.
2. That's the house. My family lived in the house.
3. The bedroom was painted blue. I slept in the bedroom.
4. The garden was behind the house. I played in the garden.
5. That's the hospital. My father worked at the hospital.
6. This is the school. I first studied English at the school.

B. Rewrite the sentences using a relative pronoun that's the object of a preposition. Show all the patterns.

1. This is the cabin where we spent a night.

   This is the cabin in which we spent a night.
   This is the cabin which we spent a night in.
   This is the cabin that we spent a night in.
   This is the cabin we spent a night in.

2. The lake where we swam was very cold.

3. Do you remember the place where we met?

7 Adjective Clauses with *When*; Combining Sentences: Memories of Times

A. Combine the sentences. Use the second sentence to make a clause with *when*, omitting the unnecessary words.

1. I remember the time. We lived in that house at that time.

   I remember the time when we lived in that house.

2. I remember the day. We moved into the house on that day.

3. There was a month. It rained constantly during that month.

4. That was the year. I started school in that year.

5. The week was exciting. We went to the mountains in that week.

6. There was one summer. The weather was unusually hot during that summer.

B. Rewrite the sentences using a relative pronoun that is the object of a preposition. Show all the patterns. Omit the preposition where appropriate.

1. I remember the morning. I left home (on that morning).

   I remember the morning on which I left home.
   I remember the morning which I left home on.
   I remember the morning that I left home.
   I remember the morning I left home.

2. That was the year. We started school (in that year).

3. Do you remember the day? We met (on that day).

8 Using Adjective Clauses with *Where* and *When*: Describing Places and Remembering Times

A. Work with a partner. Tell each other about places that you remember from your childhood. Describe things like their location, appearance, or size. Use *where* and the following pairs of cues.

Example:
Student A: Tell me about the city where you lived.
Student B: The city where I lived is near the ocean/full of people and traffic/beautiful.

city or town : live	room : sleep	places : play
house or apartment : live	school : study	place : mother or father work

B. Now ask and answer questions about memories of events and your feelings about them. Follow the pattern in the example. Use *when* and the following cues.

Example:
Student A: Do you remember a time when you felt excited?
Student B: I felt excited on the day when I started school.

excited	frightened	happy	sad	disappointed	adventurous

9 Relative Pronouns, *Where*, and *When*: A Childhood Experience I

Complete the sentences with any appropriate relative pronoun (*who, that, which, [0], whose*), *where*, or *when*.

When I was three years old, my parents took me on the first long trip _that_
₁

I had ever been on. I was very little, but I remember the details clearly. My parents were the kind of

people _____ daily routines didn't change much, so going on a trip
₂

was an experience _____ was very exciting for me. I remember that we
₃

took the trip at a time _____ the weather was very hot. We traveled
₄

for two days by car from the town _____ we lived to a big city. The hotel
₅

_____ we stayed in seemed huge, and the room
₆

_____ I slept was cool, comfortable, and much nicer than my
₇

bedroom at home. I didn't know how to read yet, but the waiters _____
₈

worked in the hotel restaurant always gave me a menu. I pretended to read it and felt very grown-up.

We ate in other restaurants, too, and the food in every one _____ we

                                                                9

went to was new, different, and delicious. I wanted that trip to last forever. Now, years later, I'm the

kind of person _____ likes change and new experiences. I also like to

                          10

get to know people _____ lives are very different from mine. The days

                               11

_____ I'm traveling are the best days of my life.

                  12

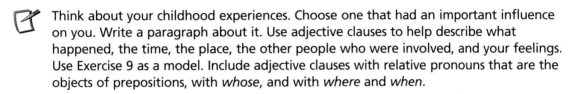

10 Using Adjective Clauses: A Childhood Experience II

Think about your childhood experiences. Choose one that had an important influence
on you. Write a paragraph about it. Use adjective clauses to help describe what
happened, the time, the place, the other people who were involved, and your feelings.
Use Exercise 9 as a model. Include adjective clauses with relative pronouns that are the
objects of prepositions, with *whose*, and with *where* and *when*.

See the *Grammar Links* Website for another model paragraph for this assignment.

**Check your progress! Go to the Self-Test for
Chapter 11 on the *Grammar Links* Website.**

Wrap-up Activities

1 **Another Theory:** EDITING

Correct the 11 errors in the passage. There are errors with in relative pronouns and adjective clauses. Some errors can be corrected in more than one way. The first error is corrected for you.

Your Blood Type and Your Personality

T here are people ~~which~~ *who* think your blood type reveals your personality. These people believe in the blood type theory of personality.

According to people who believes in the blood type theory, you can use your blood type to discover your natural talents and tendencies: Blood type is something what can help you find the right job or the right boyfriend or girlfriend.

The blood type that is most common is Type O. What are the characteristics that a Type O person has them? According to a book which explains the theory, people are optimistic that have Type O blood. Business is a field in that they are successful.

A person who his blood type is A usually has a good sense of order. He keeps the place where he lives in very neat. A Type A is also a person that tends to be patient, hard-working, and sensitive.

People whom have Type B blood are the most likely to be creative. They are people who's nature is to be flexible and full of new ideas. Some jobs that Type B people are suited for are artist, designer, and golfer.

Type AB is the rarest blood type. It was the blood type of John F. Kennedy. Kennedy was a man whom many Americans admired. The book describes Type AB people as natural leaders with characteristics that includes logical thinking and honesty.

2 The Category Game: SPEAKING

Step 1 Work in teams of two or three. Decide on a category for each group of words. Then express the category in a sentence containing an adjective clause.

1. creativity, bravery, shyness, generosity, optimism

   They're all personality characteristics which people can have.

2. the sun, an egg yolk, a school bus, a lemon, a dandelion

   They're all things that are yellow.

3. milk, gasoline, alcohol, blood, water

4. a robber, a murderer, a kidnapper, a burglar, a smuggler

5. a house, a bottle, a box, a backpack, a refrigerator

6. flood, flavor, flexible, flower, flip

7. birthday, wedding, anniversary, holiday, graduation

8. a court, an arena, a course, a field, a stadium

9. a nurse, an X-ray technician, a surgeon, a physical therapist, a dietician

10. ears, chopsticks, dice, stereo speakers, ice skates

11. a blanket, a stove, the sun, love, a bath

12. fish, frogs, humans, ducks, polar bears

Step 2 Now each team thinks of three groups of five words that somehow fit into categories like those above. The team reads its lists to the other teams. The other teams try to be the first to guess the category. Each guess must be in the form of a question containing an adjective clause, for example, *Are they all things that are yellow?* Keep score. The winner is the team that guesses the most categories correctly.

3 Making Up Definitions: WRITING

Imagine that the following nonsense words are real English nouns for people, animals, places, times, and things, including activities and feelings. Think of a possible meaning for each word and write a definition for it. Each definition should include at least two adjective clauses. Try to use all types of adjective clauses. You can be as creative as you wish.

Example: *A bowpam is an animal that has short pink fur, a fat body, and a long tail that drags on the ground. Bowpams live in countries where the weather is cold and wet. OR Bluther is a feeling people have at times when they're confused or nervous.*

1. bowpam	3. gyrgot	5. morokoves	7. termunter	9. strolth
2. bluther	4. plonkist	6. quingle	8. zenvidix	10. exmiants

4 | What Are Your Preferences? WRITING

Your preferences, that is, your likes, dislikes, and interests, can tell someone a lot about your personality type. Imagine that a person you've never met has asked you to describe yourself. Write one paragraph about your preferences. You can include your preferences in
> —people
> —work and school
> —free-time activities
> —places and times
> —movies, music, books, etc.

Use a variety of types of adjective clauses, including clauses with relative pronouns that are the objects of prepositions, with *whose*, and with *where* and *when*.

Example: I can describe myself best by telling you some of my likes, dislikes, and interests. I like to be around people who are calm and logical. People whose lives are disorganized make me a little nervous, so I prefer not to spend much time with them. The classes that I enjoy the most are math and science. In the future, I want to have a job in which I can work with numbers and computers. At times when I don't have to work or study, I like to be outdoors. I love going to places where it's quiet and the air is clean and fresh. . . .

 See the *Grammar Links* Website for a complete model paragraph for this assignment.

Exercise Pages

Introductory Task: Quiz: What Is Your Time Type?

Scoring for Quiz

16–18 points = a very "fast" person (tends to be extremely aware of time and speed)

12–15 points = a "fast" person (tends to be somewhat concerned about time and speed)

9–11 points = a "slow" person (tends not to be concerned about time or speed)

6–8 points = a very "slow" person (tends to be extremely relaxed about time and speed)

6 **Using Present Perfect Progressive:** What Have People Been Doing? II

For Student B.

College Campus

10 **Future Time with Simple Present:** An Outdoor Vacation—
Yellowstone National Park

Information for Student B.

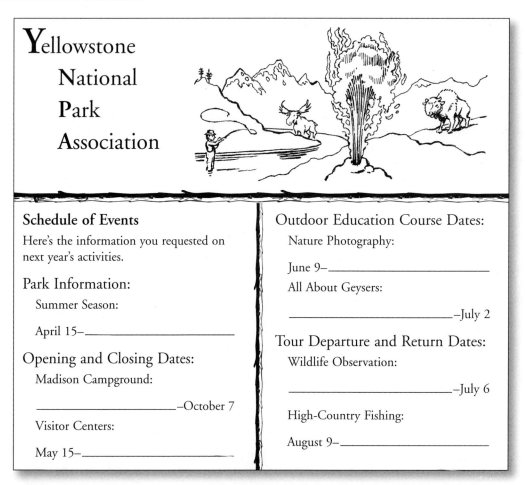

Yellowstone
National
Park
Association

Schedule of Events

Here's the information you requested on
next year's activities.

Park Information:

Summer Season:

April 15–_____

Opening and Closing Dates:

Madison Campground:

_____–October 7

Visitor Centers:

May 15–_____

Outdoor Education Course Dates:

Nature Photography:

June 9–_____

All About Geysers:

_____–July 2

Tour Departure and Return Dates:

Wildlife Observation:

_____–July 6

High-Country Fishing:

August 9–_____

12 **Listening to Tag Questions:** Christopher Columbus

Part B: Information About Columbus

Columbus set out on his first voyage in 1492. He and his crew were not the first
Europeans to arrive in North America. The Vikings had landed on the northern coast of
the continent around the year 1000. Columbus made a contract, or agreement, with the
king and queen of Spain to pay for his expedition, but he was an Italian, not a Spaniard.
Before he arrived in America, no one in Europe knew that North and South America
existed. Columbus believed that he could sail west from Europe directly to Asia.
Columbus made a total of four voyages to America. He landed on several islands off the
coast of North America, and he reached the coasts of Central and South America on two
of his voyages. But he never landed on the coast of North America. Columbus believed
that Cuba was Japan, and he never realized that he hadn't reached Asia. For this reason,
he didn't give the land a new name. A German mapmaker named it America after

Amerigo Vespucci, who explored the coast of South America. Columbus's contract made him viceroy and governor of all the lands he discovered and gave him 10 percent of the profits from his discoveries. At first he became rich, but later he had troubles and lost his titles and all his money.

> *viceroy* = person who represents the king.

UNIT 3 ■ Wrap-up

4 Ask the Oracle

Instructions for the oracle: Copy each answer in the following list on a small slip of paper. Put the slips into an empty container, such as a box or jar. After each question is asked, draw out an answer (without peeking) and read it aloud. After each answer, return the slip of paper to the container and mix it in with the rest.

The oracle's answers:

1. Yes, definitely.
2. No, definitely not.
3. It's certain.
4. It isn't certain.
5. It's possible.
6. It's probable.
7. The answer isn't clear yet.
8. It will happen.
9. It won't happen.
10. The chances are good.

5 Acting Out the Verbs

Lists of Phrasal Verbs for Skits

Telephoning the travel agent:

   call back, call up, hang up, look up, take down, talk over

At the hotel desk:

   add up, check in, check out, hand over, settle in, show up

In a restaurant:

   fill up, pass around, run out of, take back, think over, sit down

Dressing for an expedition:

   have on, pick out, put on, take off, try on, wear out

On a tour:

   find out, finish up, look over, point out, speak up, start off

UNIT 5 ■ Chapter 10

Introductory Task: The Birth-Order Theory of Personality Development—A Test

According to the birth-order theory, firstborns tend to be practical and follow rules, while laterborns are more likely to be creative and willing to bend or break rules. If you circled **a** four or more times, you show the personality characteristics of a firstborn child; if you circled **b** four or more times, you show the characteristics of a laterborn child. (An only child usually has characteristics similar to those of a firstborn.)

Now turn back to page 192 and go on to Part B of the task.

Introductory Task: Sports Trivia

1. b   5. h
2. a   6. g
3. d   7. f
4. e   8. c

4 Passive Sentences with Verbs in Different Tenses— Questions and Answers: Stadiums

Invesco Field at Mile High

1. 2001
2. football and soccer
3. yes
4. to monitor the water needed for the grass and heat the field in winter
5. by selling seats from the old Mile High Stadium

The Skydome

1. 1989
2. football, baseball, basketball, other events
3. no; on artificial grass called "Astroturf"
4. with three panels that take 20 minutes to open or close
5. eight miles of zippers

Introductory Task: The Things Fans Do

Answers: All the statements are true!

4–9

Professor Wendell's solution: The police inspector was about to arrest John Small for the murder of Mrs. Pierson. He said that Small had poisoned her to obtain money that he otherwise might not have gotten for many years. Professor Wendell stepped in and told the inspector that he was making a serious mistake. He said that the real murderers had been Mr. and Mrs. Niles Pierson. He explained that Niles Pierson had been in serious financial difficulty: Hard times meant that people were spending less on luxuries like art. Pierson had tried to raise money by gambling and had wound up deeply in debt. Several months before the murder, Pierson had begun to slowly poison his aunt. He thought that it would look like she had died of an illness and that he would inherit her money. Suddenly, however, she had written a new will, leaving her money to John Small. Feeling desperate after Mr. Torrance had told him that there was nothing he could do about the new will, Pierson had come up with another plan. He would poison his aunt in a more obvious way and make it look as if Small had been the murderer. If Small were found guilty and sent to jail, Pierson would inherit the money after all, and his troubles would be at an end. He got his wife to help him, and on Sunday night, he pretended to be an intruder in the garden, and when everyone left the house, his wife was able to slip the poison in a new bottle of Mrs. Pierson's special Swiss organic grape juice. On Monday, when Niles Pierson and his wife were miles away, old Mrs. Pierson drank the poisoned juice and died.

Appendixes

APPENDIX 1

Spelling Rules for the Third Person Singular Form of the Simple Present Tense

1. Most verbs: Add -s.	work → works play → plays
2. Verbs that end in *ch*, *sh*, *s*, *x*, or *z*: Add -es.	teach → teaches miss → misses
3. Verbs that end in a consonant + *y*: Drop *y*. Add -ies.	try → tries
4. The third person singular forms of *do*, *go*, and *have* are irregular.	does, goes, has

APPENDIX 2

Pronunciation Rules for the Third Person Singular Form of the Simple Present Tense

The -s ending is pronounced as:

- /s/ after the voiceless sounds /p/, /t/, /k/, and /f/.

  stops   gets   takes   laughs

- /z/ after the voiced sounds /b/, /d/, /g/, /v/, /*th*/, /m/, /n/, /ng/, /l/, /r/, and all vowel sounds.

robs	gives	remains	hears
adds	bathes	sings	agrees
begs	seems	tells	knows

- /ĭz/ after the sounds /s/, /z/, /sh/, /zh/, /ch/, /j/, and /ks/.

passes	catches
freezes	judges (ge = /j/)
rushes	relaxes (x = /ks/)
massages (ge = /zh/)	

Spelling Rules for the *-ing* Form of the Verb

1. Most verbs: Base form of verb + *-ing*.	work → work**ing**	play → play**ing**
2. Verbs that end in *e*: Drop *e*. Add *-ing*.	write → writ**ing**	live → liv**ing**
3. Verbs that end in *ie*: Change *ie* to *y*. Add *-ing*.	**tie → tying**	**lie → lying**
4. Verbs that end in consonant + vowel + consonant: Double the final consonant. Add *-ing*.	**run → ru**n**ning**	**be**gin → begin**ning**

BUT: Do not double the final consonant when:

• The last syllable is not stressed.	lísten → listen**ing**	háppen → happen**ing**
• The final consonant is *w* or *x*.	allow → allow**ing**	fix → fix**ing**

Adverbs of Frequency

1. Adverbs of frequency tell how often something happens—from all of the time to none of the time:

100%

0%

AFFIRMATIVE	
always, constantly, continually	We **always** eat breakfast.
almost always	
usually, generally, normally	
frequently, often	
sometimes	
occasionally	
NEGATIVE*	
seldom, rarely, hardly ever	
almost never	I **almost never** go to bed before midnight.
never	

*Negative adverbs of frequency are not used in sentences with *not*.

(continued on next page)

2. Adverbs of frequency usually occur:

   • Before main verbs (except *be*).

   | We **often go** on vacation in the summer. |

   • After *be*.*

   | They **are rarely** home in the evenings. |

   • After the first auxiliary.*

   | I **will never** forget how nice they were. |
   | We **weren't usually** allowed to leave. |

   • After the subject in questions.

   | Does **he ever** take the bus? |
   | Are **your parents always** so nice? |

   • Before negatives (except *always* and *ever*, which usually come after the negative).

   | He **often didn't** get home until late at night. |
   | Our friends **usually aren't** late. |
   | They **won't ever** call here again! |

   *Adverbs can also precede *be* and a first auxiliary, especially for emphasis (e.g., *We **usually weren't** allowed to leave*).

3. Some adverbs of frequency can often occur at the beginning and/or end of the sentence. These include *frequently, generally, normally, occasionally, often, sometimes,* and *usually.*

   | **Sometimes** we need to take a break. |
   | We need to take a break **sometimes.** |
   | **Often** he works late. |
   | He works late **often.** |

APPENDIX 5

Spelling Rules for the *-ed* Form of the Verb

1. Most verbs: Add *-ed.*

   | work → work**ed** | play → play**ed** |

2. Verbs that end in *e*: Add *-d.*

   | live → live**d** | decide → decide**d** |

3. Verbs that end in a consonant + *y*: Change *y* to *i*. Add *-ed.*

   | try → tr**ied** |

4. Verbs that end in consonant + vowel + consonant: Double the final consonant. Add *-ed.*

   | stop → stop**ped** | permit → permit**ted** |

   BUT: Do not double the final consonant when:

   • The last syllable is not stressed.

   | lísten → listen**ed** | háppen → happen**ed** |

   • The last consonant is *w* or *x.*

   | allow → allow**ed** | box → box**ed** |

Pronunciation Rules for the *-ed* Form of the Verb

The *-ed* ending is pronounced as:

- /t/ after the voiceless sounds /p/, /k/, /f/, /s/, /sh/, /ch/, and /ks/.

clapped	wished
talked	watched
laughed	waxed
passed	

- /d/ after the voiced sounds /b/, /g/, /v/, /*th*/, /z/, /zh/, /j/, /m/, /n/, /ng/, /l/, /r/, and all vowel sounds.

robbed	remained
begged	banged
waved	called
bathed	ordered
surprised	played
massaged (ge = /zh/)	enjoyed
judged (ge = /j/)	cried
seemed	

- /ĭd/ after the sounds /t/ and /d/.

started	needed

Irregular Verbs

BASE FORM	PAST	PAST PARTICIPLE	BASE FORM	PAST	PAST PARTICIPLE
be	was, were	been	broadcast	broadcast	broadcast
beat	beat	beaten	build	built	built
become	became	become	burn	burned/burnt	burned/burnt
begin	began	begun	burst	burst	burst
bend	bent	bent	buy	bought	bought
bet	bet	bet	catch	caught	caught
bind	bound	bound	choose	chose	chosen
bite	bit	bitten	come	came	come
bleed	bled	bled	cost	cost	cost
blow	blew	blown	creep	crept	crept
break	broke	broken	cut	cut	cut
bring	brought	brought	deal	dealt	dealt

(continued on next page)

BASE FORM	PAST	PAST PARTICIPLE	BASE FORM	PAST	PAST PARTICIPLE
dig	dug	dug	know	knew	known
dive	dived/dove	dived	lay	laid	laid
do	did	done	lead	led	led
draw	drew	drawn	leap	leaped/leapt	leaped/leapt
dream	dreamed/dreamt	dreamed/dreamt	learn	learned/learnt	learned/learnt
drink	drank	drunk	leave	left	left
drive	drove	driven	lend	lent	lent
eat	ate	eaten	let	let	let
fall	fell	fallen	lie	lay	lain
feed	fed	fed	light	lit/lighted	lit/lighted
feel	felt	felt	lose	lost	lost
fight	fought	fought	make	made	made
find	found	found	mean	meant	meant
fit	fit	fit	meet	met	met
flee	fled	fled	mistake	mistook	mistaken
fly	flew	flown	pay	paid	paid
forbid	forbade	forbidden	prove	proved	proved/proven
forecast	forecast/forecasted	forecast/forecasted	put	put	put
forget	forgot	forgotten	quit	quit	quit
forgive	forgave	forgiven	read	read	read
freeze	froze	frozen	rid	rid	rid
get	got	gotten	ride	rode	ridden
give	gave	given	ring	rang	rung
go	went	gone	rise	rose	risen
grind	ground	ground	run	ran	run
grow	grew	grown	say	said	said
hang	hung	hung	see	saw	seen
have	had	had	seek	sought	sought
hear	heard	heard	sell	sold	sold
hide	hid	hidden	send	sent	sent
hit	hit	hit	set	set	set
hold	held	held	sew	sewed	sewed/sewn
hurt	hurt	hurt	shake	shook	shaken
keep	kept	kept	shave	shaved	shaved/shaven

(continued on next page)

Irregular Verbs (continued)

BASE FORM	PAST	PAST PARTICIPLE	BASE FORM	PAST	PAST PARTICIPLE
shine	shined/shone	shined/shone	sweep	swept	swept
shoot	shot	shot	swell	swelled	swelled/swollen
show	showed	showed/shown	swim	swam	swum
shut	shut	shut	swing	swung	swung
sing	sang	sung	take	took	taken
sink	sank	sunk	teach	taught	taught
sit	sat	sat	tear	tore	torn
sleep	slept	slept	tell	told	told
slide	slid	slid	think	thought	thought
speak	spoke	spoken	throw	threw	thrown
speed	sped	sped	understand	understood	understood
spend	spent	spent	upset	upset	upset
spin	spun	spun	wake	woke	woken
split	split	split	wear	wore	worn
spread	spread	spread	weave	wove	woven
spring	sprang	sprung	weep	wept	wept
stand	stood	stood	wet	wet	wet
steal	stole	stolen	win	won	won
stick	stuck	stuck	wind	wound	wound
sting	stung	stung	withdraw	withdrew	withdrawn
strike	struck	struck	write	wrote	written
swear	swore	sworn			

Common Phrasal Verbs and Their Meanings

Phrasal Verbs Without Objects

blow up	1. come into being or happen suddenly (as in weather) 2. express anger suddenly and forcefully	catch up	reach the same place as others who are ahead
		check in	1. register 2. see or talk to somebody briefly
break down	fail to function	check out	leave (as a hotel)
break up	1. come apart 2. come to an end	come along	progress
		come back	return
		come out	result, end up, turn out

(continued on next page)

Common Phrasal Verbs and Their Meanings (continued)

Phrasal Verbs Without Objects (continued)

come over	visit		set off	start on a journey
come up	appear or arise		settle in	move comfortably into
drop out	leave an activity or group		show up	appear
get along	1. have a friendly relationship 2. manage with reasonable success		sit down	be seated
			slow down	become slower
			speak up	speak more loudly
go back	return		stand out	1. be better or the best 2. be different
go on	continue			
grow up	become adult		start off	begin a journey
head back	start to return		start out	begin
head out	leave a place		take off	start (to fly or move); leave
keep up	continue at the same level or pace		turn in	go to bed
			turn out	end or result
let out	end (for classes)		turn up	be found; arrive or appear, often unexpectedly
let up	slow down or stop			
pay off	be successful		watch out	be careful
push on	continue despite difficulty		work out	1. exercise 2. succeed
set in	begin to happen (for weather)			

Phrasal Verbs with Objects

add up	total (a bill)		build up	make stronger
blow up	1. explode 2. fill with air 3. make (a photograph) larger		burn down	destroy by fire
			call back	return a telephone call
			call off	cancel (a plan or an event)
break up	separate into smaller pieces		call up	telephone
bring back	return with		carry out	do as planned
bring down	cause somebody or something to lose power		check in	1. register someone (at a hotel, etc.) 2. return (as a book or equipment)
bring in	earn profits or income		check out	1. find information about 2. take something and record what is being taken (as a book or equipment)
bring off	accomplish			
bring on	cause something to appear or happen			
			drive back	force to return
bring out	produce or publish something		figure out	discover by thinking
			fill up	make or become completely full
bring up	take care of and educate (a child)		find out	discover (an answer)

(continued on next page)

finish up	end (something)		put up	1. provide (money); invest or pay in advance 2. assemble or build
get through	finish successfully		run off	print or copy
give up	stop doing (an activity)		run up	make an expense larger
hand over	give (something) to someone else		set back	slow down progress
hang up	end a telephone conversation		set off	1. make different from others 2. cause to explode 3. make angry
have on	wear		set up	1. assemble or build 2. create or establish
hold up	stop or delay		show off	display proudly
keep back	1. discourage 2. keep from advancing		sign up	register someone for an activity; add (a name) to a list
keep up	continue something at the same level		stick out	continue to the end of something difficult
leave behind	abandon		take back	return something
let down	disappoint		take down	write (pieces of) information
look over	examine quickly		take off	1. remove 2. make (time) free
look up	search in a dictionary or other reference		take on	accept responsibility for (e.g., a project)
make up	1. invent 2. replace; compensate		take over	get control or ownership of
pass around	give to others in order to share		take up	begin an activity
pass over	disregard		talk over	discuss
pick out	choose or select		think over	consider carefully
pick up	get; collect		think up	create
play down	make something seem unimportant		tire out	cause to be exhausted
play up	make something seem more important		try on	put on (clothing) to test its fit
point out	tell		try out	test
pull along	drag something		turn down	1. make quieter 2. say no to (an invitation)
put down	insult		turn in	1. give to an authority 2. inform an authority about
put off	delay; postpone		turn off	stop from working
put on	1. host 2. dress (a part of) the body in something		turn up	make louder
			wear out	make unusable through long or heavy use
put together	assemble		work out	solve (a problem)

Common Verb–Preposition Combinations

agree with	confide in	know about	pay for	rely on	wait for
believe in	depend on	learn from	plan for	search for	write about
belong to	dream of	listen to	play with	succeed in	worry about
care about	forget about	live on	prepare for	suffer from	
care for	happen to	look after	prevent from	talk about	
check in	hear about	look for	protect from	talk to	
come from	hear of	look over	read about	think about	
concentrate on	hope for	pass over	recover from	think of	

Common Phrasal Verb–Preposition Combinations and Their Meanings

catch up with	come up from behind and reach the same level	keep up with	go at the same speed as
close in on	surround	look forward to	think of (a future event) with pleasure
come out against	1. oppose 2. end with a bad result	meet up with	meet unexpectedly
come up with	discover (an idea)	miss out on	lose a chance for something
cut down on	use or have less	put up with	tolerate
drop in on	visit unexpectedly	run out of	use all the supply of
face up to	confront, meet bravely	run up against	meet and have to deal with
get along with	enjoy the company of	stand up to	1. confront somebody or something 2. tolerate or endure harsh conditions
get back from	return from		
get down to	begin (work)		
get through with	finish	start out for	begin a journey toward a particular place
give up on	admit defeat and stop trying	watch out for	be careful of
keep on at	continue		

Some Proper Nouns with *The*

1. Names of countries and islands:

the Bahamas	the Falkland Islands	the Philippines/the Philippine Islands
the British Isles	the Hawaiian Islands	the United Arab Emirates
the Czech Republic	the Netherlands	the United Kingdom
the Dominican Republic	the People's Republic of China	the United States of America

2. Regions:

the East/West/North/South	the East/West Coast	the Midwest	the Near/Middle/Far East

3. Geographical features:

- Map features:

the Eastern/Western/Northern/Southern Hemisphere	the Occident/the Orient
the North/South Pole	the Tropic of Cancer/Capricorn

- Canals, channels, gulfs:

the Suez Canal	the English Channel	the Arabian Gulf	the Gulf of Mexico

- Deserts:

the Gobi (Desert)	the Mojave (Desert)	the Sahara (Desert)	the Sinai (Desert)

- Mountain ranges:

the Alps	the Caucasus (Mountains)
the Andes (Mountains)	the Himalaya Mountains (the Himalayas)
the Atlas Mountains	the Rocky Mountains (the Rockies)

- Oceans and seas:

the Arctic Ocean	the Indian Ocean	the Sea of Japan
the Atlantic (Ocean)	the Mediterranean (Sea)	the South China Sea
the Black Sea	the Pacific (Ocean)	
the Caribbean (Sea)	the Red Sea	

- Peninsulas:

the Iberian Peninsula	the Yucatan Peninsula

(continued on next page)

3. Geographical features: (continued)

- Rivers:

the Amazon (River)	the Mississippi (River)	the Rio Grande	the Thames (River)
the Congo (River)	the Nile (River)	the Seine (River)	the Tigris (River)

- Names with *of*:

the Bay of Naples	the Cape of Good Hope	the Strait of Gibraltar	the Strait of Magellan

4. Buildings and other structures:

the Brooklyn Bridge	the Museum of Modern Art	the Statue of Liberty
the Eiffel Tower	the Ritz-Carlton Hotel	the White House

5. Ships, trains, and airplanes:

the *Mayflower*	the *Titanic*	the *Orient Express*	the *Spirit of St. Louis*

6. Newspapers and periodicals:

the *New York Times*	the *Washington Post*	the *Atlantic Monthly*	the *Economist*

Spelling Rules for Regular Plural Count Nouns

1. Most verbs: Add -s.

room → rooms	studio → studios

2. Nouns that end in *ch, sh, s, x,* or *z*: Add -*es*.

lunch → lunches	box → box**es**
brush → brush**es**	buzz → buzz**es**
kiss → kiss**es**	

   If a noun ending in one *s* or *z* has one syllable or stress on the last syllable, double the *s* or *z*.

bus → bus**ses**	**quiz** → quiz**zes**

3. Nouns ending in a consonant + *y*: Change *y* to *i*. Add -*es*.

sto**ry** → stor**ies**	universi**ty** → universit**ies**

4. Nouns ending in *f* or *fe*: Change *f* to *v*. Add -*es* or -*s*.

lea**f** → lea**ves**	kni**fe** → kni**ves**

   Exceptions: belief → beliefs, chief → chiefs, roof → roofs

5. A few nouns ending in a consonant + *o*: Add -*es*.

hero → hero**es**	potato → potato**es**
mosqui**to** → mosquito**es**	toma**to** → tomato**es**

Pronunciation Rules for Regular Plural Count Nouns

The -*s* ending is pronounced as:

- /s/ after the voiceless sounds /p/, /t/, /k/, /f/, and /th/.

cups	cuffs
hats	paths
books	

- /z/ after the voiced sounds /b/, /d/, /g/, /v/, /*th*/, /m/, /n/, /ng/, /l/, /r/, and all vowel sounds.

jobs	bones
kids	things
legs	bells
knives	bears
lathes	days
dreams	potatoes

- /ĭz/ after the sounds /s/, /z/, /sh/, /zh/, /ch/, /j/, and /ks/.

classes	churches
breezes	judges (ge = /j/)
dishes	taxes (x = /ks/)
massages (ge = /zh/)	

Irregular Plural Count Nouns

1. Nouns that have different forms in the singular and plural:

SINGULAR	PLURAL	SINGULAR	PLURAL	SINGULAR	PLURAL	SINGULAR	PLURAL
child	children	goose	geese	mouse	mice	tooth	teeth
foot	feet	man	men	person	people	woman	women

2. Nouns that have the same form in the singular and plural:

SINGULAR	PLURAL	SINGULAR	PLURAL	SINGULAR	PLURAL
fish	fish	moose	moose	sheep	sheep
means	means	series	series	species	species

3. Nouns from Latin and Greek that have kept their original plural forms:

SINGULAR	PLURAL	SINGULAR	PLURAL
alumnus (alumna)	alumni (alumnae)	medium	media
analysis	analyses	memorandum	memoranda (memorandums)
basis	bases	parenthesis	parentheses
crisis	crises	phenomenon	phenomena
curriculum	curricula (curriculums)	stimulus	stimuli
datum	data	syllabus	syllabi (syllabuses)
hypothesis	hypotheses	thesis	theses

4. Nouns with no singular form:

cattle	police

5. Nouns with only a plural form:

belongings	clothes	congratulations	goods	groceries	tropics

6. Nouns for things in pairs with only a plural form:

jeans	pajamas	pants	scissors	shorts	(sun)glasses	tongs	trousers

Common Noncount Nouns

1. Names of groups of similar items:

cash	equipment	furniture	jewelry	mail	stuff
change (i.e., money)	food	garbage	luggage	money	trash
clothing	fruit	homework	machinery	scenery	traffic

(These groups often have individual parts that can be counted, e.g., clothing is made up of dresses, shirts, coats, etc.)

2. Liquids:

coffee	gasoline	honey	juice	lotion	milk	oil	sauce	soup	tea	water

(continued on next page)

Common Noncount Nouns (continued)

3. Foods:

bacon	cabbage	chicken	food	lettuce	pie	seafood	vitamin
beef	cake	chocolate	garlic	meat	pizza	spaghetti	wheat
bread	candy	corn	hamburger	pasta	pork	spice	
broccoli	celery	fish	ice cream	pastry	rice	spinach	
butter	cheese	flour	jelly	pepper	salt	sugar	

4. Other solids:

aspirin	detergent	glass	hair	paper	silk	toothpaste
chalk	dirt	gold	ice	rope	silver	wood
cotton	film	grass	nylon	sand	soap	wool

5. Gases:

air	carbon dioxide	hydrogen	nitrogen	oxygen	smoke	steam

6. Natural phenomena:

cold	fire	hail	light	smog	sunshine	warmth
darkness	fog	heat	lightning	snow	temperature	weather
electricity	gravity	humidity	rain	space	thunder	wind

7. Abstract ideas:

advice	education	help	law	permission	tradition
art	energy	history	life	practice	travel
beauty	entertainment	honesty	love	pride	trouble
behavior	freedom	importance	luck	progress	truth
business	friendship	information	music	quiet	variety
competition	fun	insurance	news*	responsibility	violence
confidence	grammar	intelligence	noise	slang	vocabulary
courage	hatred	interest	opportunity	sleep	wealth
crime	happiness	knowledge	patience	space	work
democracy	health	laughter	peace	time	

8. Fields of study:

accounting	business	engineering	journalism	music	psychology	writing
art	chemistry	geography	literature	nutrition	science	
biology	economics	history	mathematics*	physics*	sociology	

*Some noncount nouns, such as *news*, *mathematics*, and *physics*, end in *s*. These nouns look plural, but they are not; they always take a singular verb.

Common Noncount Nouns (continued)

9. Activities

baseball	cards	dancing	running	skating	studying	traveling
basketball	conversation	golf	sailing	skiing	surfing	
bowling	cooking	hiking	shopping	snowboarding	swimming	
camping	cycling	reading	singing	soccer	tennis	

10. Languages:

Arabic	English	German	Japanese	Portuguese	Spanish	Turkish
Chinese	French	Indonesian	Korean	Russian	Thai	Urdu

APPENDIX 16

Pronouns

SINGULAR	SUBJECT	OBJECT	REFLEXIVE	POSSESSIVE DETERMINER	POSSESSIVE PRONOUN
First person	I	me	myself	my	mine
Second person	you	you	yourself	your	yours
Third person	he	him	himself	his	his
	she	her	herself	her	hers
	it	it	itself	its	its
PLURAL					
First person	we	us	ourselves	our	ours
Second person	you	you	yourselves	your	yours
Third person	they	them	themselves	their	theirs

APPENDIX 17

Common Adjective + Preposition Combinations That Are Followed by Gerunds

accustomed to	critical of	good at	responsible for	used to
afraid of	discouraged about	happy about	sad about	useful for
angry at/about	enthusiastic about	interested in	sorry about	worried about
ashamed of	familiar with	known for	successful in	
(in)capable of	famous for	nervous about	tired of	
certain of/about	fond of	perfect for	tolerant of	
concerned about	glad about	proud of	upset about	

Some Verbs That Can Be Followed by Gerunds

acknowledge	complete	encourage*	forgive	mind	recollect	start*
admit	consider	endure	hate	miss	recommend	stop**
advise*	continue*	enjoy	imagine	permit*	regret*	suggest
allow*	defend	escape	include	postpone	remember**	support
anticipate	defer	excuse	involve	practice	report	tolerate
appreciate	delay	explain	justify	prefer*	require*	try**
avoid	deny	feel like	keep	prevent	resent	understand
begin*	detest	finish	like*	prohibit	resist	urge*
can't help	discuss	forbid*	love*	quit	resume	
celebrate	dislike	forget**	mention	recall	risk	

*Verbs that can take either a gerund or an infinitive.
**Verbs that can take either a gerund or an infinitive but with a difference in meaning.

Some Verbs That Can Be Followed by Infinitives

1. Verb + infinitive:

agree	claim	don't/didn't care	manage	refuse	try**
aim	consent	fail	mean	remember**	wait
appear	continue*	forget**	offer	seem	
attempt	decide	hesitate	plan	start*	
begin*	decline	hope	pledge	stop**	
can't/couldn't afford	demand	intend	pretend	struggle	
can't/couldn't wait	deserve	learn	promise	tend	

2. Verb + noun phrase + infinitive:

advise*	command	forbid*	invite	persuade	teach	urge*
allow*	convince	force	order	remind	tell	warn
cause	encourage*	hire	permit*	require*	trust	

3. Verb + (noun phrase) + infinitive:

ask	choose	expect	hate*	love*	need	prefer	want	would like
beg	dare	get	like*	know	pay	prepare	wish	

*Verbs that can take either a gerund or an infinitive.
**Verbs that can take either a gerund or an infinitive but with a difference in meaning.

Grammar Glossary

active sentence   A sentence that is not in passive form; often, the subject is the performer of the action of the verb.

Millions of people watch the World Cup.

adjective   A type of noun modifier; often describes a noun.

He drinks **strong, black** coffee.

adjective clause (also called *relative clause*)   A clause that modifies a noun.

A scientist **who studies personality** has developed a new theory.

adverb   A word that describes or otherwise modifies a verb, an adjective, another adverb, or a sentence.

They worked **quickly** and **carefully** on the project.

adverb clause   A clause that functions like an adverb, modifying the main clause verb or the main clause.

Because they want their product to sell, companies do market research.

adverb of frequency   An adverb that tells how often an action occurs.

"Night owls" **usually** do their best work at night.

agent   The performer of the action of the verb. In a passive sentence, the agent, if included, is in a *by* phrase.

The goalie stopped the ball.
The ball was stopped by **the goalie.**

article   The words *a/an* and *the*, which are used to introduce or identify a noun.

a cook   **an** orange
the menu   **the** recipes

auxiliary verb   A verb that is used with a main verb to make questions and negative sentences and to help make tenses and express meaning (*do, be, have,* and modals).

Are you working?
We **did**n't finish the exam.

She **has** traveled a lot.
They **should** get out more.

base form of a verb (also called *the simple form of a verb*)   A verb without *to* in front of it or any endings.

play   work   be   do

causative verb   A verb (e.g., *have, let, make*) used to mean to cause or allow someone to do something.

John **had** us buy the concert tickets.

clause   A group of related words that has a subject and a verb.

Before he leaves, . . .
We're back!
. . . because it sells well.

collective noun   A noun that refers to a group.

committee   family
audience   team

common noun   A noun that does not name a particular person, place, or thing.

cat   coffee   students
buildings   loyalty

conditional sentence   A sentence that contains a condition clause and a result clause and expresses a relationship between the condition and result.

If a storm comes up, you should go inside.

connector   A word that shows how ideas are related.

because   but
also   nevertheless

■ **coordinating conjunction** A word—*and, but, or, nor, so, for, yet*—that connects clauses and, in some cases, also phrases or words.

> We wrote the proposal, **and** they accepted it.
> I tried **but** didn't succeed.

■ **count noun** A noun that can be counted.

> a **restaurant**   two **restaurants**
> an **apple**   three **apples**

■ **definite article** *The*; used to identify nouns that refer to something specific and are known to both the speaker and listener.

> **The** chef in this restaurant wrote a best-selling cookbook.

■ **demonstrative** *This, that, these, those*; demonstratives can be pronouns or determiners.

> **That** is really good.
> **These** days, dining out is popular.

■ **determiner** A word that comes before a common noun; determiners can be articles, quantifiers, demonstratives, and possessives.

> **the** salad   **many** desserts
> **this** table   **your** order

■ **future** *Will/be going to* + base form of the verb; used to talk about future events; sometimes also expressed with simple present, present progressive, *be about to*, and modals such as *can* and *may*.

> The weather **will be** nice tomorrow.
> They**'re going to see** a movie tonight.

■ **future perfect** *Will/be going to* + *have* + past participle; tense used to talk about an action or state that will occur before a future action, state, or time.

> I **will have finished** my work by then.

■ **future perfect progressive** (also called *future perfect continuous*) *Will/be going to* + *have* + *been* + verb + *-ing*; tense used to talk about an action that will continue to a future action, state, or time.

> They **will have been traveling** for many days when they get there.

■ **future progressive** (also called *future continuous*) *Will/be going to* + *be* + verb + *-ing*; tense used to talk about actions that will be in progress in the future.

> He **is going to be flying** to Hawaii next week.

■ **gerund** Formed from verb + *-ing*; often functions as a noun.

> We enjoy **dancing** and **singing**.

■ **indefinite article** *A/an*; used to introduce a noun that doesn't refer to something specific or that the speaker and listener don't both know.

> **a** banana   **an** author

■ **indefinite pronoun** A pronoun that is used to talk about unspecified people or things or about people or things in general.

> Is **anybody** out there?

■ **infinitive** Formed from *to* + base form of the verb; often functions as a noun.

> We wanted **to go** to the circus.
> **To climb** Mount Everest is our dream.

■ **intensifier** A word that is used before an adjective or adverb to strengthen the meaning of the adjective or adverb.

> That restaurant is **very** expensive.
> We got our food **quite** quickly.

■ **intransitive verb** A verb that does not take an object.

> We **stood** in line for football tickets.

■ **main clause** (also called *independent clause*) A clause that is, or could be, a complete sentence.

> **We arrived late.**
> When we got there, **he had to leave.**

■ **main verb** The verb in a sentence in the simple present or simple past and, in sentences in other tenses, the verb that carries the primary verbal meaning (i.e., not an auxiliary verb).

> We **traveled** to Japan.
> We had **gone** there once before.

modal An auxiliary verb that expresses ideas related to degrees of certainty, social functions, and/or ability.

> She **might** be at home.
> They **must** leave soon.
> We **can** sing well.

modifier A word, phrase, or clause that describes and gives more information about another word, phrase, or clause.

> You look **happy**.
> The man **in white** is the chef.

noncount noun A noun that cannot be counted.

> **rain**   **sand**   **happiness**
> **physics**   **swimming**

noun A word that names a person, place, or thing.

> **Albert Einstein**   **ocean**   **table**

noun clause A clause that functions like a noun.

> We think **that they will get married and live happily ever after.**

noun phrase A noun and its determiners and modifiers, if any.

> We ate at **that very charming new restaurant.**

object A noun, pronoun, or noun phrase that receives the action of the verb.

> Paul called **us**.
> The chef prepared **a delicious meal**.

object of a preposition A noun, pronoun, or noun phrase that comes after a preposition.

> for **Mary**   to **them**
> with **my best friend's mother**

particle An adverb that is part of a phrasal verb.

> They set **out** late.

passive causative A structure, with *get/have* + object + past participle, that expresses the idea that someone "causes" someone else to perform a service.

> The players **had** their uniforms **cleaned**.

passive sentence A sentence that has *be* followed by the past participle of the main verb; the subject of the sentence is the receiver of the action of the verb.

> **The World Cup is watched by millions of people.**

past perfect *Had* + past participle; tense used to talk about past actions or states that occurred before another past action, state, or time.

> I **had read** the book before I saw the movie.

past perfect progressive (also called *past perfect continuous*) *Had* + *been* + present participle; tense used to talk about an action that began before and continued to another past action, state, or time.

> They **had been working** for hours when he arrived.

past progressive (also called *past continuous*) *Was/Were* + present participle; tense used to talk about an action in progress in the past.

> He **was sleeping** when the phone rang.

phrasal verb A verb + adverb (particle); its meaning is different from the meaning of the verb + the meaning of the particle.

> They **kept on** despite the difficulties.
> She **called** him **up**.

phrasal verb with preposition (also called a *three-word verb*) The combination of a phrasal verb + a preposition.

> We **ran out of** time.

phrase A group of related words that does not contain both a subject and a verb.

> **on the street**   **the people upstairs**
> **had already gone**

possessive   A word or structure that shows ownership; may be a determiner, noun, pronoun, or phrase.

> **our** homework   **David's** house
> It's **theirs**.   the corner **of the table**

preposition   A function word such as *at, from, in,* or *to* that takes a noun, pronoun, or noun phrase as an object to form a prepositional phrase; often helps express meanings related to time, location, or direction.

> **in** the classroom   **around** the same time
> **with** my friends

prepositional phrase   A preposition plus a noun, pronoun, or noun phrase.

> **in the classroom**   **around the same time**
> **with my friends**

present perfect   *Have* + past participle; tense used to talk about actions or states that occurred at an unspecified time in the past or, with a time expression of duration, to talk about actions or states that began in the past and continue to the present.

> They **have written** a book.
> They **have lived** there for many years.

present perfect progressive (also called *present perfect continuous*)   *Have* + *been* + present participle; tense used to talk about actions that began in the past and continue to the present; it often emphasizes that the action is ongoing.

> They **have been cleaning** all morning.

present progressive (also called *present continuous*)   *Am/Is/Are* + present participle; tense used to talk about actions in progress at this moment or through a period of time including the present.

> Look! It**'s snowing**.
> He **is studying** in the United States this year.

pronoun   A word that replaces a noun or noun phrase that has already been mentioned or that is clear from context.

> **I** need to talk to **you**.
> Al is looking at **himself** in the mirror.

proper noun   A noun that names a particular person, place, or thing.

> **Molly Brown**   **Denver, Colorado**
> **the** *Titanic*

quantifier   A word or phrase that indicates the quantity of a noun.

> **some** potatoes   **a few** choices
> **not much** oil

quoted speech   A way of reporting speech that uses the exact words of the speaker.

> **"I'll love you forever!"** he promised.

reciprocal pronoun   A pronoun (*each other* or *one another*) that is used when two or more people or things give and receive the same feelings or actions.

> They stared at **each other** from across the restaurant.

reflexive pronoun   A pronoun that is used instead of an object pronoun when the object refers to the same person or thing as the subject of the sentence.

> They bought **themselves** a new car.

relative pronoun   A pronoun that begins an adjective clause.

> The author **who** wrote the book gave a speech.
> I like the book **that** we saw in the store.

reported speech   A way of reporting speech that does not use the speaker's exact words.

> He told her **that he would love her forever**.

simple past   Verb + *-ed*; tense used to talk about actions and states that began and ended in the past.

> We **walked** to school.
> He **looked** healthy.

simple present   Verb (+ *-s*); tense used to talk about habitual or repeated actions in the present and about things that are generally accepted as true.

> I **work** in a restaurant.
> Water **freezes** at 32°F.

stative passive *-ed* adjective following *be* or *get*; unlike true passives, expresses states rather than actions.

> The door **is closed**.
> We **got excited** about the team.

subject The noun, pronoun, or noun phrase that comes before the verb in a statement and that generally is what the statement is about.

> **Kate** went to the restaurant.
> **The woman in the white hat** ordered coffee.

subject complement A noun, pronoun, noun phrase, or adjective that renames, identifies, or describes the subject of a sentence.

> He is **a superb chef**.
> They looked like **professionals**.

subordinate clause (also called *dependent clause*) A clause that cannot stand alone but must be used with a main clause.

> **When we met**, we discussed the ad campaign.

subordinating conjunction A word (*when, where, because, although, if*, etc.) that begins an adverb clause.

> **Although** they advertised the product, it didn't sell well.

tag question A statement with a short question ("tag") added at the end.

> You haven't been to London, **have you?**
> He lives here, **doesn't he?**

time clause A clause that begins with a time word like *when, while, before,* or *after*.

> **After this class ends**, I'm going home.
> They came **while she was working**.

transition A word (*also, however, in addition, therefore,* etc.) that connects main clauses, sentences, or larger units, such as paragraphs.

> The clients were pleased. **Therefore**, they accepted our design.

transitive verb A verb that takes an object in an active sentence.

> The golfer **hit** the ball.

verb A word that shows an action or state.

> **do**   **come**   **be**   **have**

verb–preposition combination A combination formed by certain verbs and certain prepositions.

> We **looked for** the cat.
> They **heard from** him.

verb with stative meaning A verb that refers to a state, not an action.

> She **has known** him for years.
> He **is** a good lawyer.

wh- question (also called *information question*) A question that begins with a *wh-* word (*who, what, where, when, why, how,* etc.) and asks for information.

> **Who will win the game?**
> **How far did you travel last night?**

yes/no question A question that can be answered with *yes* or *no*.

> **Do you like chocolate?**
> **Was he at the game?**

[0] article (called the "zero" article) used instead of *a/an* with indefinite plural count nouns and noncount nouns.

> I bought **[0]** bananas at the store.
> I put **[0]** fruit in the pie.

Index